RESUME & LinkedIn Strategies for New College GRADUATES

What Works to Launch a Gen-Z Career

MASTER RESUME WRITERS

Jan Melnik &

Louise Kursmark

RESUME & LINKEDIN STRATEGIES FOR NEW COLLEGE GRADUATES

Copyright © 2023 by Jan Melnik and Louise Kursmark

ISBN 978-0-9966803-9-4

Publisher: Emerald Career Publishing
              www.emeraldcareerpublishing.com

Cover & Interior Design: Deb Tremper, Six Penny Graphics
http://sixpennygraphics.com

Distributor: Cardinal Publishers Group
www.cardinalpub.com

Printed in the United States of America

CONTENTS

What Works

Portfolio

Thanks to Our Contributors!

Career Center Professionals

Throughout the book you will see "Career Centers Say" boxes that share the wisdom of these professionals who work every day to assist students and graduates advance their careers.

- Career Center Staff, Western Washington University
- Sharon Belden Castonguay, EdD, Executive Director, Gordon Career Center, Wesleyan University
- Kate Chroust, MA, Senior Director of Career Services, Endicott College
- Carla Coury, MA, Interim Executive Director, Career Management Center, A.B. Freeman School of Business, Tulane University
- Helen Eaton, MBA, Associate Director of Career Services, Endicott College
- Gretchen Heaton, MA, Dean of Career Development, Bay Path University
- Cheryl Minnick, EdD, Career Success Director, College of Humanities & Sciences, University of Montana
- Cara Mitnick, JD, Director of Professional Development, University of Rhode Island Graduate School
- Toni Ripo, MA, Coordinator of Career Services, University of South Florida Sarasota-Manatee
- Amanda Schagane, MSEd, Associate Director of Alumni Career Services, University of Kentucky
- Micall Searles, MA, Career Coach, University of Montana
- Chaim Shapiro, MEd, Director of the Office for Student Success, Touro University

Resume Writers

The Portfolio beginning on page 115 features the work of 36 professional resume writers in addition to the two book authors. You can find the name and contact information of each writer on the resume page. We encourage you to reach out if you would like to put their talents to work for you!

Kaljah Adams	Phyllis Houston	Birgitta Moller
Andrea Adamski	Teresa Hutton	Zakiyyah Mussallihullah
Jean Austin	Michelle McCann Kelley	Chelsey Opare-Addo
Linda Bartone	Michelle King	Ruth Pankratz
Beverly Baskin	Carolyn Kleiman	Barb Penney
Brenda Bernstein	Cathy Lanzalaco	Robert Rosales
Norine Dagliano	Ed Lawrence	Donna Tucker
Wendy Enelow	Kasindra Maharaj	Vivian Van Lier
Sandra Flippo	Gabrielle Maury	Kate Williamson
Jill Grindle	Jheneal McDuffie	Chelsea Wiltse
Roshael Hanna	Kristi Meenan	Julie Wyckoff
Erika Harrigan	Cheryl Milmoe	Lucie Yeomans

INTRO

Congratulations! You've graduated from college or are seeking an important internship—both critical steps in launching your professional career. This book will give you all the strategies you'll need to jump-start your job search.

It all begins with a super resume. Chapter 1 outlines exactly the steps to take for building an authentic, accomplishment-focused resume that presents you as a qualified candidate *and* differentiates you from other applicants. You'll find approaches for addressing many questions, such as: "What if I have only a few (or no) extracurriculars?" "How do I handle minimal experience?"

LinkedIn is today's must-have social/professional medium for networking and job search. Chapter 2 explains how to craft an effective Headline for your profile and describes great strategies for creating About and Experience content that is compelling, packs the right punch, and gets readers (hiring managers!) to click "See more" to read your marketing message and story.

Next up: Your e-note/cover letter. Chapter 3 breaks down an easy-to-follow formula for concisely writing a short email message or cover letter that helps you stand out from the competition. At the same time, it's exactly what you'll need for people to use in telling your story when introducing you to others.

The tools are all set—now Chapter 4 walks through key recommendations for maximizing your job-search success. From scripting your networking messages and tapping into your network of contacts in the most appropriate way to sharing timelines for when and how to follow up on leads, you'll learn best practices to power your search.

You've landed the interview! Here's the game plan to prep the right way. Chapter 5 highlights everything you'll need to most effectively plan for every interview—both virtual and in person. You'll learn how to prep for behavior-based and other types of interview questions, "tell something about yourself," recover from false steps, and respond when asked if *you* have any questions (yes, you do have questions!).

Finally, "a picture's worth a thousand words." In a comprehensive Portfolio, we share more than 90 great examples of resumes for college students and new graduates to give you fresh ideas on resume design and all-important content strategies. Pick and choose from many effective approaches for deciding the best way to craft *your* story and present yourself as an attractive candidate.

Most importantly, the strategies and tactics we share in this book will serve you now—as you launch your career—and at every point in the future as you navigate the world of work. You'll be an informed, well-prepared job seeker who knows how to express your value to potential employers.

This is your first step in your lifelong career journey. We will help you make a successful leap and create momentum for every future career transition. Let's get started!

CHAPTER 1:
Write a Great Resume

Your resume: It's the universal door-opener in networking and job search. You reach out to a connection who might have a lead on a job … What's the first thing she asks? *"Send me your resume."* A contact on LinkedIn responds to your inquiry, and what does he say? *"Please email your resume."* With every job application you make, you are required to upload, email, or otherwise submit your resume.

The document you share needs to tell these people—your existing contacts, new connections, and potential employers—who you are, what you can do, and where you fit into the vast world of work.

We're here to tell you and show you how to do that.

What Matters Most on Your Resume?

Start with the basics: You must quickly present your qualifications for the job opportunity you are targeting. Going deeper, show how you can step into a company or organization and rapidly come up to speed, provide solutions, add value, and make a difference.

That's your challenge in writing your resume: Giving readers the information they need to evaluate you as a potential employee by showcasing the unique combination of knowledge, skills, expertise, and personal attributes—also known as your "brand" or your "value proposition"—that sets you apart from other candidates.

A Word About Branding

Branding is what defines you. While people across the country in big advertising and marketing jobs make lots of money creating the branding you see behind some of the top Super Bowl ads, there's not a whole lot of magic when it comes to *your* brand.

What differentiates you? What distinguishes you—as a candidate … as an intern (if you've held an internship or two) … as an employee (if you've had any part- or full-time jobs, even in fields unrelated to your studies and future career interests)?

A resume that is simply a list of where you've been and what you've done (school and job activities) will not differentiate you from every other new-graduate candidate. But when you share what makes you special and unique, and provide evidence to back it up, you create a resume that is distinctive and interesting—and that expresses your unique brand. What's more, it speaks to the needs of the employer because it conveys *what* you can do, *how* you do it, and *where*, *why*, and *how* you have made a difference.

As well, understanding your unique brand will help you tell a consistent, cohesive, complementary story about yourself in all of your career communications—your resume, LinkedIn profile, cover letters/e-notes, and interviews. Think of it as 3D: Not just what appears on paper, but who you are IRL.

We'll start with the resume. In this chapter we walk you step-by-step through creating all of the different sections of this foundational career document. Beyond the nuts-and-bolts, though, we share strategies for making your resume stand out—in a good way!

Meet the CAR Story

Let us introduce you to our favorite technique for illustrating what you do, how you do it, and why it is valuable in the workplace: the CAR story.

C = Challenge … You can also think of this as a *problem* or even an *opportunity*.

A = Action … What did you do? What initiative and what steps did you take?

R = Result … What was the outcome? What resulted from what you did? What were the short- and long-term results from the action or initiative you took?

The CAR story is valuable because it reveals specifics, not generalities. The CAR structure is helpful to you as it keeps your narrative on track—whether sharing verbally or in writing, you can move smoothly through the three story phases in a way that is clear and logical, uncovers things that *you* have done, and ends on a positive note with outcomes or results.

We encourage you to follow the CAR format in crafting mini success stories that provide evidence of your unique skills, talents, activities, and accomplishments. You might be thinking: *"Well, I haven't worked (yet) in this field … I don't have any CAR stories that are relevant."* And that might be true.

However, as a college student or new graduate, you *have* had successes, and probably more than a few. They might have come from your experiences in the classroom, during a co-op or internship or part-time job, through extracurricular or volunteer activities, or any other ways you have spent your time. Now is the time to recall those successes and, as you create content for your resume, integrate stories that will give readers evidence of your potential and your value.

Before you dive into the actual writing process, use the following questions to jump-start your thinking.

Initial Questions to Ask Yourself
In the Classroom

- Have you completed a capstone paper?
- Have you contributed to a significant group project?
- Have you assisted a professor or TA in one of your classes?
- Have you done any field work or study?
- Have you coached or mentored (formally or informally) another student or group of students?

Outside the Classroom

- Have you been involved in any extracurricular activities or athletics?

- Have you been part of any clubs or groups on campus?
- Have you held any elected or appointed leadership roles? Examples might be captain of the band or an athletic team, officer of a club or organization, committee or event chairperson.
- Have you volunteered for any events or organizations?
- Have you been a member of a fraternity or sorority?
- Do you have personal circumstances that have presented challenges you've had to overcome?

On the Job

- Have you worked at your college or university?
- Have you held part-time or full-time employment during the academic year, throughout summer and winter breaks, or while in high school?
- Have you started any type of business enterprise (babysitting, lawncare, tutoring, web design, band, given lessons of any type)?

Very likely you have been able to answer "yes" to several or even many of these questions. Every experience—even if seemingly unrelated to your future profession—can provide rich material for your resume, LinkedIn profile, cover letters, and interview responses.

We'll show you how it's done as we move into the details of creating all of these important career messages. And, in worksheets later in this chapter, we'll guide you through the process of capturing your CAR stories and converting them into relevant, meaningful content.

Let's begin with some fundamentals.

The Real Estate of Your Resume

More than a half dozen core components make up most resumes:

1) Contact Info
2) Profile-Summary
3) Skills and Expertise (technology skills and other specific competencies)
4) Education
5) Work Experience
6) Military (if you have military or ROTC experience)
7) Additional: Extracurriculars, Volunteerism/Community, Certifications, Credentials, Licenses, Affiliations, Memberships, Languages, Personal Details

As we delve into each of these core components, we share with you our strategies and recommendations for making each section of your resume clear, compelling, and relevant.

To give you an idea of how all this information might come together, here's a quick picture of the different sections on a resume. Keep in mind, you don't need to include them *all* and you don't need to position them where they are in this sample.

Douglas Cornwall

Chicago, IL 60601 | doug.cornwall@mail.com | 312-222-5412 | LinkedI

[Name and Contact Info]

[Profile-Summary (Includes Headline)]

...ive Marketing and Project Management Professional

- ...n in accurately interpreting and conveying client intentions to achieve exceptional results.
- ...study, learning and mastering new technology and skills to make contribution to organizations.
- Solid work ethic complemented by employing an "above-and-beyond" approach to every assignment and project

Advertising & Digital Marketing | Project Management | Content Creation | Team L...
Social Media Marketing | Brand & Marketing Strategy | Photography

[Skills and Expertise]

[Education (Includes Courses and Projects)]

Education

Select Marketing Projects

NORTHWESTERN UNIVER...
Bachelor of Sci...e Degree (2023)
Major: Mark...ing | Minor: English

GLOBAL MARKETING RESEARCH PROJECT: Led team that analyzed market and competition for new Indian soap launch in Egypt and created comprehensive marketing plan, distribution and pricing strategy, and multipronged promotional tactics.

Course Highlights

Advertising, Sports Marketing, International Marketing, Consumer Behavior, News Writing, Social Media, Digital Journalism, Music Industry

- **SOUTH SIDE DELI:** Collaborated with Chicago-area business to develop expanded social media presence on Instagram/Twitter/Facebook to increase local patronage among university students in the vicinity.

Technology

[Skills and Expertise]

...a (Instagram, Twitter, Facebook),
...t Office (PowerPoint, Excel, Word),
...n, Sony a7R II camera, ABBYY FlexiCapture

- **JACK'S:** Designed radio and print advertising that boosted traffic and attracted more customers for Evanston restaurant/bar.

Internship Experience

[Work Experience (Separate Sections for Internships and Additional Employment)]

...Chicago, IL   **Jan—May 2023**

...ng exposure to numerous real estate management transactions. Shadowed company president ...corporate property visits. A privately owned real estate development and private equity ...roup specializes in commercial and industrial acquisitions.
- ...first digital marketing strategy and detailed plan for execution (to launch Fall 2023).
- Organized ...estate documents for Vice President, Facilities; proofed transactions in Excel spreadsheets.
- Attended w...ly President's meetings discussing companywide project status.

Intern | SOUTH BEN... CUBS | South Bend, IN   **Mar—Sep 2022**

Proactively targeted and cr...ated own internship with the High-A affiliate of the Chicago Cubs.
- Shadowed Assistant ...neral Manager and other staff, gaining experience in front-office operations.
- Assisted Marketing Man...ger by writing ad copy, designing flyers, and brainstorming promotional ideas.

Additional Work Experience

Accounts Payable Clerk | MIDWEST FINANCIAL SERVICES | Chicago, IL   **Summer 2022**
- Captured invoice data using ABBYY FlexiCapture, then organized and recorded data using Excel.
- Tested in top percentage of employees on mandated Excel test—scored a full 10 points above average.

Front End Supervisor | DEAL$ DISCOUNT STORES | Chicago, IL   **Summer 2021**
- Managed 5 cashiers, delegated work assignments, and handled a broad range of customer service issues.
- Developed problem-solving skills and worked effectively to defuse angry customer situations.

Activities

[Extracurriculars, Volunteerism]

Activity Chair, Northwestern Marketing Club | **Captain,** Club Volleyball | **Volunteer,** Greater Ch...

1) CONTACT INFO

Make it easy for employers to connect with you by positioning your all-important contact information at the top of your resume. Don't create a resume style that throws email and phone number into a footer, at the bottom of the page, or in an unexpected location.

What's essential?

Name

If you use something other than your given name, include that as well.

Eduardo "Ed" Perez
Damon (DJ) Bartelli

To make it easy for someone to reach out to you, eliminate confusion on gender—if applicable—with:

Ms. Taylor L. Symington
-or-
Alex J. Fischer (she, her, hers)
-or-
Jerry Gambardella (they, them, theirs)

Contact Number

Provide one phone number with area code. No need to say home/cell/mobile.

This would be a good time to create a personal voicemail greeting that is brief, clear, and professional. And … be certain to check your messages regularly during your job search!

Email

Provide one email address.

Should you continue to use your college email address? It's okay to do so *if* you will have access to this email indefinitely or for at least a year or two after graduation. However, we suggest that you move immediately to your post-college identity with a permanent email that identifies *you* and does not overly emphasize where you went to school.

We recommend a well-branded gmail address. Try:
> first name-hyphen-last name: Susan-Delmonico@gmail.com
> -or-
> first name-period-last name: Susan.Delmonico@gmail.com

If you have a name that's frequently used, try adding your middle initial:
> first name-initial-last name: RobertTWilson@gmail.com
> -or-
> first name-hyphen-initial-hyphen-last name: Robert-T-Wilson@gmail.com

If necessary, use any one of the above protocols and try adding a single number. Don't use your birth year, and try to avoid birth month and date. Try selecting your favorite single digit and add it to the end of one of the options described.

Another option, useful if you have a popular name, is to add a word or two to convey your professional identity. For example:

AlexSmith-UXdesigner@gmail.com

ChrisWaters.Engineer@gmail.com

Address

Best practice today is *not* to include your full home (or college) address. Rather, simply list a zip code *or* a metro area *or* city-state-zip code.

It makes sense to include your location if:

- You want to remain in the same geographic area as your hometown or college. Having a local address can give you an advantage with some employers.
- You are targeting a particular geography different from where you reside. For instance, you can live in the Greater Chicago area and be seeking an opportunity in Boston. You could show *Boston, MA 02108* or *Greater Boston Area* for the address on your resume.

If your search is geographically broad, or if you strongly prefer to work remotely, don't tie yourself to one area by including a location.

LinkedIn

Be sure to include your LinkedIn URL on your resume (and any other communications, including the signature block on all of your emails). Chapter 2, Build a Powerful LinkedIn Profile, describes how to create a vanity URL.

SAMPLE RESUME HEADERS

As shown in the following samples, you can be creative in selecting and presenting the information that reflects *you*—the brand you are creating, the look you are seeking—while being professional and clear. Don't mix in too many fonts or special effects in the header of your resume or in the overall document.

D'JANA E. MESSIER *(she/her/hers)*
Boston, MA 02134 | 555-193-2222 | djemessier@gmail.com
https://www.linkedin.com/in/djanamessier

Stephen J. Wilkinson, MS
Greater New York City – 518-388-0538
stephen.j.wilkinson@gmail.com – https://www.linkedin.com/in/sjwilkinson3

Marie D. Lipscomb
mdlipscomb@gmail.com • 692-399-2005
https://www.linkedin.com/in/mdlipscomb

julia perrone   digital branding | customer experience
miami fl 33137 | 786.299.3772 | julia.perrone@gmail.com | www.linkedin.com/in/julia.perrone

DJ Andrews *(they, them, theirs)*
419-381-6755 ■ djandrews@gmail.com ■ https://www.linkedin.com/in/dj-andrews6

2) PROFILE-SUMMARY

This is the content that appears directly below your contact info in the top quarter to top third of page one of your resume. It includes both a **Headline** with keywords and a concise **Profile** or **Summary**—a brief overview of your most relevant qualifications and an introduction to the detailed resume content that will follow.

The Headline and Profile are extremely important resume sections because oftentimes what you say (or *don't* say) here influences whether the reader moves on to the remainder of your resume—your key Education and Experience sections.

This top section of the resume is where you market yourself, promote your strengths and capabilities, show proof of performance (or competency), and give the reader the answer to the question: **Why should they be interested in *you*?**

First of all, they need to know what kind of jobs you're interested in. Are you an aspiring Accountant, a newly qualified Civil Engineer, a Digital Marketing Strategist, or a candidate for jobs in Criminal Justice? Your Headline and subheadings should put readers in the picture and create the appropriate professional framework for everything that follows.

Don't waste valuable real estate by using a heading such as Summary of Qualifications, Profile, or Objective. Instead, announce your professional identity—a piece of information that is much more valuable to your audience and beneficial to you.

Next, create a brief overview that highlights the professional skills and personal attributes that will make you a great employee—*and that differentiate you from other job seekers.*

So how do you choose the right information … and how do you frame this information on your resume?

In this chapter you will find two Worksheets that we designed as helpful tools for pulling out the many different bits of information that you can use in your resume—and in other career messages, too.

Before you dive in, take some time to think about what describes and differentiates you—the capabilities, knowledge, and descriptors that you instantly think of when characterizing yourself. Sometimes it's helpful to consider how others describe you:

- What did a past employer or internship supervisor say about you? Even in part-time jobs or short-term assignments, you likely exhibited characteristics that will carry over to your professional career.
- What have your favorite professors said about your skills, your work in class, maybe even your presentation abilities on a group project?
- How are you known to your friends, family, and other people in your life? What's your reputation? What can you be relied upon to do (or not do)?

Assessments are another very helpful tool for identifying your traits. Beginning on page 32 we provide a list of several assessments, some free of charge, that you can take online to generate many different strengths and descriptors.

The worksheets that follow will help you in considering your strengths and experiences from a number of different perspectives. When you've completed all of your pre-work, think of all the information and insights you'll have for writing your Profile-Summary—and, in fact, *all* of the sections of your resume!

- Worksheet responses

- Your answers to the questions on pages 2, 3, and 8 of this chapter

- Findings and insights from any assessment tools you completed

You'll find that the insights and information you uncovered will also help you with your LinkedIn and cover letter. The framework we recommend, and that we share with you in dozens of examples throughout this book, focuses on areas to emphasize when telling your story about what you have done. These are the things that will help you stand out in the eyes of someone who might be in a position to refer you, introduce you, or—yes—even hire you.

Worksheet #1 for Creating Your Resume HEADLINE and PROFILE-SUMMARY

To get you started, we have provided prompts for a number of questions. Feel free to take your answers in any direction you choose!

Related to Your Target Jobs
- **What kind of job are you looking for? Be specific!** *(Auditor position with a Big 4 accounting firm … Entry-level sales job in the medical or pharmaceutical industry … U/X designer role with an e-commerce company … Journalist, digital marketing, or other writing job … Internship in government, ideally in Washington DC … Elementary teacher in an inner-city public school, etc.)*

PRO TIP: If you are unsure of what you'd like to do, take a step back from writing your resume. Investigate different types of jobs that interest you. Talk to people who hold a variety of jobs and ask them what they do, what they like, what they find frustrating. (Your parents' friends who are well established in different careers can be great sources for this information.) Review job postings and see how you match up against the required skills. Talk to career advisors in your college career or success center—they can help you with assessments, career guidance, and contacts with alumni who can be good information sources for you.

When you've made even a tentative career decision (you're not locking yourself into one career forever! You just need a place to start), come back and complete this worksheet with that particular goal in mind.

- **What alternative job titles might be used for similar roles?** *(This question can help you broaden your headline/subheadings to appeal to a larger audience.)*

_____

_____

_____

Related to Strengths/Characteristics

- **If I were to call your supervisor and ask what stood out to them about you, what would they say?** *(Very reliable, dependable—could always be counted on to take an extra shift or stay late when needed … worked well independently … quickly learned new skills, etc.)*

_____

_____

_____

- **If you were introducing yourself to a prospective employer and you could tell her just *three key strengths* you believe accurately describe you, what would you say?** *(Think of such modifiers as hard working, caring, detail oriented, "no quit," competitive, determined, and so forth—and then know the examples you'd share to demonstrate these strengths.)*

_____

_____

_____

- **What's one positive thing people have always said about you that you know is absolutely true?** *("She can always be counted on to do what she says—if she makes a commitment, she honors it." "He is very detail oriented with an incredible need to do anything he touches accurately and with excellence.")*

_____

_____

_____

- **What would people be surprised to know about you?** *(This is not a trick question! Sometimes it evokes responses that may interest an employer or illuminate job skills. Two examples: "As a hobby when I was in middle school, I took my interest in HTML/tech and started building websites for my friends—one* *of them had a landscaping business for the neighborhood and another had a garage band." Or: "I have a photographic memory for baseball stats for my favorite team.")*

_____

_____

_____

Related to Work, Class, Athletics, or Extracurricular Experience
- **What impact did your work have on the team, organization, and/or customers?**

_____

_____

_____

> **PRO TIP: Use the CAR story format described on pages 2–3 as you address these questions.** Following the structure of Challenge-Action-Result, you'll be prompted to tell a complete story that includes helpful details and often ends with a specific result. You'll find your CAR stories incredibly useful not only in writing your resume and other career documents, but in interviewing. You'll have a leg up on other candidates who only talk in generalities, and you'll be providing evidence that you are a problem solver who gets results.

- **In what ways did you contribute to the team?** *(Were you assigned to a project or specific role where what you did brought value to the overall objective? Did you step up to fill an unexpected need? Did you find ways to make other team members more successful?)*

_____

_____

_____

- **How did the organization benefit from your work?** *(Did the company make a big sale as a result of a proposal that you helped put together? Did your research help identify a new market for the company's products? Did you solve a technical problem that was causing staff to lose valuable time?)*

_____

_____

_____

- **What was the overall purpose behind the work you did?** *(Talk about **how** and **why** you did something, not just what you did.)*

_____

_____

_____

- **What problems did you solve?** *(Be specific. "Two months of backfiling had piled up when a staff member went on maternity leave. I organized all the files and then came up with a simple method for tracking documents in process throughout the department that helped improve efficiency." "The department wanted to increase its visibility on social media, but there was always a last-minute rush to get things out. I started using Hootsuite to pre-schedule social media postings, and I trained 2 staff members to do it after I left. As a result, they avoided last-minute rushes and were able to maintain a consistent online presence.")*

_____

_____

_____

- **How was success measured in your role?** *(Were you expected to meet specific goals? Did a supervisor share results with you or let you know that you had done a good job—or where you needed improvement?)*

_____

_____

_____

PRO TIP: Don't be too humble when describing something you've done or accomplished. Include details that will make your story credible, and take credit for results that you achieved or *helped* achieve. It's the fine art of "tooting your own horn, not blowing it"—a subtle difference. In other words, you want to share honestly what you have achieved without bragging about yourself.

- **What would fall apart at your job if you weren't there? How would it impact the organization?** *(Think of the work you were doing. Would there have been a consequence—for instance, lack of response to customer emails or improper call routing or handling—if you weren't there doing the work?)*

_____

_____

_____

- **Looking back at your XYZ position/internship, what are you most proud of accomplishing?** *(What mattered most about this experience? This can align with what you liked most about the position.)*

_____

_____

_____

- **How would your internship supervisor describe your contributions?** *(This could relate to specific details of assignments/projects you were involved with.)*

_____

_____

_____

- **What did you learn about yourself through that experience?** *(Your response can be positive or not— i.e., "I thought I'd like the field of architecture—but from this internship, I learned that about 90% of their work is inside an office, handling tons of paper and files … I want to be outside more, working with people.")*

_____

_____

_____

- **Quantify statements as much as possible.** *(Include numbers and percentages to help tell the story. You won't always know specific numbers for results, but details make your stories more memorable and credible.)*

_____

_____

_____

- **Were there ways you went above and beyond your job description?** *(This can relate to taking on extra responsibilities, helping other employees, etc.)*

_____

_____

_____

- **How did you select your major?**

_____

_____

_____

- **When you were a senior in high school, what did you think you wanted to do after completing college? Has that changed?**

_____

_____

_____

Related to Activities
- **What do you do in your free time, outside of school?** *(Many times, responses to questions in this section create openings that are useful in your LinkedIn profile or e-notes/cover letters.)*

_____

_____

_____

- **What's your favorite interest or hobby?**

_____

_____

_____

- **If you could "do anything" for work, what would the ideal job be (no matter how unrealistic)?**

_____

_____

_____

Career Centers Say ...

"When I ask, 'what did you do and how well did you do it?', I'll often get, 'they asked me to do this ...' But that's not what we want to know. Instead, 'what were you able to accomplish for the organization and, most importantly, how well did you do it?'

"I'll push for a description of the challenges they faced ... what actions they took ... and what the outcomes or results were (even if they weren't good)—the classic CAR story information. But because many students haven't begun to think of telling their story like that, they need to be encouraged to tell the story of how they brought value to the organization, because that's why someone may want to hire them. I also advise that while they should include things such as being a lifeguard or camp counselor or yearbook editor on their resumes, that's not where they need to go into a lot of detail."

— Carla Coury, Interim Executive Director, Career Management Center, A.B. Freeman School of Business, Tulane University

Examples of Resume Headline and Profile-Summary

You have many options for the style and format of your resume Profile-Summary. We share several examples below, and you'll find 90+ additional samples in the Portfolio beginning on page 115.

Things to keep in mind: Your **Headline** should typically be one or two lines at most and, as discussed previously, authentically present possible title(s), target role(s), keywords depicting possible fields or industries of interest, and a few words that describe your value proposition: what makes you uniquely qualified.

The **Profile-Summary** itself is fairly short—perhaps a brief paragraph or two and/or a few quick bullet points. Again, you'll find many examples in this book to get you thinking of some of the skills, strengths, capabilities, experiences, or success stories you might choose to highlight.

As you write and edit your headline and profile, continuously ask yourself: **What will be of greatest interest to employers for the jobs I'm targeting?** You do want to express your authentic strengths and personality, but don't forget that the ultimate purpose of your resume is to interest an employer and land an interview. Keeping this focus in mind will help you pare down unnecessary or less-relevant details so that your profile is sharp and succinct.

PRO TIP: A resume is never a one-size-fits-all document, but you don't have to start from scratch every time. Once you've created your **foundational resume,** you can easily tweak it to fit a specific job target or audience—often with just a few adjustments to the headline and possibly the profile. Save and label all of these multiple versions so that you can quickly put them into action whenever needed.

SAMPLE RESUME PROFILE-SUMMARIES

The eight samples on the following pages showcase very different content, chosen to represent the diverse job targets, fields of study, and unique strengths and value of each new graduate.

Candidate: <u>Art Sales</u> — Customer-Centric & Results-Oriented Professional
Capitalizing on Extensive Art & Interior Design Experience: Modern & Trend-Conscious, Yet Classic

Goal-driven design professional with exceptional record of cultivating and building productive relationships—essential in pivoting to **Professional Art & Design Sales** position. Deep experience working with clients and the trades with particular expertise working with contemporary and abstract art. Reputation for inspiring confidence in clients, establishing rapport quickly, and being easy to work with.

➤ Strong account management background—"professionally persistent" in getting to the "yes!"
➤ Methodical and accountable—with outstanding follow-through skills.
➤ Technology: AutoCAD, Adobe Photoshop, Indesign, Microsoft Office, Mac Pages/Keynote, Filemaker Pro.

GRADUATE NURSE

Targeting: New RN Residency — Med-Surg Nurse — Oncology Unit Nurse

Newly Qualified Nurse (BSN December 2022) eager to begin professional nursing career.
Nurses' Aide since 2020, with 2 years of front-line service to patients on an oncology unit and a reputation for above-and-beyond assistance to both patients and clinical staff.

Registered Nurse status—NCLEX planned for early 2023
Certified Nurse Aide, State of Colorado—2020–Present

Full resume shown on page 149.

Candidate: Entry-level Software Developer with Aspirant Technologies

Deep interest in joining Aspirant—transitioning ability to quickly learn/master new skills with proven background in web development and experience using Javascript and Linux.

✓ **Demonstrated record** of quick immersion in challenging projects and delivering solutions—whether in software development (designed/developed web application to track $80K in rental gear for Northwestern U. Outing Club) or engineering (played instrumental role as engineering intern with several manufacturing companies—developing solutions to challenging problems).

✓ **BSME** (Northwestern University) complemented by 9+ months of intensive programming/web development learning with Dynamic Tech Industries.

Targeting Role as Summer Associate / Legal Intern | 2nd Year Law Student
Areas of Interest: Risk Compliance – Litigation – Real Estate – Corporate/In-house Counsel

Highly motivated law student with range of experiences including U.S. Attorney's office, Attorney General's office, and District Court internships. Detail-oriented and methodical—ardent in pursuit of solutions to complex problems.

Creative catalyst and innovative problem-solver with a deeply collaborative leadership style. Expertly draw in all stakeholders and coalesce ideas to determine best courses of action.

Aspiring
DATA ANALYST | ECONOMIC ANALYST
Recent graduate (BS Economics) with skill and passion for identifying, analyzing, and communicating data insights—using data to tell a story that informs and influences organizational strategy and decision-making.

Skills and Strengths
- **Data Research, Analysis, Visualization, and Presentation:** Experienced at identifying and mining data sources to develop accurate and meaningful analyses for businesses and nonprofits.
- **Technology:** Skilled and experienced in using Excel, PowerPoint, R, SQL, Stata, and SAS.
- **Communication:** Effective in sales roles (including cold-calling) and team projects, using both data and persuasion to influence opinions and drive action.

Full resume shown on page 218.

Engineering Project Manager | Mechanical Engineer

Results-oriented and hard-working Mechanical Engineer and Professional Designer with solid internship experiences, exceptional work ethic, and proven ability to quickly learn and contribute to organizational goals.

- ❖ Expertise includes schematic design and engineered solutions, customizing add-on mounting/installation of systems to optimize equipment utilization in manufacturing environment.
- ❖ Technology: Microsoft Office, SOLIDWORKS, Arduino, Quartus, MATLAB, Mastercam 9; Language: C++.

Digital Marketing | Project Management | Content Creation | Brand Strategy | Social Media

Creative Project Management & Marketing Professional with background that combines innovative approaches and experience in accurately interpreting and translating client intentions with effective results.

Quick study in mastering new technology | Solid work ethic and "above-and-beyond" approach to every assignment

Select Marketing Projects
- **GLOBAL MARKETING** … Led team that analyzed market/competition for new soap launch in Brazil and created comprehensive marketing plan, distribution/pricing strategy, and multipronged promotional tactics (Spring 2023).
- **DONALD & SONS DELI** … Collaborated with Boston, MA, business to develop expanded social media presence on Instagram/Twitter/Facebook designed to increase local patronage among area university students (Spring 2023).
- **THE PLACE** … Designed radio and print advertising for Wakefield, MA, restaurant/bar. Boosted traffic and attracted more customers (Fall 2022).

──ASPIRING AUDITOR/ACCOUNTANT──
Competitive | Disciplined | Hard Working | Accountable
- → **Academic and athletic high performer** known for determination, work ethic, and dedication to continuous improvement.
- → **Goal achiever** who approaches challenges with discipline, effective time management, and a daily commitment to accomplishing small details that are the foundation for major wins.
- → **Quiet leader** able to inspire teammates to work together, work hard, and improve performance.

Full resume shown on page 211.

3) SKILLS AND EXPERTISE

In reviewing resumes, employers—and, just as importantly, resume-scanning programs—look for specific skills that match the job description. You will probably find it natural to incorporate those skills into your descriptions of jobs and internships, achievements, and class projects. But it can be helpful to also include a list of specific skills, knowledge, and expertise you possess that make you a great fit for the job you're pursuing.

As well, a Skills list offers you an opportunity to quickly tweak your resume to precisely match the skills called for in a job posting. Of course, you want to be totally truthful. We're not suggesting that you include skills you don't possess, but we do recommend that you take the time to compare your wording with the job posting and see if light editing can improve the match.

Several of the Profile-Summary samples on the previous pages include skills in a variety of formats—as a subheading, in a bullet point, or as a footer to the summary. Another option would be for you to segment your skills into a specific, separate list, as shown in the following samples.

SAMPLE SKILLS LISTS

TECHNICAL PROFILE

Programming Languages: Python, Java, Powershell | **Operating Systems:** Windows, Linux, VMWare ESXi
Development Tools: Pycharm, IntelliJIdea, Git
Defensive Sofware: CrowdStrike Falcon, Splunk, ProofPoint, Phantom, Logrhythm, Palo Alto, Firewall, Varonis, Securonix, Microsoft ATA | **Offensive Software:** Metasploit, CrackMapExec, Bloodhound, Burpsuite, John The Ripper

---

Technology Skills:

▶ Ruby, Ruby on Rails, Git, Heroku, AWS, SQL (MySQL, PostgreSQL), Javascript, Angular, HTML, CSS, SASS, REST API, Agile, Test Driven Development, Bootstrap, Linux (from Open Source Web Development Curriculum/The Odin Project)

▶ MATLAB, Python, Java, SOLIDWORKS | Microsoft Office Suite | Arduino Electronic Prototyping

---

Demonstrated Skills
- **Competent, Compassionate Care**—Blending professional skill with kindness and empathy.
- **Critical Thinking**—Demonstrating good judgment and providing solutions to identified problems.
- **Teamwork**—Supporting ultimate goal of patient care by assisting teammates and volunteering for extra duties.
- **Verbal and Written Communication**—Emphasizing clarity and timeliness.
- **Process Efficiency and Effectiveness**—Removing obstacles and saving time to focus on critical care functions.

Full resume shown on page 149.

> ### *Career Centers Say ...*
>
> "Something I remind students: They can't solve all of the problems in the world immediately. In other words, be realistic *(they aren't able to leap tall buildings in a single bound)*. I say to them, 'keep in mind that you are a student, and a prospective employer is not expecting the expertise of someone who has been working in the field with many years of experience."
>
> — *Chaim Shapiro, Director of the Office for Student Success, Touro University*

4) EDUCATION

Because you are a new or soon-to-be graduate, your education is likely your strongest qualification and what employers are most interested in. For that reason, we recommend positioning your Education immediately after your Summary-Profile. Later, when you have one or more professional roles under your belt, you can elevate Experience to this prominent position and move Education toward the bottom of the resume.

Academic Information

Start with your college/university name and degree information, including:

- Full name of the university; city and state
- Name of the college (if relevant) within the university
- Full name of degree
- Major; Minor (if any); Concentration (if any)
- Date of graduation (year or month/year) *or* anticipated date of graduation
- Honors (i.e., *Summa cum Laude, With Honors, With Highest Honors, With Distinction, Dean's List*)
- GPA (if 3.3 or higher, as discussed on page 22)

SAMPLE DEGREE FORMAT

> **UNIVERSITY OF TEXAS,** Austin, TX | **Bachelor of Science, Business Management**
> - **Minor: Accounting** | Dean's List Standing (all semesters) | GPA: 3.8
> - **Anticipated Completion:** May 2024

Projects and Courses

Many college students gain valuable experience through team projects, capstones, special research studies, and other in-depth academic experiences. It can be especially valuable to include these details on your resume if you don't have relevant internship or co-op experience.

While it's not necessary to list courses in your major, you might want to do so as a way to authentically embed keywords related to your target job or industry—especially if you don't yet have relevant work experience where you can include these terms.

SAMPLE PROJECTS LIST

EDUCATION

BS Economics | University of Colorado, Boulder, CO | 2023

SENIOR CAPSTONE PROJECT: Senior Seminar in Economics
- Independently identified study topic—the effects of climate change on the Colorado ski industry—and created project plan encompassing data research, analysis, and presentation.
- Researched and identified statistical sources (ski-town tax income and CO_2 emissions) and transformed into data using regressions in R and Excel.
- Analyzed findings, prepared report, and presented to the university Economics Department.
- *Of note: Earned "Best Presentation" recognition and grade of A.*

EXECUTIVE CASE STUDY: Entrepreneurship (Amazon Prime)
- Member of 4-person team conducting semester-long research and SWOT analysis to identify potential new markets and services to expand market share for Amazon Prime.
- Brainstormed ideas and analyzed economics to determine viability and profitability.
- Created and delivered presentation to local business executives.
- *Of note: Our concept—live-streamed remote concerts—became an offering for Amazon Prime and other broadcasters in response to the COVID crisis. Entire team received A grade.*

Full resume shown on page 218.

SAMPLE COURSES LIST

BENTLEY UNIVERSITY • Waltham, MA — **Bachelor of Science Degree** *(antic. graduation: 2023); GPA: 3.72*

Major: **Economics** || Minor: **Finance** || Annual Scholarship Recipient

Coursework in Major:

– Financial Accounting	– Quantitative Methods in Business	– Legal Foundations
– Business & Global Economy	– Organizational Behavior in Business	– Real Estate and Society
– Marketing Management	– Functions of the Capitalist Enterprise	– Introduction to Ethics
– Introduction to Economics	– Introduction to Psychology	– Introduction to Finance

---

Extracurriculars

Extracurriculars and other academic involvement can be included here, in the Education section. Or, if your activities are extensive, they may warrant a dedicated section that can be positioned further down in the resume. You'll find further discussion and examples of this on pages 29–30.

SAMPLE EXTRACURRICULARS

Education

BS Business | MICHIGAN STATE UNIVERSITY, East Lansing, MI   Anticipated December 2023
Major: Business Management • Minor: Marketing • GPA: 3.3/4.0

Athletics: 3-year Starter, MSU Soccer Team
- Instrumental performer on 2020 and 2021 teams that advanced to the NCAA tournament.
- Honed individual skills and motivated teammates to reach top performance.
- Maintained a high grade point average while balancing academic schedule and 20+ hours of weekly soccer activities.

Leadership: Member of MSU Soccer Leadership Group
- One of 8 teammates selected by head coach as part of inaugural Leadership Group.
- Met weekly and provided input on a range of topics—game strategy, team relationship building, team management.

Full resume shown on page 193.

Study Abroad

Study abroad is an invaluable learning experience and often a topic for ice-breaking conversation during interviews. Here is an example of study abroad experience featured in the Education section.

SAMPLE STUDY ABROAD

Education & Professional Development

DUKE UNIVERSITY | Durham, NC
Bachelor of Arts degree (2023)

➤ **Triple Major:** International Political Economy — Spanish Language — Literature
➤ **GPA:** Cumulative 3.7; Spanish 3.9
➤ **Honors:** Duke Dean's List; Eduardo D. Perrone Spanish Achievement Award (2022)

STUDY ABROAD, Institute for the International Education of Students (IES) | Madrid, Spain

➤ Spring 2021; also served as IES Ambassador to the Madrid Program.

Multiple Colleges

What if you attended more than one college? Perhaps you transferred from another institution or completed an associate's degree at another school. You certainly aren't required to show all of your institutions on your resume. The choice is yours. If the information will be beneficial to you in any way, include it. If it's not really relevant, feel free to omit it. Here are a few general guidelines:

- If you completed an associate's degree at another school, consider including it if it expands your technical or professional knowledge *or* if you earned it at a highly regarded institution *or* if the school is located in your target region.

- If you completed only a semester or so of credits, you don't need to take up space on your resume with this information. Again, though, if the details add value to your qualifications, feel free to include them.
- In either case, if you had a stellar GPA or earned other recognition or commendations, don't hesitate to include these details on your resume.

SAMPLE MULTIPLE COLLEGES

EDUCATION

UNIVERSITY OF MICHIGAN | Ann Arbor, MI
- Candidate, **Bachelor of Science, Computer Science** *(May 2024 graduation)* | GPA: 3.74

WASHTENAW COMMUNITY COLLEGE | Ann Arbor, MI
- **Associate in Applied Science, Computer Science and Information Technology** *(May 2022)* | GPA: 3.87
- Earned **Computer Systems Technology (CTCSTC) Certificate**

PRO TIP: Wondering whether or not to show your GPA? Generally, include your GPA if it is higher than 3.3 or 3.5. If it's lower, omit it altogether. Consider showing your **GPA in major** if it is higher than your overall GPA.

You may be asked about your GPA during the interview process, but it's better to be invited to interview—based on your strong resume—than eliminated before you even get in the door. We address how to answer this interview question in Chapter 5.

Additional Tips for Education

- **If you didn't finish college and are no longer studying,** show all of the same information as described for this section, but be clear about the level of education you completed.
  - *Example:*
    UNIVERSITY OF MICHIGAN | Ann Arbor, MI — Matriculated in **Bachelor of Science degree program, Computer Science** (completed 2 years) | GPA: 3.4
  - *Example:*
    Northeastern University, Boston, MA
    Completed 80% of credits toward **BFA in Game Art and Animation** • 3.8 GPA
- **Do NOT show the range of actual years that you were in college.** Rather, show only the year that you graduated (or anticipate graduating). However, if you completed your degree in less than four years, consider mentioning that as a bullet point under the degree/major/minor:
  - *Example:*
    Completed 4-year degree program in 3.5 years
- **What about SAT/ACT scores?** If you are a current student seeking an internship, your standardized test scores may be valuable to include—provided they are strong. Once you've graduated, there is no need to list these scores.

- *Example:*

Standardized Test Scores:
SAT ... Total   **1520** || *Math: 740* | *Evidence-Based Reading/Writing: 780*
ACT ... Composite   **33** || *English: 34* | *Math: 33* | *Reading: 33* | *Science: 32*

- **Should you mention high school?** If your high school experiences are significant—for example, you graduated as valedictorian, earned other honors, or held leadership positions—you may want to include them, briefly, in Education after your college/university details. Just be careful that your high school accomplishments and activities don't overshadow your more recent college experiences.

  - *Example:*

MIDLAND REGIONAL HIGH SCHOOL • Austin, TX *(2019 Graduate)*

- ACADEMIC HONORS
  National Honor Roll, National Junior Classical League Latin Honor Society, National Spanish Honor Society, National Society of High School Scholars, National Who's Who High School Registry

- ATHLETICS
  Captain, Outdoor Track Team; Indoor/Outdoor Track Team; Midland Football; 6 varsity letters
  Most Valuable Player, All-Area Third Team Indoor Track, Athlete-of-the-Month, Coach's Award

---

5) WORK EXPERIENCE

Create a section under Education for Experience. You might subdivide this into Work Experience and Internship Experience (or Co-op Experience)—or you can group everything (paid, unpaid, and internship experience) in reverse-chronological order under a single Professional Experience heading.

Worksheet #2 for Creating Your Resume EXPERIENCE Section

Use the following framework to capture details of each job, internship, co-op role, and volunteer position (including summer and part-time). The examples that follow show different approaches for presenting this information on your resume.

Before you begin, look back to Worksheet #1 in this chapter. Those questions and your responses—including your CAR stories—are likely to prove helpful as you flesh out details of each of your experiences.

Company Name

City

State

Month and Year of Employment or Volunteer Position

Title

What was the company's primary business? *(insurance, retail store, restaurant, bank, real estate, technology, manufacturer/product, etc.)*

_____

What department or aspect of the business did you work in? *(customer service, call handling, administration/paperwork, assembly, shadowing broker/principal, etc.)*

_____

What were the top two or three things you were asked to do? Were they ongoing projects or assignments? Did every day look the same, or were the responsibilities varied? Be as specific as possible. *(If it is obvious what your job was—Server in a family restaurant—include only exceptional details: "Selected to train all new team members.")*

_____

_____

_____

_____

_____

Are there any specific achievements you can claim? Did you fix a problem, start a new process, contribute to a successful team project, resolve a recurring customer issue, or otherwise make a difference? Be specific and use the CAR format to describe these achievements.

_____

_____

_____

_____

_____

_____

_____

What do you think stood out positively about your performance and contributions?

_____

_____

_____

_____

What did your supervisor say about the work you did?

_____

_____

_____

_____

If you were invited back for a second (or third) summer/winter break, be sure to mention that and include the date ranges *(i.e., Summers, 2020 & 2021).*

What else would be important to know about this role? What did you love about it? What did you dislike (if anything)?

_____

_____

_____

_____

_____

_____

Repeat this information as many times as needed to cover all of your work experience, internships, co-op jobs, and volunteer roles.

SAMPLE EXPERIENCE SECTIONS
The next two pages show examples of Experience sections that integrate internship/co-op, part-time jobs, and even volunteer experience into a cohesive summary of valuable work skills.

Education & Internship Experience

UNIVERSITY OF HARTFORD, BARNEY SCHOOL OF BUSINESS | West Hartford, CT
- **Bachelor of Science, Marketing** (anticipated 2023)… *Top 10% of business schools worldwide, AACSB Accreditation*
- **Scholar-Athlete 2021–Present** (Dean's List) • **National Scholars Honor Society** • **America East Academic Honor Roll**
- **Division I Men's Varsity Cross-Country, Indoor & Outdoor Track & Field Teams;** all 4 years; set Indoor 5K record.

NBC CONNECTICUT-NBC 30/WVIT | West Hartford, CT … **June–Aug. 2022**
Sports Department Intern: Directly assisted Kevin Nathan, NBC's Sports Department Director.

Professional Marketing Internships

Marketing Intern, Marketing Communications Team	DYNAMIC | Boston, MA | May–Aug 2022

Recruited for marketing team for company providing prospecting, remarketing, and merchandising solutions for auto, travel, finance, retail, and CPG brands and agencies. Delivered cohesive, high-end, on-brand look to projects, eBooks, and blogs. Managed marketing communications and event budget.

→ **Restructured sales database, optimizing searches:** Proposed combining 3 different systems, garnered executive approval, and moved assets to Google Drive. Created consistent nomenclature and hierarchy—currently in testing for Q4 launch.
→ **Supported numerous events and conducted extensive event analysis,** identifying qualified leads, conversion rates, marketing stage, deals won, and ROI.
→ **Managed detailed content/social calendar;** designed Marketing Open House slide deck for VP, Marketing.
→ **Established new leads,** leveraging Marketo to source and prospect Dynamic event attendees.
→ **Managed social media and 4+ weekly blogs,** posting on Facebook, Twitter, and LinkedIn and designing thumbnail/banner images.

Digital Marketing & Social Media Intern	NORTH SHORE EVENTS COMPANY | Beverly, MA | May–Aug 2021

Hired to bring HubSpot Inbound Marketing expertise to event planning/marketing services firm serving Fortune 500/top corporate clients: Bvlgari Parfums, Nestle Waters, MDG Awards, Jack Brewer Foundation, United Nations.

→ **Provided comprehensive analysis of North Shore Events' digital identity.** Developed white paper and presented PowerPoint to principals.
→ **Managed social media**—Facebook, Twitter, Instagram, Pinterest, LinkedIn. Instituted hashtag trends; blogged weekly. Implemented social content calendar, instilling consistency across social media channels.
→ **Conducted extensive research** for Sr. Managing Partner on industry conferences/publications that accepted guest contributors. Submitted content/synopses to Entrepreneur, Bplans, Women Grow Business, and YFS Magazine; article published Dec. 2021, Bplans.
→ **Planned and executed** *Bankstreet Golf Invitational*, a 70-player benefit tournament. Handled event promotion and social media.

Professional Experience

EXXONMOBIL—**Process and Optimization Co-Op**   Houston, TX | January 2022–August 2022

Gained hands-on engineering experience within refinery processing units. Learned and used 2 new software programs (Tableau and Alteryx) to complete 10 projects, including:

- Performed and analyzed Cooling Water Tower efficiency and pressure survey for Blowdown line piping system.
- Conducted Trasar study and analyzed Cooling Water Tower chemical distribution.
- Developed Tableau Dashboards for Gasoline Metrics and Product Offtake.

Supervisor Endorsement: "Alex Riordan was a Day One asset to the ExxonMobil Refinery Team. His technical knowledge, attention to detail, and positive attitude helped accelerate several projects to a successful conclusion … He tackled a very challenging set of tasks with zeal." **Earned top intern rating (#1 on 5-point scale).**

PRIMO CHEMICAL—**Technical Center Co-Op**   Buenos Aires, Argentina | January 2020–July 2020

Pursued international co-op opportunity, seeking a challenging professional and cultural workplace.

- Developed the Stain Test Protocol on polymer products for the Electronic Market.
- Researched and developed a dimensional analysis study on polymers for the Electronic Market.
- Worked cross-culturally with colleagues in Argentina and at other Primo R&D centers in France, India, China, and US.

Supervisor Endorsement: "Alex displayed a maturity and autonomy that are very rare among university students … He identified very quickly the priorities and challenges of his missions and provided high quality work … Alex demonstrated an excellent ability to adapt to a multi-cultural work environment." **Invited to return for internship the following year.**

NORTHEASTERN UNIVERSITY—**Chemistry Teaching Assistant**   Fall 2020–Present

One of a handful of undergraduates chosen as Teaching Assistants, roles primarily held by graduate students.

Full resume shown on page 168.

EDUCATION & ENGINEERING EXPERIENCE

WORCESTER POLYTECHNIC INSTITUTE • Worcester, MA   May 2023 Graduate *(antic.)*
College of Engineering, Technology, and Architecture

- ➔ **Bachelor of Science Degree, Civil Engineering** (Dean's List Standing)
- ➔ Member, **Sigma Alpha Pi,** National Society of Leadership and Success
- ➔ Member, **Massachusetts Society of Civil Engineers** and **American Society of Civil Engineers**

DONOVAN & THOMAS | Pittsfield, MA   Dec. 2022–Jan. 2023
Engineering Intern | Directly supported Senior Hydrogeologist; used CAD extensively in project designs/revisions.

- ➔ Worked on **plan designs** for Massachusetts public/private schools and assisted in writing **sedimentation and erosion control plan** for Baker Quarry in Stockbridge, MA.
- ➔ **Researched maps, submitted permit applications, pulled USGS maps, corrected topographic maps,** and handled **water samples** for laboratory testing. On behalf of company, made visits to various state agencies (DOT, DEP) as well as town halls and project subcontractors. Organized bridge records for municipalities.
- ➔ Accompanied engineering teams during **water quality testing;** participated in field test of **well-yielding levels.**
- ➔ Attended **project team meetings** with engineering staff and **on-site meetings** with project/site owners.

ENGINEERS WITHOUT BORDERS USA PROJECT • Abheypur, India   Jan. 2022
Hydrology Project Engineer

- ➔ Selected as 1 of 5 engineering students who installed EWB-sanctioned rainwater harvesting and filtration project.
- ➔ Profiled in Autumn 2022 issue of In*Flow*-Line magazine (American/Massachusetts Water Works Associations).

Full resume shown on page 164.

6) MILITARY

Military experience can either appear as a separate section on the resume or can be included as a bullet point in the Profile-Summary. Military details, such as ROTC participation, may also be featured as part of the Education section, as shown in this example:

SAMPLE MILITARY INCLUDED WITH EDUCATION

EDUCATION——————————————————————————————————————

GEORGETOWN UNIVERSITY, Washington, DC
- **Bachelor of Science, Mathematics** (anticipated May 2024)
- **Midshipman, Naval ROTC** — Completed mini boot camp, Great Lakes Naval Base
- **Naval ROTC Liaison** — Georgetown University Student Veterans Association

Military Experience Attained Prior to College

Some new graduates have prior military experience that may range from a few years to a few decades. That experience can be a valuable differentiator. It may bolster professional skills and experience, if service was related to the new degree and career goals. And it undoubtedly builds character, skills, and experience—such as discipline, leadership, teamwork and collaboration, international travel, unflappability, technology skills—that add value in the workplace.

SAMPLE MILITARY SUMMARY-PROFILE AND STANDALONE SECTION

In this example, prior experience in the Air Force relates to recent education (BS in Aerospace Engineering) and current goal of a career in Avionics. Military experience is mentioned in the Headline and Summary and then expanded in a separate section further down in the resume (below Education and Experience).

Avionics Manager
Distinguished Military Background & B.S., Aerospace Engineering

Accomplished, resourceful, and highly trained/licensed **Avionics Technical Professional** with **4 years of demonstrated expertise with the US Air Force** complemented by **Bachelor of Science degree in Aerospace Engineering** *(graduating May 2023).* Deep knowledge and understanding of aircraft systems. Proven ability to quickly learn/master new skills; effective leadership background.

Education Section follows ... then Experience Section ... then Military Background:

Military Background

UNITED STATES AIR FORCE | 219th Aircraft Maintenance Squadron   Oct. 2015–Aug. 2019
Airman First Class, Electronic Warfare Systems Journeyman *(Honorable Discharge)*

Prior to commencing 4-year undergraduate program, gained deep avionics expertise complemented by proven management/supervisory background and technical experience. Recipient, Airman of the Month *(multiple occasions).*

- Effectively led, supervised, and trained other military personnel to accomplish expected skill levels as electronic warfare journeymen. Promoted into supervisory role as shift leader for shop based on exemplary performance.
- Worked effectively as a team member with broad background in environmental and electrical systems, guidance and control systems, communication systems, and navigation systems. Key skills reading schematic diagrams.
- Orchestrated Missile Warning System upgrades on 4 deploying aircraft; streamlined reconfiguration procedure utilizing existing aircraft hardware in place of overhaul of system cabling. Cut 22-hour standard modification time in half.

7) ADDITIONAL: Extracurriculars, Volunteerism/Community, Certifications, Credentials, Licenses, Affiliations, Memberships, Languages, Personal Details

All of the above categories represent potentially valuable information to include on your resume. You might create separate sections for each, or combine multiple categories into a single section.

How to decide? The more closely your extracurriculars, volunteerism, and miscellaneous information align with your current career goals, the more deserving they are of their own section on the resume. As well, if any of these categories is extensive, it is often best to present the details in its own section.

Let's consider how you might handle each of these categories.

Extracurriculars

One option is to include your extracurriculars in Education—either very briefly or in an expanded format, as shown in the sample on page 21. This approach keeps them within the college experience.

Alternatively, you might create a separate section, formatted similar to your work experience, to showcase major accomplishments, important leadership roles, and other details that bolster your qualifications in the workplace.

Volunteerism/Community

While volunteer activities may not seem to relate to your professional goals, they are important indicators of your character and show how you choose to spend your time. Similar to Extracurriculars, these activities might be included in a miscellaneous section at the bottom or featured in their own section, as you'll see in one example below.

Certifications, Credentials, Licenses

Certifications, credentials, and licenses can be grouped into one section or included in Education, as separate entries under your college details.

Affiliations, Memberships

Affiliations and memberships might be included in Education, if they are connected with your university. Or they can be listed in the miscellaneous/extras section at the bottom.

Languages

Language proficiencies are always valuable to include. You might mention them in a bullet point as part of your Summary-Profile or add them to the final section of the resume. Be clear about your level of proficiency—Bilingual, Fluent, Proficient, Conversational.

Personal Details

Resumes in the United States and Canada should not include personal information such as date of birth, marital status, or nationality; nor should they include a photo. However, you can add some interest and differentiation to your resume by including a detail or two that shows your personality or is a good conversation starter.

Personal details might include hobbies, travel experiences, or interesting activities. Keep these mentions brief—you want to spark interest, not derail an interview (or your candidacy) by over-sharing.

Even if you decide not to amplify any or all of these extras, we recommend that you include them at least briefly. You never know what tidbit will interest someone who's reading your resume, or what experience will resonate with an employer. Taken all together, these additional items round out the picture of you as a qualified candidate with a diversity of life experiences and a history of contribution, involvement, and achievement.

View these examples to get ideas for your own resume. As you'll see in one example, you can combine multiple categories into a single section both to save space and to avoid over-emphasizing these "extras" that are valuable but not as important as relevant experience, education, and professional activities.

SAMPLE EXTRAS

Community / Volunteerism

DELTA DELTA DELTA • Madison, WI   2020–2023
Service Sorority Member / Volunteer • University of Wisconsin
Worked with teams to organize and conduct successful fundraising events (from "Hoops for Hope" and "Trihop" to letter-writing campaigns). Raised as much as $65K for St. Jude Children's Research Hospital.
== One of top 10 fundraisers, individually raising >$6K by including personalized messages in campaign.

KIDS WITHOUT CANCER • Madison, WI   2021–2022
Group Leader (Fundraising) / Club Member • University of Wisconsin
Contributed creative energy to raising funds supporting research at Madison Memorial Hospital.

BAKER ELEMENTARY SCHOOL • Madison, WI   2020
English & Mathematics Tutor
As a volunteer, tutored public school students in Grades 2–4.

ADDITIONAL EXPERIENCE

French Tutor | Springfield University, Department of Modern Languages | Sept. 2021–May 2022
➢ Tutored undergraduate students at all levels of proficiency in French language and literature.

Tutor | Higher Education Opportunity Program [HEOP] | Agawam, MA | Sept. 2020–May 2021
➢ Tutored subjects including French, Philosophy, and English to 7 HEOP students.

Volunteerism

North Branford High School • North Branford, CT
Track & Field Clinic Volunteer (July 2022)

Jump Rope for Heart Day • New Haven, CT
Event Volunteer, Washington Elementary School (mid-July 2020 and 2021)

ADDITIONAL

➔ **Leadership:** Headed Concert Committee (Emory University) and Entertainment Committee (Choate Rosemary Hall High School) that raised funds to support nonprofit groups. Orchestrated ~25 events, led teams as large as 15, and managed details of large-scale performances. Donated more than $50K to worthy charities.

➔ **Languages:** Speak proficient Portuguese and conversational German—completed independent study with Syracuse University teaching assistant/German native, 2020–2021. Studied Latin for 6 years.

➔ **Activities and Interests:** Competed in 9 Olympic-length Triathlons in 2021–2023. Coached Little League baseball for 4 years. Volunteered monthly at St. Francis soup kitchen for 3 years.

Assessment Tools

As we discussed on page 8, assessments can help you identify skills and give you language to describe what you know to be true about yourself. Here's a roundup of readily available tools, including several of our favorites.

VIA Strengths Assessment

The VIA Survey of Character Strengths (VIA stands for "Values in Action") is an instrument that is free of charge and quickly (under 15 minutes) provides details that can assist students in recognizing some of their strengths and characteristics across 24 ranked criteria.

To take the VIA strengths assessment survey, go to the website (below) and set up a free account. Most people find the process to be fun, and the results are straightforward and informative—often affirming, sometimes surprising.

Website: http://www.viacharacter.org

GALLUP® CliftonStrengths

The CliftonStrengths assessment is a tool that can provide a good outline of top talents across 34 different themes along with definitions of those talents.

Website: https://www.gallup.com/cliftonstrengths/en/home.aspx

Strong Interest Inventory®

The Strong Interest Inventory is a tool that categorizes an individual's strengths across six key areas: Realistic, Artistic, Investigative, Social, Enterprising, and Conventional (RAISEC). The instrument also defines personal style preferences across the five categories of work style, learning environment, team orientation, leadership style, and risk taking.

Website: https://www.themyersbriggs.com/en-US/Products-and-Services/Strong

---

Career Centers Say …

"The Strong allows students to build self-awareness for career and life decision-making. It provides reliable and valid insight into students' interests and suggests potential careers that might be a good fit for them."

— *Micall Searles, Career Coach, University of Montana*

YouScience

YouScience is a tool that matches strengths (aptitudes: what someone is "good at") and interests (what someone likes to do) with careers where certain combinations will possibly provide a competitive advantage.

Website: https://www.youscience.com/student-aptitudes/

> ### *Career Centers Say ...*
>
> "YouScience provides students with language for resumes, cover letters, and interviews—helping to describe their strengths and value in a way that is easy for them to access and understand the results."
>
> — *Kate Chroust, Senior Director of Career Services, and Helen Eaton,*
> *Associate Director of Career Services, Endicott College*

Self-Directed Search® Assessment

Useful from the time students are incoming undergraduates until graduation, the SDS begins by helping students to be thoughtful and intentional about their choice of major as it relates to their professional goals. The assessment helps students learn and apply their "Holland Codes" (named for the creator of this theory of personality types and environmental models, John Holland), thus opening up a new library of resources, including O*NET—the U.S. Department of Labor database that is billed as "the nation's primary source of occupational information."

SDS Website: https://self-directed-search.com/53-2/

O*NET: https://www.onetonline.org/

> ### *Career Centers Say ...*
>
> "Career planning is an iterative process, and assessments are one tool that can help students gather new data that can be used to test out possible career ideas."
>
> — *Gretchen Heaton, Dean of Career Development, Bay Path University*

Myers-Briggs® Type Indicator

Endorsed by many university career services professionals, the MBTI is useful in clarifying motivation for work, communication, and leadership style by characterizing 16 distinctive personality types that result from interactions among test-takers' expressed preferences.

Website: https://www.myersbriggs.org/my-mbti-personality-type/mbti-basics/

Other Suggested Tools to Explore

Values Card Sort, Skillscan, and Imagine PhD.

FAQ: Your Questions, Our Answers

"Should my resume be one page or two?"

Take it from the experts: Your resume can be one page *or* two—whatever is needed to best present your unique story and value proposition. Don't think that just because you are a college student or new graduate you "don't have enough material" to warrant more than one page. In fact, we often find that college students have more material to warrant a two-page format than many professionals in their later 20s.

Why is that? At this stage, whether you are seeking an internship or co-op experience or your first/next employment out of school or even grad school admittance, you don't necessarily know which aspects of your background will be most appealing to the reader (decision maker!) of your document.

For example:

- Maybe a **volunteer experience** you show on the second page of your resume resonates with the reader because she, too, was involved with Habitat for Humanity as an undergrad.

- Perhaps a multiyear **summer job** as camp counselor starting in high school and continuing as a freshman or sophomore in college impresses readers with a message about your work ethic.

- **Part-time or full-time seasonal work** (i.e., winter break, summer vacation) teaches valuable work skills, and steady employment indicates that you can be counted on to show up and do your job—basics that many employers have learned not to take for granted!

- It's possible that your **study abroad** involvement is of interest to a company that looks for diverse perspectives or plans to expand internationally.

- Maybe an **extracurricular activity**—even a slightly obscure interest, hobby, or sport—is something the reader's own near-adult child does.

- It is quite likely that if you participated in **band, chorus, performing arts, fine arts, any high school or collegiate team, or an intramural or club sport,** one (or more) of these might connect with the reader in a way that garners a few seconds more of attention and serves as an ice-breaker for conversation.

- And, of course, any appointed, elected, or self-designated **leadership role** is indicative of future leadership potential, so be sure to mention it.

> **PRO TIP: Your Career Center may require a one-page resume or a specific format.** Career centers often present multiple student resumes to prospective employers, and having a similar design and single-page format is helpful. Of course you want to be eligible for opportunities sponsored by the career center, so you'll need to conform and create a resume according to their guidelines. That's fine—but don't let it stop you from creating a separate resume that is perhaps longer and deeper in content and that expresses your personality and your value proposition more clearly. Use the appropriate resume for each specific opportunity.

"What about ATS?"

Applicant Tracking Systems are frequently used by employers to screen candidate resumes. The software can be programmed to search for candidates using specific keywords and keyword phrases selected by the hiring authority. Keywords might reflect specific skills, job titles, years of experience, degrees, geographic locations, and other criteria that the hiring manager considers important for that particular job.

As a candidate, you won't know which of the many ATS is being used by a particular company or which unique keywords will be employed; therefore, the optimal strategy is to write a resume that authentically embeds keywords aligned with the role you are seeking, positioning yourself in a way that conveys your experience, education, and strengths. As well, you'll want to carefully review each job posting and tweak your resume, if necessary, to match specific keywords—assuming that you do have the specific skill or other parameter being sought.

All of the techniques we share throughout this chapter—along with the portfolio of 90+ samples in this book—are designed to work effectively with ATS. As you'll learn about job search in Chapter 4, your best bet will always be networking and being introduced for job opportunities. However, as you create your resume content and design, follow these guidelines to give yourself the greatest likelihood of sailing through a resume-scanning system.

- Do not use resume **templates** or design software such as Canva to produce your resume. While these tools can create beautiful-looking documents, in most cases they are not formatted to meet ATS restrictions. (If you love a Canva resume, create a separate text version for uploading and share your beautiful document with contacts and during interviews.)

- You may use any **font** and any **colors** that you like.

- You may use attributes such as **underscore, bold, italics, different sized fonts,** and other enhancements.

- Any **graphics** that you include will not be read by ATS but will not affect how your resume is scored—the system simply skips over the graphics and reads the text.

- If you choose to use them, understand how the system reads **tables** (from left to right across each row, one row at a time) and **columns** (down one complete column, then down the next column). Format your resume appropriately so that content is read in the correct order.

- Do not use **Text Boxes**—by this we mean using the "Insert Text Box" feature in MS Word, Apple Pages, and other word processors. Although this is a convenient way to place text on a page, the text box will be treated as a graphic and the contents will not be read.

- Position your **name and contact information** at the top of the document and not in a header or footer, which will not be read by the ATS.

"I don't really think I've got anything special to share."

Take it from us: We've written hundreds of resumes for new graduates, and every single individual had something special and unique to share. We are confident that you do, too.

Start with the facts. Plug in each of the components you do know—where you are going to school, your major, class projects, extracurricular activities, and so on. Do the same for your various experiences, starting with co-op or internship experience and even going back to high school part-time jobs and volunteer activities.

Once you have a fact-based framework, go back to pages 2–3, 9–14, and 23–25 and ask yourself all of the questions designed to elicit talents and skills, experiences, achievements, success stories, and other distinguishing details. View the 90+ samples in this book to see what others have highlighted and how they've positioned their diverse activities and experiences.

As you add flesh to the bare bones of your chronology, you'll find it easier to build relevant content and create a resume that defines and showcases *you*.

"What if I have no extracurriculars, no clubs or sports?"

Think of what you've done in each of your courses, especially the ones that are in your major and/or that you enjoyed the most. What were some of the special projects? Often they are the source of skill-building experiences that go beyond the assignment—such as developing collaboration skills, stepping up and leading the project, coming up with a great idea, solving a technical problem, assisting a professor with labs or experiments—and so much more.

Another powerful question to ask yourself is, "How do I spend my free time?" Often we find that students who have done "nothing" have, in fact, done a lot! It is simply outside the usual framework of school, sports, clubs, and part-time jobs. As an example, one of our sons was extremely active in a garage band all through high school and college. That experience, while not typical to include on a resume, became the framework for showcasing highly valuable skills in marketing, graphic design, scheduling and organizing, work ethic, creative thinking, and collaboration.

"I'm worried because I didn't have an internship or co-op experience."
What might substitute for this valuable real-world experience? Think about part-time or volunteer work, clubs or sports, or other areas of involvement.

In particular, class projects often require skills that relate to workplace projects, similar to what you'd learn and do during an internship or co-op. Take some time to think through those projects and highlight the specific skills, activities, and technologies that you had to learn or demonstrate. Use the CAR format (pages 2–3) to describe the project, your contributions, and the outcome. Several of the samples in this book show expanded project summaries that illustrate how to make these experiences a central, and valuable, part of your resume.

And as you page through the samples, you might be reminded of something you've done that you didn't think "mattered" (scouting, church group, youth activity).

"I don't have any work experience."
Everything and anything that you've done can help tell your story. Did you have great travel opportunities that let you immerse yourself in another culture? Possibly learn a new language or gain greater familiarity with a language you studied in high school or college? Travel opens your mind to different perspectives and can help you make well-thought-out decisions.

If you had family responsibilities that prevented you from taking an outside job, you might briefly mention a caretaker role or other ways that you assisted your family. Such experiences may strike a chord with employers and can illustrate your sense of responsibility and desirable soft skills such as communication and time management.

"What if the work experience I did have is totally unrelated to my field?"
That's perfectly fine! Showcase what you did—and try to draw out where you made a difference. Employers like to hire people who have been successful in learning new skills, using new software, making a contribution, "doing great work" in whatever they are doing. So tell your stories proudly (and honestly, of course).

"What if my GPA is poor?"
As we mentioned in our Pro Tip in the Education discussion in this chapter, omit your GPA altogether if it is low. In other words, don't showcase what *doesn't* add value to your candidacy. Other than when you are first launching a career after graduation (and unless you are pursuing a career in education), your GPA typically won't get more than a passing glance throughout the decades to come. What becomes more

important very quickly will be your experience, your successes, your contributions, and your accomplishments in the workplace.

"What if I changed my major?"

This really doesn't matter and is nothing you need to explain, unless it adds value to your candidacy and your story. For example, let's say you changed your major from Architecture to Construction Management. You can explain that you found you were more interested in *building* than *designing,* and you love nothing more than being on the job site, transforming the architect's vision to reality. That foundational education in Architecture will likely be an asset that not every candidate will have, so it is worth mentioning.

But for most people, there's no need to include any mention of changing majors on your resume. With our strategy that recommends you include only your date of graduation (not your entire tenure at the university), any extra time will be invisible to the reader.

"How do I address special needs or challenges?"

A disability or other challenge typically isn't a concern when developing your resume and other career materials. Focus on your education, experience, activities, and achievements, just like any other new graduate creating a resume.

A special need may become relevant if you require accommodation for interviewing and/or on the job—both of which are handled much later in the process. For instance, at the time an interview is being scheduled, you would communicate the need for a particular accommodation to address sight or hearing challenges. Necessary accommodations in the workplace would generally be addressed at the time of an offer or, possibly, when completing an application.

Your Groundwork (and Grunt Work) Will Pay Off

The work you do in developing your resume—using the questions provided, possibly taking several assessments, and completing the worksheets in this chapter—becomes the foundation for everything to follow: Your LinkedIn profile, e-notes and cover letters, scripts for job-search outreach, and interview prep.

Dive in—and good luck harvesting material that will showcase your unique talents!

CHAPTER 2:
Build a Powerful LinkedIn Profile

If you're reading this book, you are very likely a digital native. Social media and use of tech is second-hand to you, and you probably use such apps as TikTok, WhatsApp, Instagram, Twitter, YouTube, Snapchat, Pinterest, and maybe even Facebook. But as a college graduate (or student), you should be aware that LinkedIn is the #1 professional social media app for building and showcasing your brand and networking for internships and job search.

In Chapter 1 we provided several worksheets and a number of questions to consider in developing your resume Headline and Profile-Summary, as well as Experience, Education, and other categories. While much of this information is transferable to your LinkedIn site, don't make the mistake of simply copying your resume into your LinkedIn account and thinking you're done.

> **PRO TIP: Ignore LinkedIn's encouragement to "upload your resume."** Rather, create unique LinkedIn content that engages readers and prompts them to reach out to connect with you. At that time, you can share your resume, customized if need be for relevant opportunities.
>
> For your LinkedIn profile, you'll want to take the good content you've developed for your resume and change the voice and tone of your writing to better reflect the engaging and conversational language expected in social media. We'll show you how.
>
> If you do make a direct application for a job via LinkedIn, you can privately upload a job-specific resume. We'll talk all about job search in Chapter 4.

LinkedIn Subscription

For nearly every graduate or student, a free personal subscription to LinkedIn will serve most of your needs. You can upgrade to premium if you wish, especially if someone else is paying or your university makes a free premium subscription available to you for six months or a year. However, you can typically access and use the majority of useful LinkedIn features with a free account. These features support building your professional identity and branding on the web without the need for creating your own personal website.

As well, you'll be able to build a network of professional contacts. These will likely include students (from both high school and college), college professors, high school teachers, coaches and program directors, internship supervisors, employers, and others. Over time your contacts will grow and create a database that you'll be able to use when reaching out for introductions, advice, and recommendations.

In Chapter 4, we go into detail about how to make maximum use of LinkedIn for your job search—including setting up free searches for job alerts. But first, you need to create a profile that will engage readers, attract recruiters, and complement your resume.

Creating Your LinkedIn Profile

Like a resume, the LinkedIn profile is divided into several key sections where you can present specific types of information. The most important sections—just as on your resume—are:

- **Header** (including custom URL, photo, background banner, contact information, connections, and headline)
- **About** (somewhat similar to the Summary-Profile on your resume)
- **Experience**
- **Education**

In this chapter we will guide you through the process of creating content for these primary sections and share samples of diverse profiles to inspire you in building your own.

We also offer recommendations for completing several other important areas of your profile—**Skills, Recommendations,** and **Interests**—and a number of optional sections that may add value and interest.

Career Centers Say ...

"I emphasize the important basics: Create a profile with a vanity URL, have a solid headline (not 'student at University of XYZ'), use a professional headshot, write in first person, and show the college degree and graduation month and year (May 2022, not spring 2022)."

— *Cheryl Minnick, EdD, Career Success Director, College of Humanities & Sciences, University of Montana*

Now, let's get started creating your profile.

PRO TIP: As with any online tool or social media app, LinkedIn's features, navigation, guidelines, and limitations do change periodically, so when you begin to build your profile don't be surprised if some of the criteria and functionality we cite are different. Use the "Help" link (found under "Me" in the top right corner of your profile) if you need it.

Header (including Custom URL, Photo, Background Banner, Contact Information and Other Details, Connections, and Headline)

This top portion of your profile offers a quick snapshot of important information. It is easily visible and readable even on small phone screens. Here's how you can make it as effective as possible.

Custom URL
When you create an account, LinkedIn automatically assigns a lengthy alpha-numeric URL. But you can customize the URL, and we strongly recommend that you do so. It will create a more professional and branded image.

For example, LinkedIn assigned the following URL—www.linkedin.com/in/jan-melnik-ab763b2—that Jan customized to www.linkedin/com/in/janmelnik/.

To customize your URL, go to your profile and, on the menu bar at the top under "Me," choose "Help" for details on using many features of LinkedIn. Within the search bar, enter "customize URL." This opens the option to "Customize your URL."

Here's how it looks:

Click on "Customize your URL," then on "Edit URL" in the upper righthand corner of the screen.

Click on the pencil to the right of your current URL and enter a shorter, cleaner URL (without the append-age of numbers and letters). Depending on how popular your name is, you might have to insert a hyphen or period between your first and last names, add a middle initial, or perhaps add a number at the end of your name. Avoid using your birthday or birth year.

Once you have saved your selection, include the customized URL in the contact info at the top of your resume, in your cover letter/e-note, and in the signature block at the bottom of all your job-related emails.

Photo
According to LinkedIn—and we agree—your photo is critically important. In fact, LinkedIn reports that having a professional-looking headshot image of yourself on Linked increases 14 times the likelihood of your profile being viewed by others. First impressions are everything, so make sure that your photo exudes a professional image.

Check with your school to see if they offer headshot photo-taking opportunities for students for LinkedIn. A local library may also offer this free of charge as part of the programs they present for job seekers. You can opt to have a professional photographer take your headshot, at a cost anywhere from $100 to $300+.

If you opt to take it yourself with a tripod or a friend using a camera, follow these general guidelines for the best results:

- Dress as you would for an interview.

- A headshot is from the shoulders up, so your head/face should almost completely fill the LinkedIn circle.
- Try to have a natural-looking smile.
- Be careful with lighting to avoid a mug-shot look or awkward shadows.
- Be sure no lamps or trees are "growing" out of your head.
- You are the only person who should be in the picture.
- Don't use a photo from a wedding, party, or casual event.
- Once you have what you think are a few possible choices, have people who can be objective vote on the best image.

When uploading your image, you will have an option to select a LinkedIn filter. Most experts recommend using either the classic or spotlight filter for the most professional results. Remember—your picture is one of the key parts of who you are. It is a fundamental part of your brand.

Background Banner
LinkedIn's background picture panel gives you an opportunity to add dimension to your profile and "tell" more of your story—present more of your brand.

You can decide on what complements your profile photo best—a landscape image, a cityscape or skyline, a mountain or beachscape, an image that is abstract or contemporary, silhouettes of people in an office, an image that represents your profession (such as a plane for an aerospace engineer), an inspirational quote, or a favorite picture that you've taken of something.

You can find a good selection of (free) high-quality images here: https://unsplash.com/backgrounds/apps/linkedin. Another option is to create a banner using Canva. Here's a tutorial: https://www.makeuseof.com/create-professional-linkedin-banner-using-canva/.

Contact Information and Other Details (Websites, Phone, Address, Email, Instant Messaging, IG, Twitter, Birthday)
Under "Me," click "View Profile," then click the pencil icon in the top (Header) section of your profile. You can then add any of the details that you wish. Our recommendations:

- DO add your email address and phone. This will make it easier for people (especially recruiters) to contact you without having to use LinkedIn's InMail feature.
- DON'T list your street address. You may include city/state/zip if you wish.
- DO include your social media links *if* you are comfortable sharing all of your posts. If you prefer to keep them private, DON'T list the links here.
- List your birthday if you wish—it's up to you. We recommend *not* including the birth year.

Connections
Prominently shown in your LinkedIn Header is the number of connections you have. In Chapter 4 we discuss the value of connections and how to use them in your job search. For now, focus on building your connections from the ground up by sending invitations to people you know and people you get to know through your school, work, volunteer, and job-search activities.

Headline

Like the title on a book or online article, the headline is one of the most important sections on LinkedIn. It's what will ideally grab the attention of a hiring manager, maybe a recruiter, or perhaps someone in a position to recommend or refer you.

The default is your current or most recent job title (pulled from your Experience listing), but you can change that. And you should—now and throughout your career—to create a headline that will add meaning and value to your profile.

These guidelines will help.

- Include authentic keywords and descriptors. Just as with your resume, you want your profile to reflect the real you, with the genuine attributes that you bring to work.

- Don't waste space in your headline describing yourself as a student at your university. That information will be very apparent. What's more, it represents your past (or your present if you are still enrolled). Your headline should position you for your future.

- Save your in-depth branding statements and lengthier "I" narrative (storytelling) for the profile itself and make the headline keywords count.

- Avoid announcing that you are looking for a job. You *can* use your About section to share details concerning your desire for an internship or employment opportunity.

- Consider repurposing some of the content from your resume Headline and Profile-Summary.

- Look back at the assessment tools we described in Chapter 1, particularly the VIA Strengths Assessment, to capture powerful and accurate descriptors.

Career Centers Say ...

"Everyone can benefit from having a great LinkedIn profile. I just helped a student who has 'good' but not off-the-charts 'great' experience improve her LinkedIn profile to prioritize her hard UX skills and weave the platforms and skills she knows throughout her profile. Within weeks of our meeting, she was contacted through LinkedIn by multiple employers who wanted to interview her.

"It's important for students to understand that if an employer receives a student application and the student has no LinkedIn profile or other professional web presence (i.e., a research page or personal webpage) and the employer can only see this candidate's high school lacrosse statistics, for example, the employer will think the student is not 'with it' professionally. I use this argument because there are students who are still dubious about the value of a LinkedIn presence."

— *Cara Mitnick, Director of Professional Development, University of Rhode Island*

SAMPLE HEADLINES

Maximum allowable characters and spaces: 220 if created on a laptop, 240 if created on a mobile device. Recommendation: 140–200 characters to avoid an overly weighty headline that's hard to read quickly.

Candidate: Business / Financial Analyst | Customer Service | Relationship Management | Exceptional Work Ethic

Aspiring Accountant/Auditor ▶ BS in Business, Double Major in Accounting and Economics ▶ High achiever with competitive drive and exceptional work ethic

Internship Candidate: Marketing, Advertising, Public Relations & Project Management | Excellent Communication Skills

High-energy GWU business administration/international, May 2023 B.S. >> Consulting, Sales, Marketing, Project Management

Customer Service – Retail Background | Results-Oriented | Committed to Going "Above and Beyond" to Exceed Expectations

Behavioral Health and Mental Health Associate—Creating pathways to progress for people with challenges and disabilities

Talented Member Services Supervisor | Professional Event Planner | Exquisite Attention to Detail

Highly Qualified CFA Candidate ▶ Excellent Technical & Financial Analysis Skills ▶ Strong Internship Background

Tenacious Business/Finance Major | Dedicated Team Player | Creative & Honest with High EQ

High-energy, Focused Economics Major | Keen Management, Marketing, and Analytical Strengths | Driven by Success

Trend-focused Marketing Major & Automotive Enthusiast | Google Superstar with Top Analytical/Research Skills

Talented Cybertech and IT Major | Dedicated Team Player | Proven Skill Adding Organizational Value | Expert Coder

Hospitality-Hotel-Tourism Major: Motivated Food Service Professional with Fine Dining Experience and Extensive Wine Knowledge

About

Closely weighted with the value of your Headline, **About** is the other area of your LinkedIn site where you are trying to capture eyeballs and draw readers in. Who are these readers? They are the internship coordinators, hiring managers, and even recruiters who scour LinkedIn for talented candidates.

If you scan through profiles on LinkedIn, you'll see that besides the photograph and title, the first three lines (approximately) in About are visible before scrolling down into the body of a LinkedIn profile. That's why what you say here is critically important to consider strategically. You want the reader to click "see more" and move into the heart-and-soul of your About content.

Here are three examples of non-students (including both authors of this book) with what appears on the LinkedIn About section before the "see more" link. We've identified the character count for each of the samples (the LinkedIn format allows quite a range). Later in this chapter you'll find relevant student examples showing the full About sections.

Be Inspired. It's your career. It's your life. My passion is working with clients to achieve their career dreams—delivering solutions, not simply services! As a Master Resume Writer, Credentialed Career Manager, and Certified Professional Resume Writer, I work one-on-one with clients coast-to-coast to create strategic resumes and career documents that advance their candidacies—and garner attention in the right way. I specialize i ...see more **(433, Jan Melnik)**

* * * * *

As a resume writer/executive career advisor, I have a single goal for each client: Telling a career story that is memorable, meaningful, relevant, succinct, and interesting. Today, that means:

▶ Writing for today's readers—shorter, tighter, harder-hitting copy that conveys critical information q ...see more **(298, Louise Kursmark)**

* * * * *

I don't dread Mondays and neither do my clients. That's because I help women advance their careers in pursuit of their unique versions of life success. When you find the right position at the right company, Mondays are no longer the enemy... see more **(240, Kate Pozeznik)**

In writing your About section, create short, concise paragraphs and perhaps bullet points. Avoid lengthy, text-heavy content. Instead, break things up with lots of white space.

Keep in mind that on LinkedIn there are limitations with respect to design and font. You can't use bold or italics or underscores. But you can create subheadings with all capital letters. You can use certain symbols repeatedly to create visual breaks between subsections. For instance, try a series such as:

+++

or:

****

You can also cut-and-paste in some Wingdings as unique bullet points, as these samples show:

► International Business Major
► Economics Minor
► Spanish Concentration
-or-
☞ Student Government
☞ Yearbook
☞ Intramural Golf
☞ Club Rugby

Your LinkedIn About should be written in the first person. That means to freely use the word "I" … as in, "Characteristics that I'm known for include …" or "I'm passionate about …" Remember, LinkedIn is *different* from the resume. Your resume should *not* use the word "I."

By writing in the first person, you create a profile that is engaging, friendly, and like a conversation—one of the key points behind social media.

Career Centers Say …

"In the minds of many students, LinkedIn is just one more thing they have to do—and most don't like writing about themselves. Generally speaking, the Education and Experience sections line up factually with what is presented on the resume itself and don't require much creativity. However, the About section is the best opportunity they have in LinkedIn to distinguish themselves as an individual and not just another random job seeker who looks like all the others.

"I advise that LinkedIn—a great job-seeking tool—is really the place where they need to be if they're professional and serious about their careers. They'll be out there with other professionals in their target industry. It's an opportunity for them to add more color to the story their resume tells. I remind them that recruiters are going to use LI to check the legitimacy of what they say."

— Carla Coury, Interim Executive Director, Career Management Center, A.B. Freeman School of Business, Tulane University

SAMPLE ABOUT SECTIONS

From the 12 varied example that follow, you can see that the style of the About section encourages an engaging, friendly, transparent communication approach. Share what is authentic and helps to describe "what makes you you." Remember: Short and succinct paragraphs are the way to go.

Maximum allowable characters and spaces: 2,600
Recommendation: At least 1,800. It's fine to use all 2,600, especially if you include a key skills list at the end that won't be read in the same way but will increase keyword density.

ABOUT SAMPLE 1: Aerospace Engineering major seeking internship *(1,742 characters)*
Since I was a kid, I've been fascinated with transportation, especially planes. Some kids deliver newspapers for their first jobs. Others have lemonade stands. My experience? A family vacation that included jet travel

with a cockpit tour and a chance to meet the pilots paved the way for my curiosity to build, and I got my first of many summer jobs working at an airport. This turned into what became my selection of major as a mechanical engineering student with a deep desire to pursue aerospace/aviation as my target industry.

Across my internship experiences, a common denominator is having been selected based upon demonstrated strengths that include leadership abilities, collaborative working style, effective communication skills, and—of course—mechanical engineering background/coursework and aviation/aerospace interests.

For my next internship, of particular appeal would be an opportunity to design new mechanical parts, assemblies, and installations. This could include the mechanical design of complex aircraft interiors and structural modification. Working for an airline or an aerospce manufacturer would also be appealing.

My mechanical engineering/aviation education and internships have been complemented by skills that include Matrix Laboratory, Basic Python, and Sabre GDS. A native English speaker, I have intermediate German skills and also immersed fully in Spanish during my study abroad experience in the spring of 2022.

Additional characteristics include a high level of motivation and strong work ethic plus a proven ability to rapidly learn and apply new skills. I have excellent research and writing skills and am an effective presenter. Customer-centric, I am committed to bringing value to the work I do.

ABOUT SAMPLE 2: Economics major pursuing post-graduation job as an Investment Advisor/VC Associate *(1,631 characters)*

"He was extremely conscientious, intelligent, hardworking …"
"Jack delivered quality research, creative content, seasoned insight …"
"Proactive and self-starting…"

These are just some of the remarks that have been made about my performance and record of contributions working as an intern for several key investors and SMEs over the past few years while building my skill set as an investor/associate—all while completing a degree in Economics.

What I like to say about my subject matter expertise (with a deep interest and experience in the Technology Sector, Cybersecurity, Data Management, and Database Platforms): I'm hungry! I value morals over money. And I believe strongly in betting on people as a VC strategy.

I have a solid range of experience working with and interning with several well-recognized hedge funds and capital management firms.

According to manager endorsements, my key differentiating strengths include:

▶ Insight to due diligence through keen analysis and deep-dive research

▶ Strategic and visionary thinking

▶ Talent for formulating and asking the RIGHT, precise questions

▶ A track record of identifying exceptional deals and opportunities

My "hunger" extends to all areas of my work. I am eager to do whatever it takes to contribute, be successful, and make a difference. I have an unparalleled work ethic and can work very well autonomously and independently. As well, I quickly engage with others and cultivate relationships that are productive.

I'd love the opportunity to connect and engage—here on LinkedIn, via phone, or in a meeting. Please reach out via InMail or directly via email, JackPartridge@mac.com.

ABOUT SAMPLE 3: Business/Accounting graduate pursuing job as an Auditor *(2,235 characters)*
What I find most exciting about accounting and especially auditing is that the numbers tell a story. The bottom line, of course, is profit or loss, but numbers reveal so much more.

Where and how is the company investing its resources? Is it planning for the future or hanging on to the past? How does it compare to competitors? Are costs out of line with revenues? Where is new business coming from?

And—very important to a logical thinker like me—the numbers add up. If they don't, there's an interesting puzzle that needs to be examined, each strand followed to its source to identify errors and discrepancies.

The numbers tell a story of the past and create a roadmap for the future.

In a similar way, the activities and accomplishments of my past paint a clear path to success in the future.

As a recent State University graduate with a degree in Business and a double major in Accounting and Economics, I am excited to begin my professional career. And as a dedicated athlete since a young age, I see many parallels between achievement in the corporate world and on the basketball court.

Competitive drive, a winning attitude, desire for continuous learning, and the willingness to work hard to reach goals—these are the traits that have led to victory in my academic and athletic pursuits and will do the same as I begin my professional career.

My past accomplishments are indicators of my future success:

► I have maintained a high grade point average while investing more than 20 hours each week in practice, preparation, and games as an NCAA Division I basketball player.

► I have emerged as a mentor and an authentic leader-by-example among my teammates and have been chosen to participate in valuable leadership development programs.

► Having held a variety of front-line service jobs (wait staff, coach, camp counselor), I have developed excellent communication skills and demonstrated a strong work ethic.

I've gotten this far in life through meticulous preparation, hard work, and making maximum use of my abilities. I've seen how teamwork elevates and strengthens each individual member. And I've learned that there is joy in the grunt work as well as the game. I'll carry these lessons forward—and I'm ready for what's next.

ABOUT SAMPLE 4: English major pursuing Library Science master's degree *(1,227 characters)*
What do I love about libraries? The books, for one thing! From slowly flattening my TBR pile, to helping others discover a love for reading, I have always had a fondness for libraries and what they contain. This is why I will be applying to a Library Science master's program in the near future to become a librarian.

For about 2 years in high school, I volunteered in a middle school library. That experience further cemented my chosen career path.

As for education, I graduated from high school the day before my 16th birthday and earned an AA from Erie State College one year later, when I had turned 17. I now enjoy studying at Haverford College as an English/Creative Writing major with a History minor as well.

I will graduate with my bachelor's degree in May of 2023. Through my program at Haverford, I have discovered a passion for creative writing, and I am now working on my first novel.

From a young age, I have always enjoyed learning, starting at Erie at the young age of 14. Because of this love of learning, I aspire to be a lifelong learner, even when I am not enrolled in a school.

Now, as I prepare to bring my library expertise to a master's level, I'm ready and excited for the next learning adventure!

Career Centers Say ...

"LinkedIn is a powerful networking tool for the job search. I recommend creating a strong profile, following companies of interest, and joining professional interest and alumni groups as well as building your connection list as you meet new people. The job board on LinkedIn is very robust as well. We know employers are Googling candidate names for due diligence, and LinkedIn has great search power to be one of the top hits on a search."

— *Amanda Schagane, Associate Director of Alumni Career Services, University of Kentucky*

ABOUT SAMPLE 5: Psychology major pursuing opportunities in behavioral health/mental health prior to master's degree studies *(1,909 characters)*
What inspires me: Helping others to be their best.

Whether working in an addiction outreach van, helping disabled athletes participate in water sports, or inspiring my choral group to work hard and perform at our peak, I take great joy in guiding, encouraging, and supporting people to overcome barriers and achieve goals.

About to graduate with a BA in Psychology, I am pursuing career interests in behavioral health and mental health that will allow me to gain experience, insights, and perspectives that will guide further education and career direction.

My interest in the helping professions is not new. Throughout high school and college I sought volunteer and employment opportunities that served diverse groups and individuals but had one thing in common: the opportunity to interact with, and help, people facing challenges. For example:

== As an intern at Midwest Health System, I participated in direct services to people addicted to opioids and often homeless as a result. I saw how little things had a big impact, and how being present at the right time can be the catalyst for change.

== Most recently, in completing my senior thesis I conducted research and then compiled customized music playlists for seniors with dementia. I observed how music sparks memories and offers comfort.

== Previously I worked with children with disabilities in educational settings. Through positive reinforcement I helped students persevere in difficult tasks and experience the joy of personal achievement.

My other great love is music. I've been a member of bands and choral groups in high school and college.

How does this interest affect my career goals? Music creates common points of interest and allows people, no matter their disability or challenge, to express themselves and participate in a joyous activity. I love bringing music into care settings and using it to unlock barriers and build connections.

ABOUT SAMPLE 6: Information Technology major pursuing full-time job after graduation *(1,850 characters)*
A dedicated Help Desk professional, I am currently a Junior majoring in Cybersecurity and Information Technology at the University of Illinois Chicago.

WHAT I DO: I help people and businesses with technical assistance and support related to computer systems, hardware, and software. I am responsible for answering queries and addressing system and user issues in a timely and professional manner. I work with an IT team and will often interact with system and computer users across the company. My key strengths include understanding and maintaining daily system performance, having the ability to troubleshoot customer problems, and applying innate follow-up and follow-through skills.

WHO I'VE WORKED WITH: My first IT job began at I-Net Consulting. I started as an intern, made my way to part time, full time, and then a salaried employee in less than 3 years—while continuing to complete credits toward my bachelor's degree (maintaining a 3.8 GPA). I learned my first steps in this firm thanks to the diligent training and work of the staff and the owner, who treated me like family. I-Net is a multiple service provider for small to mid-sized businesses. I learned how to do simple tasks as a help desk professional by having duties as a Network Administrator.

Now, as I prepare to begin my senior year at UI, I am completing a 3-month internship as a remote Help Desk Analyst at Cornerstone Building Brands, an enterprise company. The firm has 25,000 employees, and here I have learned to thrive in a high-intensity and fast-paced work culture.

HOW I CAN HELP: In addition to my technical abilities, my greatest strengths are being an honest and caring person with excellent leadership and organizational skills. I care for my customers and my colleagues. I have ambition and I always encourage people around me to see the brighter side of themselves.

ABOUT SAMPLE 7: Business Administration major seeking post-graduation job in sales *(2,432 characters)*

"Sales is a numbers game." That might be the conventional wisdom, but I have to disagree. To me, sales is all about people—their needs and problems, the issues that keep them up at night.

My interest in people is what attracts me to a career in sales as I complete my bachelor's degree in Business Administration. I'm excited to put into practice all that I've learned—in school, in athletic competition, at jobs, and in volunteer roles—to help companies meet their goals and solve their problems.

Of course, numbers are important too. I love numbers—I was a Finance major before I switched to Business. But I quickly learned that it's the stories behind the data that fascinated me.

For example …

► A young fitness company, struggling to find clients, was assigned to my team as a Marketing project. When we looked at their marketing plans and programs, we noticed that they hadn't clearly defined their target market. We helped them zero in on the people most likely to use their services, then invest their small marketing budget appealing to those people. The results were above expectations.

► As a summer intern for a commercial real estate development company, I used my research and analytical skills to help clients properly evaluate potential purchases. But most of all, what I observed was how important it was to reach out to the right people for a referral, a piece of information, or an insider perspective. Networking and relationship building were critical in every aspect of the business.

► As a trainer and a referee for youth soccer clubs, I helped drill the basics and explained the rules. And I quickly learned that it was just as important to communicate with the parents, not just the young athletes—to set the right expectations and avoid misunderstandings.

The third element that attracts me to sales—beyond the people and the numbers—is the competitive aspect of the job. As an athlete, I've channeled my desire to win into doing what's necessary to make that happen. In sales, the same fundamentals apply: plan, practice, prepare, psych up, and build on today's successes to reach even greater heights tomorrow.

If you're looking for a hard-working, competitive, people-focused professional to add to your sales/marketing/account management team, please get in touch: AJDuncan@email.com. I would love to explore what keeps you (and your customers) up at night and how I can help everyone get a good night's sleep!

ABOUT SAMPLE 8: Environmental Engineering graduate seeking full-time role *(1,693 characters)*

To make a long story short, I started out as a computer science major driven to work at some exciting startup with vibrant, naturally lit interiors and armies of sticky notes on white boards. At the beginning of 2021, I switched to Environmental Engineering. Why? I decided that I wanted my time to be spent either helping handle the effects of climate change or helping create ways we can live without disrupting the planet's natural systems.

I love engineering because it provides explanations for how the world works quantitatively. It's satisfying to me to finally be able to explain everyday occurrences. Engineering helps me appreciate and understand the complexity of the modern world.

My best subjects in school have always been math and art (and, later on, computer science). These subjects are all taught with an emphasis on problem solving. The feeling I get when I solve a math problem or finish a clay sculpture is the most satisfying feeling I know. Engineering is a career dedicated to solving problems, and I know that I can flourish in this environment.

An important value of mine is cooperation. Having been involved in many situations where others are butting heads, I've found that rarely leads to successful outcomes. I've participated in enough school projects and sports teams to understand that the best thing I can do for my team is to leave my ego behind and try to understand other people's points of view. Compromise is never perfect, but at least it maintains relationships and creates progress.

I'm excited to explore what's next as I prepare to graduate and land my first professional role in "the real world."

ABOUT SAMPLE 9: Professional Writing major pursuing roles in digital marketing *(1,299 characters)*
Who am I? A creative Freelance Digital Marketer specializing in SEO, analytics, website optimization, content, and social media marketing and advertising.

About to graduate from Juniata College with a degree in Professional Writing, I now seek a full-time role in Digital Marketing. My love for creative communication fuels my passion for digital marketing, and my history in art gives me broad perspectives in design. I study trends to understand the market, and my work as a consultant while going to school brings pragmatic experience to my skill set.

To build a successful brand, you need to understand the customer. My skill lies in identifying the customer's needs and establishing a strategy to craft the right story for the customer's brand and intended audience.

I'm at my best when working on a brand that has unrealized potential and helping to unlock it. I have helped several websites grow organically, and my experience includes building websites on Shopify and other e-commerce platforms. I'd love to help your clients level up their branding, image, websites, and go-to-market strategies.

Specialties: Digital Marketing, Digital Advertising, Web Design, Product Advertisement, SEO, SEM, Graphic Design, GoogleAnalytics, GoogleAdwords, AdobeInDesign, Social Media Management & Marketing

ABOUT SAMPLE 10: Environmental Biology major seeking research opportunities *(1,249 characters)*
I am a 3rd year Environmental Biology major at the University of Georgia. My passions include conservation biology, mammalian ecology, the study of climate change, and microbiology. I am interested in participating in research that connects topics such as microbiology, cell biology, and medicine.

My future career plans include applying to and being admitted to medical school, where I hope to perform research on epilepsy. Ultimately I aspire to be an internal medicine physician, general cardiologist, or neurologist with a specialty in epilepsy.

My interest in studying epilepsy comes from within my own family, seeing my brother afflicted with the condition for the past several years. This personal experience has inspired me to perform research and care for patients like him to improve their quality of life and reduce suffering for the patient as well as their family.

Additional skills I possess are a basic competency in statistical analysis, technical writing and communication, and problem solving. I can use various research tools such as Minitab and Excel to perform data analysis and statistical hypothesis tests. I am fluent and literate in two languages (English and Arabic) and have working knowledge of Mandarin Chinese and Spanish.

ABOUT SAMPLE 11: Finance major seeking position as investment advisor *(1,636 characters)*
Finance—while it is a topic that has been consistently linked to money and confusion, this is simply not true. The field of finance extends to every detail of a person's life or a business's operation.

I have personally gone through financial hardships that created a heavy burden on my quality of life, but with the help of my studies and persistence, I have since opened new doors for myself that I thought were not feasible (and which I plan to do for others).

Amazingly, I did not always want to pursue a career in finance. It never occurred to me that I might love it because of all the misconceptions I had. I have always been good at math and quite enjoyed it to the point that I would redo my homework repeatedly, for the fun of working with numbers! I attempted multiple career paths, such as the military, biology, and kinesiology, and although I found each to be fascinating, I never felt truly satisfied. It dawned on me while spending three days reading tax publications for my own taxes that this is what I wanted to do.

I began the finance journey and uncovered a miraculous world of budgeting, stocks, bonds, journal entries ... you name it! Although many aspects of finance have beneficial aspects, I've decided to pursue a career as a financial advisor because I can have a direct impact on individual lives. I will use all my experiences, from my childhood to now, as well as my passion for the career, to be the best financial expert for my clients.

Hard working, dedicated, and optimistic, I especially like this quote from Dolly Parton: "The way I see it, if you want the rainbow, you gotta put up with the rain."

ABOUT SAMPLE 12: English Literature major seeking full-time job after graduation *(1,937 characters)*
For many, reading and writing was a chore in school. Funnily enough, it was for me, too! I could barely pay attention in class while reading, zoning out and listening to the rumble of my peers' voices as the teacher tried to make the reading fun through playing the popcorn reading method. Going into middle school, I dreaded the concept of summer reading. It was something I only did at school, not with my own spare time!

However, that summer marked the start of the slowly turning tide of my enjoyment of reading. Selecting the book *The Mysterious Benedict Society* by Trenton Lee Stewart, I started begrudgingly, but then quickly got enveloped in the mystery the protagonists found themselves in and the Morse code used between them. I was intrigued. And I became addicted to the anticipation.

Furthering my plot along to 7th grade, at the literature fair at my school I saw a notice for a story-writing contest. I wanted to give it a shot, see if my rampant imagination could find itself a home in words and story and plot. I had to cut my story down as I furiously typed, the maximum page requirement stopping me short of the ever-expanding plot unraveling in my head. My story wasn't a winner, but it was a feat I never imagined myself accomplishing. I realized writing made me feel alive.

Words have magic. Stories provide excitement and thrills and even comfort. They are whole worlds at our fingertips. I want to help authors piece those threads together to make their wild and extravagant tales come true. I want to aid in creating stories that will help anyone at any age discover reading is not a chore.

As a bookseller at Barnes & Noble, I helped customers find new books to love. I also volunteered at Smith-field Public Library, answering patrons' questions and accurately shelving books. As I seek to put my B.A. in English Literature to work, I am confident of one thing: My pursuits will always follow where books lead.

Experience

In building out the Experience section of your LinkedIn profile, pattern how your resume is developed, positioning entries in reverse-chronological order (most recent first). Include any internships and/or co-op jobs within the experience section, treating them exactly as you would full-time employment—because it *is* valuable experience.

Consistency is important. Be sure titles of any internships or jobs you've held are correct—and match what you say on your resume. Also be sure that your dates are accurate and, again, are identical to what you present on your resume.

The details of each position or internship should be presented in a more conversational manner than how the information appears on your resume. Remember to use very short paragraphs and/or bullets to high-light information. Try to convey your personality and energy through crisp narrative that reflects branding and value proposition.

Below you'll find Experience descriptions for ten different students with a variety of majors. Notice how experience can be crafted from undergraduate studies as well as internships and co-ops, from part-time jobs in high school and/or college, from entrepreneurial work, and even from volunteer positions.

EXPERIENCE SAMPLES
Maximum allowable characters and spaces: 2,000 per entry
Recommendation: 1,800 or less

EXPERIENCE SAMPLE 1: Internship Experience
SOTHEBY'S, New York, NY
Intern, Jewelry Department
Jan.–May 2022

Because of my deep interest in the fashion industry, I was excited to secure a 5-month, full-time, paid internship working primarily in the jewelry department at the world-famous Sotheby's auction house.

ACTIVITIES: I was involved with a number of jewelry exhibitions and sales and assisted jewelry specialists with appraisals and sales.

CONTRIBUTIONS:

* I brought my organizational skills to prioritizing and promoting jewelry events.

* I maintained methodical records of high-value merchandise.

* Interacting with clients, I ascertained their needs and connected them with specialists.

* It was my idea to create Excel spreadsheets to catalog new inventories of jewelry, before merging with the larger database. As a result, we saved time and avoided duplication of effort because all entries were complete before the merge.

EXPERIENCE SAMPLE 2: Summer Job Experience (unrelated to career goals)
BOSTON SEAPORT, Boston, MA
Sailing Instructor
Summers, 2019–2022

Over the course of 4 summers, I instructed both individual students (aged 8–13) as well as families in every aspect of safely rigging, navigating, landing, and de-rigging a sailboat. I also was a volunteer at a number of events held at the Seaport.

A few things I learned …
\>> I can make a real difference, to customers and the company, by providing excellent customer service.
\>> It's often easier to help people than to tell them why you can't.
\>> Kids learn fast and are a joy to teach. Adults … not so fast, but also fun to teach!

EXPERIENCE SAMPLE 3: Summer Job Experience (related to career goals)
BLUE CROSS/BLUE SHIELD, North Haven, CT
Finance, Marketing & HR Intern
Summer 2022

In a diverse finance/business internship, I supported a recognized leader in patient/provider education to 85M+ health consumers as well as more than 780K physicians and clinicians. Most of my activity involved the company's health and wellness websites.

Highlights included:

- Gaining broad expertise interning within Finance, Marketing, and Human Resources departments.
- Being instrumental in preparing budgets as well as entering financial data into spreadsheets.
- Tracking travel and entertainment costs, reconciling receipts to recorded amounts.
- Increasing brand awareness and contributing to multimedia advertising campaigns, including selecting images for social media and Instagram posts.

EXPERIENCE SAMPLE 4: Internship Experience
SUPREME FABRICATORS, Portland, ME
Applications Engineer Intern
October 2022–March 2023

This was a great opportunity to learn a number of engineering processes with Supreme. A few examples:

>> I played a key role in the installation of a fully automated machining line. Other experience entailed operating automated cell, inspection CMM, and CNC equipment.

>> As part of my work responsibilities, I captured data, analyzed details against projections, determined variances, and identified corrections required as part of the quality control process for precision-oriented, high-tolerance machined parts.

>> I was able to enhance my technology skills using SOLIDWORKS and Mastercam to design parts and program machines for cutting.

From my supervisor's recommendation: "I would rate Joseph in the top 10% of interns over the course of 15 years … I was extremely impressed with Joseph's ability to learn."

EXPERIENCE SAMPLE 5: Summer Job Experience (unrelated to career goals)
PRIVATE LANDOWNER, Charlotte, NC
Laborer-Caretaker-Landscaper
Summers, 2018–2022

Caring for a 200-acre estate, I managed a variety of responsibilities ranging from lawn seeding/reseeding, fertilizing, mulching, weed-whacking, and mowing to trimming hedgerows.

Other highlights:

== I handled matters related to commercial tenants as well as cared for livestock (herds of bison and elk). Maintenance work included painting agricultural buildings and maintaining vehicles.

== I helped to clear new-growth forest, handled lawn restoration and seeding, and maintained land-scaping at the property owner's commercial rental storage facility in the same town (125+ units). I was involved in constructing an on-site windmill.

== During special on-site events for 100+ people, I oversaw a staff of 4 handling valet parking.

== Most of my work was performed completely autonomously; I managed my own work time without supervision, coordinating my work around high school/college classes and my schedule as a Division I athlete.

EXPERIENCE SAMPLE 6: Class Project Experience
PGA TOUR, Gainesville, FL
Marketing Campaign Developer (PGA's "Birdies for the Brave" Initiative)
Jan.–Apr. 2023

As a component of one of my sport marketing classes at UCF, I co-wrote a marketing plan for the PGA program, "Birdies for the Brave." This particular program, designed to create awareness among military families, had stalled and the PGA was seeking new strategies to boost overall image and reach.

I crafted creative social media techniques, designed family-friendly tie-in events, and provided fundraising ideas.

My marketing plan earned 2nd place in the class competition.

EXPERIENCE SAMPLE 7: Internship Experience
AVERY ARCHITECTURAL AND FINE ARTS LIBRARY, Columbia University, New York, NY
Assistant to the Lead Audiovisual Photographic Cataloguer
May–Aug. 2022

This internship provided extensive insight into the work of a cataloguer and archivist at a renowned institution. In particular, I was able to capitalize on my role to learn as much as possible about preservation of materials in the prominent women's historic archive—the acquisition process, selection and stewardship of historical images/documents, naming conventions, and digitizing and cataloguing materials.

Other highlights included the following:

>> I digitized and catalogued photographic and audiovisual materials, working with materials from various collections, including records of the National Organization for Women/papers of Betty Friedan. From this experience I expanded my knowledge of the archival aspect of history while furthering my understanding of the relevance of and access to materials in a research environment.

>> I learned the Columbia library system's computer cataloguing programs and created digital records of library holdings.

>> Additionally, I labeled/organized/photographed materials for library records, digitally repaired damaged photographs (using Adobe Photoshop), and provided front-desk coverage as needed.

EXPERIENCE SAMPLE 8: Class Project Experience
SYSTEMBIO CONTROLS, San Diego, CA
Senior Design Project
Fall 2021–Spring 2022

In this role, I functioned as leader of our team of 3 seniors and spearheaded project design to focus on one deliverable at the conclusion of our engagement for this resource recovery company: We presented energy content findings and delivered our recommendation for waste-heat utilization.

Highlights:

** Performed thermodynamic analysis on biomass fuel furnace to increase efficiency and effectively recycle waste heat from the furnace.

** Optimized fuel-drying system for biomass fuels of various compositions (from 85% moisture to 35% moisture by weight). Measured biomass fuel energy density with oxygen bomb calorimeter testing.

EXPERIENCE SAMPLE 9: Entrepreneurial Experience (throughout high school and college)
MATT PINEDA LAWN CARE, Pittsburgh, PA
Entrepreneur/Business Operator
Summers, High School & College

Recognizing a need in my own neighborhood, as an eighth grader I established a successful lawn care business. I was able to expand my base of accounts through word-of-mouth referrals of satisfied clients.

— I launched a business spanning all seasons, from providing lawn care, mowing, and trimming in the summer and leaf removal in the fall to winter snow removal and spring clean-up.

— In addition to handling marketing, quoting, and accounting for the business, I maintained equipment and supplies.

EXPERIENCE SAMPLE 10: College Coursework Experience
CLEMSON UNIVERSITY
Scholar/Athlete
Aug 2020–May 2023

In 2020 I transferred to Clemson for one key reason: I wanted the more competitive experience I could get at a Division I school. And while I found—and greatly valued—that experience, I also found an exciting educational environment and many opportunities to learn and demonstrate leadership.

Skills mastered and lessons learned …

► ACCOUNTING AND AUDITING—through major coursework in Financial Accounting, Auditing, Accounting Information Systems, Tax Accounting, Cost Accounting, and Tax Research

► ECONOMICS—through dual-major studies that included Microeconomic Theory, Economics of Sports, World Economic Development, Labor Economics, and Industrial Relations

► TIME MANAGEMENT—balancing the heavy coursework of a double major with an intense athletic commitment (20+ hours per week)

► TEAMWORK—experiencing the camaraderie and shared accomplishment that comes from working together, working hard, and achieving common goals

► LEADERSHIP—stepping up after a losing season to turn things around by mentoring and inspiring my teammates; being chosen to attend an elite leadership class and a teambuilding experiential program

Education

This section of your LinkedIn is straightforward. The following examples show various ways of depicting information. You will notice that some of the samples are brief while others expand on courses, projects, honors, extracurriculars, and other activities and achievements. Choose the details that will impress readers and round out your profile. There is no need to repeat items (such as projects, internships, or courses) that you have already included under Experience.

When entering the name of your college or university, use the drop-down menu to select the appropriate school. That will pull the school's logo into your profile and create instant visual communication and distinction.

As we've previously discussed, a good rule of thumb is to show your GPA if it is higher than a 3.3 or 3.5. Consider showing your GPA in major if it is higher than your overall GPA. If it's lower, omit altogether. You'll see how to respond to interview questions about your GPA in Chapter 5.

EDUCATION SAMPLE 1
UNIVERSITY OF TEXAS, Austin, TX
Bachelor of Science, Business Management
• Minor: Accounting
• Dean's List Standing (all semesters) — GPA: 3.8
• Anticipated Completion: May 2024

EDUCATION SAMPLE 2
MASSACHUSETTS INSTITUTE OF TECHNOLOGY, Cambridge, MA
Candidate, Bachelor of Science in Mechanical Engineering (anticipated Dec. 2023)

== GPA: 4.8/5.00
== Study Abroad: ETH Zurich … Completed semester in Switzerland through MechE Semester Academic Exchange program (Spring 2023); immersed in European culture and various languages.
== International Leadership Community … Selected as member of on-campus, living-learning community for students interested in current/global affairs; participated in Global Leadership course featuring study of the 17 UN Sustainable Development Goals (SDGs).

EDUCATION SAMPLE 3
WEST POINT MILITARY ACADEMY, West Point, NY
B.S., Political Science (May 2023 Graduate)
• Minor: Psychology
• GPA: 3.75
• Co-Captain, Men's Varsity Basketball Team (soph., jr., sr. years)

EDUCATION SAMPLE 4
NORTHEASTERN UNIVERSITY, Boston, MA
MBA, 2023
>> Leadership: Volunteered as a mentor in the Asian-American Center, helping undergraduates with classwork and career decisions.

UNIVERSITY OF MINNESOTA, Minneapolis, MN
BSBA, 2019
>> Extracurriculars: Elected president of the Student Marketing Association. Helped plan events and the organization's first international exchange with Canadian marketing students.

Additional Profile Sections

Now that you've written the all-important Headline, About, Experience, and Education content, spend just a few more minutes filling out your profile to round out your presentation and take advantage of LinkedIn's powerful search and networking functions.

First, let's consider additional (optional) sections that you might include:

- **Volunteer Experience:** If your volunteer activities relate to your career goals, we recommend that you include volunteer work in the primary Experience section. But a separate Volunteer section is also available to you and may be a good way to present a diversity of activities and a record of contribution.

- **Courses:** Just as on your resume, it may be beneficial to list at least your major coursework to increase the keyword density of your profile.

- **Projects:** Again, projects may be better positioned under Experience, but this category allows you to expand on key projects if they are relevant and showcase additional skills and knowledge.

- **Honors & Awards:** Academic honors are more naturally included under Education, but this separate section can be valuable if you have earned recognition from a variety of organizations for different reasons. Go ahead and list them all!

- **Test Scores:** If your standardized test scores are exceptional, you may wish to list them here.

- **Languages:** We highly recommend that you list all languages with which you have at least some proficiency. Be honest about your level of skill, though—unless you are truly fluent, you don't want to claim to speak Spanish and then have that tested in an interview!

- **Organizations:** Membership in relevant professional organizations indicates a strong career interest. You may wish to add other groups, unrelated to your career goals, if you had a leadership position or a major accomplishment.

- **Causes:** It's fine to share causes you support, but we advise against anything that is overtly political, religious, or otherwise controversial—unless the cause is central to your career goals. For example, if you are an environmental scientist, your involvement with "green" causes may be beneficial.

The following three categories—**Skills, Recommendations,** and **Interests**—are important final pieces for maximizing the value of your profile. Your efforts here will pay off in greater opportunities for interaction, more connections, and increased attention from recruiters.

SKILLS

Using the drop-down menu in the Skills section, choose up to 50 skills that reflect the talent, knowledge, expertise, and interpersonal strengths you have to offer. Over time your contacts will endorse you for these skills, and the top three "vote getters" will be listed prominently on your profile, followed by the option to click to "show all skills."

You can—and should—rearrange the top three, if necessary, to make sure they reflect your primary skills and career interests. Click the pencil icon in the Skills section, then on the three dots in the top right corner. Select "reorder" and drag your top skills into the top three spots.

While in the Skills section, take the time to assign skills to each of your listings in Experience and Education. Click the pencil icon next to a skill and follow the prompts to assign that skill where you learned it or demonstrated it. These skills will then populate at the bottom of that entry.

A reminder: Skills are prime keywords used by recruiters and hiring managers to find candidates with specific knowledge and talents. Populating your profile with skills—in multiple sections—will increase your chances of being found.

RECOMMENDATIONS

Recommendations are powerful because they are third-party endorsements: Someone else has taken the time to write a testimonial for you. Think of people you might ask to recommend you:

- Managers from your internships or co-ops
- Supervisors from part-time jobs
- Professors, especially those in your major subject areas or in classes where you held a leadership role or otherwise stood out
- Community leaders, if they know you from your volunteer activities
- College/university faculty or administrators, if you've interacted with them through an extracurricular group or activity

To appear on your LinkedIn page, recommendations must be written and submitted by others. Make a list and reach out to people who know you and like you. Send them an invitation to connect on LinkedIn, and tell them you'd really appreciate a recommendation. If they write something, you'll be notified and can then approve the recommendation before it's posted to your profile.

Recommendations that you write for others also appear on your profile (as well as theirs). If you can write a genuine and thoughtful recommendation for a fellow student, a professor, a manager or supervisor, a community leader, or someone who's been helpful in your early career journey, do it! They will be pleased and your own profile will be richer.

INTERESTS

The "Companies," "Groups," and "Schools" that you are following are important because they are an opportunity to branch into new industries or reinforce your interest in one industry. They open you to new connections, and posts from these contacts will populate your daily LinkedIn feed. As well, Alumni Groups can be a particularly rich source of contacts and potential referral sources.

Leveraging LinkedIn in Your Job Search or Quest for an Internship

In Chapter 4, we'll present the best strategies for connecting with people on LinkedIn and using the robust features of LinkedIn to advance your search for the right internship or full-time employment following graduation. You'll also find other job-search tools, including Handshake, discussed in Chapter 4.

CHAPTER 3:

Open Doors With Cover Letters/E-Notes

Consistent with our counsel throughout this book to be concise, we're kicking off this chapter with succinct advice for cover letters/e-notes from two Career Center professionals.

> ### *Career Centers Say …*
>
> "Write them."
>
> — *Cheryl Minnick, EdD, Career Success Director, College of Humanities & Sciences, University of Montana*
>
> "Both are necessary and taken as evidence of your ability to write in a professional setting."
>
> — *Sharon Belden Castonguay, EdD, Executive Director, Gordon Career Center, Wesleyan University*

To Write, or Not To Write?

Some hiring managers report they never read cover letters. Others say they heavily weigh the message and tone of a cover letter when evaluating a candidate, especially if the resume has caught their attention and they want to know more.

Many job application sites as well as company sites where you can apply directly for a job will say, "Cover letter optional." Here's what we say: There is absolutely zero evidence that *including* a cover letter (even when not requested) *hurts* an applicant's chances. And there is plenty of evidence supporting that at least two-thirds of hiring managers and recruiters view a cover letter as a positive.

From our vantage point, if you skip including a letter because it is not required, you label yourself as someone who is content skipping steps or not giving 100%—taking the easy way out. A candidate who sees the word "optional" as permission to not bother might be perceived as average, run-of-the-mill, or mediocre. Clearly, that's not what you want.

We'll provide another reason for including a cover letter with every single resume you submit. Even when you are emailing your resume to someone with whom you've had a conversation and who knows your background, you want to make their job easier when passing your resume along as a candidate. You don't want to make them have to work to tell your story in the body of the email *they write* when forwarding your resume.

Instead, if you provide a short e-note or cover letter with every resume, you are giving the recipient the background details, the "why" and the "what": Why you are interested in the company ... why you wish to be a candidate for a particular job ... what qualifications you bring to the position ... what makes you a good choice as a person to interview.

Career Centers Say ...

"Tailored cover letters are an important part of your application. While a resume can indicate the specific skills, experiences, and knowledge you bring to a role, a cover letter allows you to expand on those areas, add additional value proposition, and speak specifically to why you are drawn to the organization/agency/company. Research indicates that candidates who include a cover letter yield more interviews than those who do not."

— *Micall Searles, Career Coach, University of Montana*

In this chapter, we'll give you all the tools you need to quickly put together the right type of short cover letter or e-note we recommend using every time you apply.

PRO TIP: Once you've taken the time to craft a really good cover letter, you generally won't need to reinvent the wheel each time you apply for an internship or job. You can simply edit and tweak the content to fit each role without starting from scratch.

Over time, it is efficient to build a small library of customized cover letters (and resumes, for that matter, as we mentioned in Chapter 1). Save each tweaked cover letter and resume version with a few words that label the audience and content so that you can quickly retrieve and customize for each future opportunity.

What's the Difference Between a Cover Letter and an E-note?

Great question! Generally speaking, an e-note is simply your cover letter pasted into the body of your email—it is the message.

A cover letter can be that same message, formatted as a traditional business letter on letterhead that matches your resume.

The differences relate to the way the document is set up and some opening and closing content and format. You'll find many examples of both e-notes and cover letters in this chapter, and our guidelines spell out just a few differences in these substantially similar documents.

> ## *Career Centers Say ...*
>
> "For cover letters, I tell students they have won a third of the battle if their cover letter 'looks like' a cover letter (i.e., has a header that matches their resume, a date, and an internal address of an employer), has a proper salutation and is addressed to the right person if they can find it or to 'Dear Hiring Manager' or 'Dear Selection Committee,' has three to four easily readable and grammatically correct paragraphs, and includes a signature block.
>
> "If it 'looks like' a cover letter, an employer knows that this person will be able to write proper communication once hired."
>
> *— Cara Mitnick, Director of Professional Development, University of Rhode Island*

Short and Sweet

Keep your cover letter short—a brief introduction followed by two, maybe three, short paragraphs and possibly a few bullet points, then a concise closing. When viewed on an 8.5" x 11" page, your letter should take up about half to two-thirds of the page—at most, three-quarters.

Your e-note should be just as short if not shorter than your cover letter. And just as we recommend for your resume and your LinkedIn profile, in both documents all of your paragraphs and bullet points should be quite concise, ideally no more than two or three lines long. You want to engage your readers, not turn them off with overly dense, lengthy copy.

> ## *Career Centers Say ...*
>
> "We emphasize that cover letters are students' opportunities to humanize themselves for employers and to emphasize their enthusiasm/passion for the specific job and specific employer. They should be only one page."
>
> *— Gretchen Heaton, Dean of Career Development, Bay Path University*

A Winning Formula for Writing E-notes and Cover Letters

As you begin to write letters for a variety of opportunities, simply follow these prompts that will guide you from start to finish. Once you've practiced the formula a few times, you'll be able to quickly craft a letter, or modify an existing letter, for each opportunity you encounter.

You'll see this formula in action in the many examples that follow.

> ### *Career Centers Say ...*
>
> "Make the 'why' stand out: Why that company? Why that industry? Then relate it back to experience. Think of your resume as *the facts*, the cover letter as *the story*. Even if the job posting doesn't require a letter, the candidate should submit one anyway—it's an opportunity to stand out and it helps to validate 'why them.'"
>
> — *Career Center Staff, Western Washington University*

Getting Started

- **Cover Letter:** Copy the heading (name and contact information along with any design elements) from your resume and use that as the letterhead for your cover letters. At the left margin, a few spaces below the header, type the date and then, a few spaces down, the "inside address"—the name and address of the person you're writing to.

- **E-note:** Open a new email message and enter the email address of the person or organization you're writing to.

Subject Line

- **Cover Letter:** A subject line, positioned two lines below the date, is optional but is a good way to immediately clue readers in to the reason you're writing. It also allows you to avoid the somewhat formulaic and stilted opening found in many cover letters: "I am interested in the position of Job Title and attaching my resume for your review." Instead, you can start your letter with information that's more interesting and unique to you.

- **E-note:** Mention the reason you're writing in the email subject line.

Salutation

- **Cover Letter:** Use a formal salutation (*Dear Mr. Lastname:* or *Dear Ms. Lastname:*), two lines below the inside address or subject line. For a job application that is not sent to a specific person, you may use *Dear Hiring Manager:* or *Dear Selection Committee:*.

- **E-note:** Skip the formal inside address that you would use on a traditional letter and go right to the salutation—the same type of formal greeting as in a letter: *Dear Mr. Lastname:* or *Dear Ms. Lastname:*. For a job application that is uploaded and not sent to a specific person, you may use *Dear Hiring Manager:* or *Dear Selection Committee:*.

  NOTE: Punctuation after the salutation should be a colon—Dear Ms. Jones: or Dear Hiring Manager:—not a comma.

Body—Both Cover Letter and E-note

Write or paste in your content—3 or 4 short paragraphs and perhaps bullet points. More specifically:

- **Opening Paragraph:** Express what you are applying for or why you are writing. If you have already referenced the job posting or other specific reason for your letter in a subject line, you do not need to repeat that information in your opening paragraph.

  Include a few key points—that you are graduating with a degree in 'x' and that you have internship and/or work experience that's relevant. If you want to get creative, you might include a quote by someone (famous or not) that is applicable to your philosophy, work ethic, or approach. You might also mention what, specifically, about the opportunity is particularly interesting or exciting to you. If you were referred by someone, be certain to mention that person's name right up front!

- **Second Paragraph:** This is where you connect your experience, knowledge, and skills to what is being sought or where you think your skills best line up. Be specific—whether mentioning software skills, social media background, or relevant experience you've had in an internship or through a class. If you have a number of things to share, consider breaking into two shorter paragraphs.

- **Consider Supporting Bullet Points:** See if you can share 3–4 brief bullet points that convey key interests/skills/experiences that match up with what is being sought in the job description.

- **Final Paragraph:** In a short paragraph, reiterate your interest in the role and/or the company and express your enthusiasm for being considered as a candidate. Also convey thanks.

If you are writing to an individual, it is ideal for you to indicate that *you* will follow up rather than simply waiting to hear from them. Of course, with a blind posting or other message where you don't have an individual's name, you cannot do this.

Closing

- **Cover Letter:** End with a formal closing: *Sincerely,* followed by a blank line and then your name. You do not need to add your other contact details (phone, email, and LinkedIn URL) because they appear at the top of your letterhead.

- **E-note:** End with a formal closing: *Sincerely,* followed by your email signature block—standard information that should close out every message you send throughout your job search and in other professional communications. Include your email address, phone number, and LinkedIn URL in your signature block.

> ### *Career Centers Say …*
>
> "Cover letters can be a great addition to a resume submission. However, it's important to take the time to carefully ensure that the letter is individualized, specific to the targeted role, and demonstrates why the candidate is a good fit for the position. Otherwise, a poorly written letter could tend to hurt the applicant's chances."
>
> — *Chaim Shapiro, Director of the Office for Student Success, Touro University*

Cover Letter / E-note Examples

Take a look at various ways you might introduce yourself as a candidate, express personality, and stand out in a creative way as you review the following examples. For instance:

- A short, meaningful quote
- Bullet points
- Comments from internship supervisors or employers
- A thought-provoking question
- An interesting (but brief!) story that illustrates your key qualities, reason for pursuing a specific career, reason you're interested in a company, or other pertinent facts.

SAMPLE 1: E-note in response to a job posting

Subject: Health Instructor (TeacherJobs.com posting #A742)

Dear Selection Committee:

The British poet Edward Bulwer-Lytton wrote, **"The best teacher is the one who suggests rather than dogmatizes, and inspires his listener with the wish to teach himself."**

This quote aptly describes one of my philosophies of teaching. Health education is more than simply developing lesson plans and implementing curriculum: It is instilling in each student tools and practices that can serve over the course of a lifetime.

I have worked with children from kindergarten to Grade 12 through student teaching, internship, and field placement experiences as part of my BS program in Health Education at Purdue (May 2023 graduate). You will find me to be someone who talks the talk *and* walks the walk with respect to health education, nutrition, and fitness. Passionate about imparting my knowledge and enthusiasm to students, I am committed to making a difference. I know I can do that as a health educator.

As you consider my candidacy, please also be aware that I would also be very interested in assisting as a coach—either a field hockey coach for girls or a soccer coach for boys or girls.

I would value the opportunity to speak with you about this teaching position. I am confident I can bring the knowledge, enthusiasm, and energy to contribute to the learning environment at your school. Thank you for your consideration.

Sincerely,

Eduardo Duran
eduardoduran@email.com
555-432-1234
linkedin.com/in/eduardo-duran

SAMPLE 2: E-note in response to a job posting

Subject: Product Marketing position—LinkedIn Job Posting #143115

Dear Hiring Manager:

As a Marketing major at Bryant University (I will graduate in May), I am eager to begin my professional career with an industry leader such as Lipton Tea. I bring a strong record of experience through 3 Marketing and Social Media internships that complement my theoretical studies in marketing.

These select accomplishments illustrate valuable skills I bring to your marketing team:

- **Established cohesive database of assets on Google Drive,** instilling consistent nomenclature and hierarchy that supports efficient searches.
- **Directed social content calendars for 2 different companies;** managed social media across multiple channels (Instagram, TikTok, Snapchat, Pinterest, Twitter, Facebook, LinkedIn).
- **Orchestrated off-site events for up to 100 people** (company picnic and 3-day client conferences); supervised all arrangements and managed vendor selection/negotiation, venue, and catering to ensure success.
- **Conducted marketing research and competitive analysis;** prepared white papers and presented PowerPoints that captured key findings.

In addition to these capabilities, I am a high-energy and creative professional, recognized as a sincere and perceptive "people person" who relates effectively to people at all levels. My track record reflects a proven ability to manage time well—I successfully balance a demanding academic schedule with a varsity sport.

I am confident of my ability to contribute significantly to Lipton Tea and will quickly prove that I can learn new skills and come up to speed rapidly. I am very enthusiastic about relocating to the Hoboken area. I would value the opportunity to discuss your hiring objectives and how my background and experience might represent the right fit. Thank you for your consideration.

Sincerely,

Liam O'Hara
liam.ohara@gmail.com I 555-229-3670
www.linkedin.com/in/liam.ohara

SAMPLE 3: Cover letter uploaded with resume to company job site

Ayesha Montgomery

555-678-1234

ayeshamontgomery@mail.com

LinkedIn Profile

April 25, 2023

Dear Hiring Manager:

The position of **Collections Care Coordinator** for Stanford University's Cantor Arts Center is an exciting opportunity that I believe is an excellent fit for my background and experience.

I am currently interning as a Collections Inventory Technician as part of a 4-person team for a 9-month project at Harvard University's Radcliffe Institute and The Arthur and Elizabeth Schlesinger Library. We are carefully preparing the institution's 40,000-piece collection of ancient Egyptian artifacts for relocation to offsite storage during a major 3- to 5-year construction project on campus.

Some of my responsibilities that will prove transferable to Stanford include:

- Implementing a new barcode system with use of accession numbers as a component of inventory control
- Inventorying artifacts and providing photography as well as documentation for handling, packing, and storing materials
- Writing a procedures manual for large-scale movement of collections
- Collaborating effectively with cross-functional/cross-organizational staff

In each of my roles, I have quickly acclimated to fast-paced environments and rapidly transferred my skills while learning new processes and software (I am experienced using both TMS and KE EMu collections management systems). I will graduate with a Bachelor of Arts degree from Villanova University; I majored in Archival Studies.

I am confident of my ability to contribute to Stanford University as a Collections Care Coordinator. I look forward to speaking with you about this opportunity. Thank you for your consideration.

Sincerely,

Ayesha Montgomery

SAMPLE 4: Cover letter uploaded with resume to company job site

Robert Tavares

SPORTS MANAGEMENT

555-872-1110
robert-tavares@email.com
LinkedIn.com/in/robert-tavares

March 29, 2003

Dear Selection Team:

Please consider my candidacy for the role of **Marketing Associate** for which you are currently recruiting. I bring a strong record of field, Bowl game, and NFL internship sports experience to this opportunity, augmented by a degree in Sport Management this coming spring **(Bachelor of Science, University of Florida).**

My interest in the business side of sports was aroused when I attended a sport management conference in Indianapolis during the 2021 NFL Draft Combine. That interest led me to pursue (and win) a coveted internship with the Indianapolis Colts.

I offer both relevant experience and proven skills and strengths that align with your requirements:

Sports Management & Promotions Experience
- ➢ **Marketing & Events Internship** with the Indianapolis Colts
- ➢ **Events Marketing Internship** with the Poinsettia and Holiday Bowl Games in San Diego
- ➢ **Marketing, Hospitality, and Customer Service Roles** with Florida Citrus Sports (2 Bowl Games), University Athletic Association, Walt Disney World, and PGA Tour (through marketing class)

Strengths
- ➢ **A dedicated, high-energy, and creative professional** who has gained experience with brainstorming and idea generation to deepen fan engagement, enhance sport-focused events, and solidify fan base.
- ➢ **A sincere and perceptive "people person"** who relates effectively to people at all levels. Skilled in defusing stress and conflict and maintaining calm and competence in the frenzied chaos of game day.
- ➢ **Someone who goes above and beyond in meeting commitments and deadlines,** taking initiative and meticulously organizing detailed notes and action plans that produce results.

I am confident of my ability to contribute significantly to your organization and would value the opportunity to speak with your hiring team. Thanks for considering my application.

Sincerely,

Robert Tavares

SAMPLE 5: E-note in response to a job posting

Subject: Medical Marketing/Sales Associate

Dear Selection Committee:

What interests me most about your posting for a Marketing/Sales Associate is the requirement for both research/analytical skills and people/customer skills. This "sweet spot" is the perfect definition of the value I offer.

Specifically:

▶ I'm a new graduate with a BS in Business who formerly majored in Finance. I have a good grasp of numbers, but I'm even more interested in the stories and the people behind the data.

▶ My senior marketing project was a deep dive into marketing opportunities for an innovative medical device company. My team and I came up with creative, inexpensive, and highly practical ideas that earned us an A+ and a "best in show" award from the review team.

▶ I love to solve problems for customers and colleagues, but I understand the importance of listening and learning before jumping to the answer.

▶ As a competitive athlete, I have an inner drive to improve and excel. I actually enjoy the grunt work because I know it builds the strong foundation I need for sustained performance.

From what I've read, Drexel Medical is a great place to work. I am very interested in learning more about this opportunity and how I can bring value to your company and your customers. Thank you for considering my application. I am excited to take the next steps.

Sincerely,

Rebecca Hofstatter
rebecca.hofstatter@email.com ▶ 555-345-2670 ▶ linkedin.com/in/rebecca-hofstatter

SAMPLE 6: E-note in response to a job posting

Subject: Mechanical Engineer, Indeed Posting #74A2321

Dear Hiring Manager:

Your posting for a Mechanical Engineer is of great interest to me, as I am relocating to the Chicago area in June following my graduation (BSME) from Rensselaer Polytechnic Institute.

Briefly, my qualifications include:
- 3+ years of engineering work experiences, including summer internships.
- A track record that reflects an especially strong work ethic, a deep determination and drive to excel, and a committed sense of personal self-discipline.
- An ability to work well both autonomously and as a very effective team member.
- A creative and solutions-focused approach to solving problems, with good experience brainstorming and a reputation for stepping into a leadership role.

Consistent with my tenacious approach, I have earned praise from my supervisors in every job. In my current role with Trilogy, my manager lauded my "above and beyond" performance and cited my work as "delivering value" in design/schematics for customized installations, testing, and development of documentation.

In addition to my undergraduate coursework in engineering, my on-the-job experience exposed me to a number of mechanical engineering processes while working on machines, collecting and analyzing data, handling quality control work, and operating automated cell, inspection CMM, and CNC equipment. My training and experience also includes Mastercam and SOLIDWORKS in addition to Microsoft Office, Arduino, Quartus, and MATLAB as well as C++.

I am confident of my ability to quickly integrate and make a significant contribution to your team. I look forward to discussing how my background might be the right fit with what you are seeking. Thank you for your consideration.

Sincerely,

Kendra Williams
555-772-7818 • kendrawilliams@gmail.com
www.linkedin.com/in/kendrajwilliams

SAMPLE 7: Cover letter uploaded with resume to company job site

Germaine West

555-887-2209 ▶ GermaineWest@email.com ▶ LinkedIn.com/in/GermaineWest

Dear Selection Committee:

I am excited to submit my application for a Behavioral Health Specialist with Medina Health.

As a soon-to-graduate Psychology major, I offer a strong educational foundation in human behavior. And with several years of experience working with diverse populations in medical and educational settings, I have demonstrated key skills that will be important in working with clients at your facility:

- ▶ Ability to connect with, teach, influence, and direct people with physical and developmental disabilities.

- ▶ Comfort and confidence working with challenging populations—including seniors with dementia, severely disabled children, homeless individuals, and people suffering from addiction.

- ▶ Inspirational leadership skills. I have encouraged students and athletes to stretch beyond their comfort zones and have been a leader and role model to build tight-knit, hard-working, deeply engaged music and theater groups.

As you will note from my resume, I have a long history of hands-on involvement with organizations dedicated to helping others grow and improve. I would like to continue this track record with an organization like yours that shares my values and provides essential services to people deeply in need.

May we schedule an interview soon? I would enjoy learning more about your programs and sharing how my experience relates to the needs of your organization and your clients.

Sincerely,

Germaine West

SAMPLE 8: E-note application for a referred opportunity

Dear Ms. Monahan:

My neighbor, Rick Madison (a senior software developer with Murphy Technologies), suggested that I contact you regarding your current search for a Junior Developer.

In addition to earning a BS in Engineering from the University of Massachusetts (May 2023), I have acquired software development skills through intensive self-education via The Odin Project over the last 9 months. My studies have included extensive learning about object-oriented programming in Ruby and the various technologies required to build modern web applications, including SQL, HTML, CSS, Javascript, Angular, Bootstrap, and Git.

Through my experience with Odin's Open Source Web Development Curriculum, I have built a strong foundation of programming concepts and development tools to supplement my existing math background, problem-solving ability, and computer science coursework. I am confident I have the necessary toolset and exceptional desire to learn if selected as a Junior Developer—I am eager to contribute in a development role.

This brief example illustrates my initiative and problem-solving skills.

As an undergraduate member of the Outing Club (UMass's largest club with 550 members), I identified a problem with the lack of a system to manage about $70K in rental equipment/outdoor gear. I designed and developed a web application using Ruby on Rails and a SQL database to accurately track rental gear and preserve the club's rental fleet. Application development is nearly complete, with anticipated go-live for rental management in the fall.

May we schedule a brief meeting (in person or Zoom) to discuss how my experience can enable me to quickly add value to your team? I will follow up with you next week and appreciate your consideration.

Sincerely,

Trayvon Adams
tvadams@gmail.com — 555-347-1121 — LinkedIn.com/in/trayvon-adams

SAMPLE 9: Cover letter uploaded with resume to company job site

Alison Dockery | 555-412-8819 | alisondockery@gmail.com | LinkedIn.com/in/alison-dockery

Re: **Audit Associate**

I am interested in an entry-level audit position with Marks & Bailey and believe I have the education, skills, aptitude, and attitude you seek.

Growing up, I always knew I wanted to be a professional soccer player. I devoted myself to this goal with a great deal of energy, enthusiasm, dedication, and passion. I succeeded in club play, in high school, and in college—as a Division I starting athlete—not because I had more talent than others, but because I had more commitment and an unbeatable work ethic.

When a series of injuries led me to realize that professional soccer was not in my future, I devoted all of my energy and passion to achieving other goals. I set my sights on a professional career in auditing/accounting—a field that might seem the complete opposite from professional sports but in fact has many parallels:

➜ **Solid foundation of skills.**
Success takes hard work, but it is built on fundamentals. As a double major in Accounting and Economics at Texas A&M University, I have created a strong base of knowledge in accounting and auditing, business, and information systems. My strong GPA (3.5) shows my ability to master challenging subjects while devoting more than 20 hours each week to my athletic responsibilities.

➜ **Continuous learning and improvement.**
Even world-class athletes don't rest on their laurels—they always strive for more. Similarly, in business, every project and every engagement is an opportunity to gain more knowledge, more insight, and more expertise. I love learning, and I get great satisfaction from improving my performance in any arena.

➜ **Discipline and work ethic.**
From a very early age, I saw how hard work and a disciplined approach produced results I wanted. Strong planning, organization, and time management skills have been the keys to high productivity and top performance in every area of my life.

➜ **Teamwork.**
Michael Jordan said, "Talent wins games, but teamwork and intelligence win championships." I have seen first-hand, many times, how teams become more than the sum of the individual parts. I enjoy collaborating with my teammates, working together toward a common goal, and finding solutions to challenging problems.

Nearing graduation, I am excited to begin my professional career and would be honored to do so with Marks & Bailey. I would appreciate the opportunity for an interview to learn more about your specific needs and share further details of my background, qualifications, and sincere interest in joining your firm. Thank you for your consideration.

Sincerely,

Alison Dockery

SAMPLE 10: Note sent with resume to someone who is referring/introducing you

Dear Mr. Kirchman:

I appreciate your willingness to introduce me to your contacts at Superior Technology. To assist you in making this referral, I've attached my resume and summarized a few details below.

Throughout my undergraduate studies at Emory University, I have taken advantage of every opportunity to assist in the biochemical laboratory, work with different professors and graduate students, and support the lab staff. I've been able to participate in such activities as gathering information from various assays, inventorying supplies, and caring for test animals.

I will complete my B.S. in Biochemical Sciences this May and am eager to bring my skillset and keen interest in healthcare science and biomedicine to a pharmaceutical company or testing laboratory.

Additional background on my resume reflects a commitment to continual learning (I've augmented my undergraduate work with a number of certification and badge programs) and a strong work ethic (I've held two part-time jobs through my high school and college studies).

Thank you, again, for making this introduction and helping to advance my candidacy.

Sincerely,

Josiah Bateman
josiahbateman@mail.com >> 555-781-1101 >> LinkedIn.com/josiah-bateman

---

Career Centers Say ...

"Never underestimate the power of a well-written cover letter. Some hiring managers tell us they do not review them, and others review every detail. If the job requires some writing ability, you can bet they will be reviewing the cover letter critically. Follow professional business format. Do some research and find the hiring manager's name and address to include in your draft. Candidates that take time to research the organization and demonstrate that research through the application and interview process will be more successful."

— *Amanda Schagane, Associate Director of Alumni Career Services, University of Kentucky*

CHAPTER 4:

Jump Into Your Job Search

Now that you've written your resume, drafted an e-note/cover letter, and polished and uploaded your LinkedIn profile, you are ready to launch your job search.

What's first? Of course you'll want to provide your material to anyone you've been in conversation with—employers, family or friends who have offered to help, professors, your university's Career Center, and so forth. But that's just the beginning.

In this chapter we go into detail on the top methods of conducting your job search. Keep in mind that the best—quickest!—results are likely to come from pursuing multiple approaches simultaneously.

How to Find a Job

1. **Apply to posted openings.** This is certainly the easiest method, and it can be quite effective for new graduates. On page 88 we give you some tips to increase your chances of getting a response and an interview.

2. **Talk to people you know.** Again, easy! See the section on Networking, beginning on page 90, so that your conversations are as productive as possible.

3. **Meet new people**—not randomly, but with a plan and a purpose. We explain how to go about it beginning on page 90.

4. **Follow companies and influencers on social media** to gain insights and, sometimes, alerts to opportunities. Beginning on page 95 we share recommendations around this strategy.

Career Centers Say ...

"Be methodical—one thing at a time, so you don't get overwhelmed. Have a master resume or CV complete, polish your LinkedIn profile, do informational interviews, and let everyone know you are looking. Make sure your family and friends know what you're studying, what your selling points are (internships, top grades, projects, research), and what you are seeking professionally, as they can be your biggest sources of connections and potential jobs. I tell students many, many things, but one thing I always tell them is, 'You shouldn't be your own surgeon, and you shouldn't edit your own resume (CV) or cover letter.' Reach out for help to a career advisor, mentor, alumni, professor."

— *Cara Mitnick, Director of Professional Development, University of Rhode Island*

Before You Begin

In Chapter 1 we discussed the importance of identifying a clear career goal before writing your resume. Similarly, as you launch your job search, take a few minutes to further clarify your hopes for this, your first post-college job or an important internship.

While you may not achieve a perfect fit in every aspect, you will be creating a framework that will help you in communicating with contacts, reaching out to employers, and evaluating opportunities that come your way.

You will want to review and edit these details as your search progresses. For example, you may have a short list of "Companies of Interest" right now, but that list will change (expand *and* shrink) as you learn of new opportunities, gain insights from contacts, and start interviewing. Consider these responses a working draft.

Worksheet #3 for Defining and Refining Your Job Targets

Target Job Title(s): _____

_____

_____

Industries of Interest: _____

_____

_____

Type of Work Challenges You Most Enjoy: _____

_____

_____

_____

Environment/Culture/Location Preferences: _____

_____

_____

Companies of Interest: _____

_____

_____

Career Centers Say ...

"Start a running list of potential job titles as well as target companies for the job search. Think critically about the type of organization and team you want to join before you apply. Students and recent graduates might find themselves attracted to the flashy names of Fortune 500 organizations. If candidates are looking for more of a family-oriented culture, consider small to medium-sized companies. Networking with alumni is always recommended. Alumni are semi-warm contacts and typically reply to students via LinkedIn. Using the LinkedIn alumni feature, it's easy to find alumni in a target industry or location."

— *Amanda Schagane, Associate Director of Alumni Career Services, University of Kentucky*

Job-Search Tools and Resources

You may be familiar with **Handshake** through your university, and **LinkedIn** is another exceptionally valuable tool for managing your career. In this section we share details of how to use these and other tools in multiple stages of your job search.

Tools to Manage Your Search Activities

First, you'll need to get organized. Job search involves many written communications and phone calls, a lot of contacts, important follow-up activities, and a great deal of information-gathering regarding specific jobs, employers, and connections. You need a system for keeping track of all these details.

Once you choose your system, commit to entering all the data that's necessary to keep your search humming along. Options include:

- **Spreadsheet** (Excel, Google Sheets, Apple Numbers, or similar): Set up your spreadsheet so that you can sort by many different categories—employer name, source of opportunity, referral contact name, job title, industry, name of cover letter and resume you sent, location, work environment (remote, hybrid, 100% in-office), follow-up dates and actions, interview notes, and other categories that will help you keep tabs on different opportunities and stay on top of various referrals and recommendations.

- **JibberJobber, Huntr:** These tools are customized CRM (customer relationship management) software specifically designed for job search. Both offer free and more robust premium memberships. You can set reminders for follow-up—a very useful tool!

Other Technology Tools and Considerations

More and more, **Artificial Intelligence (AI)** is being used to scan resumes, compare contents to job descriptions, identify top matches (and weed out all others), and even conduct initial screening interviews.

AI is embedded, of course, in **Applicant Tracking Systems (ATS),** the resume-scanning software that is used by most employers. There are many different systems, and each can be customized to the employer's needs and preferences. So there is no one-size-fits-all strategy for conforming to ATS.

As we discussed in Chapter 1, your best approach to "beat" the ATS is to use all appropriate keywords in your resume, focus on your unique accomplishments, and tweak the content as necessary to match a particular job description. Here are a few tools that can help you do that. The first two—Jobscan and VMock—are extensively used by higher education, so you may be able to access them through your Career Center.

- **Jobscan** allows you to upload your resume and a job description to test how well they align.
- **VMock** uses machine learning (ML), data analytics, and language assessment to analyze your resume online and then compare it to information provided by employers.
- **LinkedIn** offers another excellent tool to improve keyword matching. After you've completed your profile, click on the "More" button just below your name and headline. Click "Build a Resume," "Create from Profile." You'll be prompted to add a Job Title. On the right you'll see a list of keywords that appear in your resume and, below that, "suggested keywords."

After using any or all of these tools, see if you can honestly add any of the recommended or missing keywords into your resume, cover letters, and LinkedIn profile. You still should take the time to customize your documents for every application, but a big-picture review and editing at this stage should help to minimize future customization efforts.

> **PRO TIP: Be authentic.** As you are beefing up the keyword density in your resume, and tweaking to conform to specific postings, be honest about what you have to offer. *Do* claim skills and experience that you own, that you can discuss in an interview, and that you can bring to an employer. *Don't* add keywords that sound great but don't represent your skills and knowledge. Employers are sure to find out—either in the interview process or when you can't perform essential job duties. Either way, your reputation will suffer and your career will be off to a bad start.

While it's important to consider AI, ATS, and the increasing use of technology in the hiring process, don't be overly concerned. If you follow our guidelines for Job Search and Networking—both coming right up!—you will focus your attention on the much more important activities that will help you get in front of the right contact or hiring manager (via email, phone, Zoom, or, ideally, in person) to make the case for your candidacy based on much more than keyword matching.

> ## *Career Centers Say ...*
>
> "I still believe that the best job-search tool is networking, via LinkedIn, professional associations, or contacts. We are also increasingly emphasizing the development of polished professional e-portfolios that demonstrate skills and competencies in real-life examples."
>
> — *Gretchen Heaton, Dean of Career Development, Bay Path University*

Handshake

There is probably not a university today that isn't introducing its students to Handshake (https://joinhandshake.com). The robust website provides students with job-search tools, a way to explore career options as well as internships, and a portal for connecting with employers.

> ### *Career Centers Say ...*
>
> "I believe that internships are the key to helping students land the job of their dreams. That's our main goal—career readiness—and making sure that students have all the tools and resources that they need to find a job. My staff and I work to create campaigns promoting internships and increasing placements. It's essential to capture this experience in a compelling way on the resume. This helps to give our graduates a competitive edge."
>
> — *Toni Ripo, Coordinator of Career Services, University of South Florida*

The steps are simple for getting onto Handshake if you haven't already.

1) Sign up on Handshake and download the app.

2) Create a profile. You can do this quickly if you follow the same process you used to craft your resume and LinkedIn, and even some of the same content. Once your profile is established, you will receive personalized job recommendations.

3) Meet with prospective employers through the chat feature, by attending webinars, and by participating in other activities. Ask questions and gain insight into the hiring needs and practices of companies of possible interest, explore company culture, and see actual job opportunities. Some postings will include details such as salary, if the position is remote or not, whether the role can be used for work study, if a paid internship is available, and other helpful information.

4) Sign up for career fairs, other events, and information of interest.

5) Upload your resume and cover letter, and apply to positions of interest in just a few clicks. (Be sure to read our tips beginning on page 88 for ways to maximize your chances of earning an interview.)

6) Schedule appointments with your Career Center.

Handshake allows users to explore opportunities in many different career paths—from tech, media, and finance to marketing, education, and government. Companies range from early-stage startups and mom-and-pop enterprises to companies in the Fortune 500. For students interested in exploring opportunities in locations other than their home state or in the area where their university is located, Handshake can be a great gateway.

Because most campuses are using Handshake, your Career Center is your best resource for specific questions you may have for this tool.

LinkedIn

One of the reasons we recommend LinkedIn as the #1 tool for job search is because it's a perfect way to get established for making career connections, pursuing job opportunities, and managing your career today and for years to come. While we all know that technology is constantly changing, LinkedIn has consistently provided exceptional value for more than 15 years. At the time of publication, its reputation and influence show no sign of waning.

There are other fundamental reasons for encouraging you to get familiar with and use LinkedIn in your job search:

- The people who will want to talk to you (and hire you) are likely on LI and using it regularly.
- The people you will possibly be contacting for recommendations or references are also likely to be on LI.
- And, as your career becomes established, the people (recruiters!) who are hired or retained to search for good candidates like you are definitely using LI to source and vet candidates. Building a robust LinkedIn site for yourself can pay strong dividends over time—starting with right now.

Your Roadmap for Optimizing LinkedIn
LinkedIn offers many features that you can explore at your leisure. Here, we'll focus on the essential activities and strategies that most effectively support your search as a newer LI user.

1. Create Your LinkedIn Profile
Most likely, you've completed your profile following the guidelines in Chapter 2. If you haven't, now is the time. Your LinkedIn activities won't be effective without a robust, keyword-rich profile that lets people know who you are, what excites you professionally, and what you're looking for.

2. Build Your Connection Network
You have three paths to building this network.

First, see if you have any outstanding invitations from people wishing to connect. We recommend that you accept all invitations, unless the person has a reputation that is not as professional as you think it should be, or if their LinkedIn site features anything that would detract from a professional image. Pass on those invitations and save social media interactions with those friends for IG and Snapchat.

When you accept an invitation, you'll be given an opportunity to respond with a message. This is courteous and professional and we recommend sending a message—"Thanks for connecting!"—along with a brief personal note.

- To a fellow new graduate, you might say, "Hope your search is going well!"
- To a graduate who has landed a role, you can say, "Congrats on the exciting gig! Way to go!"
- To a professor or other contact from your university, you might wish to say, "Thanks so much for connecting. I'd like to reach out to you shortly to ask for a recommendation."
- To someone affiliated with an industry or company of interest, you'll want to be very mindful and take the time to compose a careful reply. See the tips in the Networking section, beginning on page 90, for message ideas.

PRO TIP: Spam and telemarketers exist on LinkedIn. You may receive offers for services or products. You can simply ignore these invitations and messages.

Your **second** path to building your network is to extend invitations to people you know. Your goal is to build your number of connections, but an equally important objective is to build **quality connections** with people who have some professional knowledge or contacts that can be helpful during your job search and throughout your career.

Certainly reach out to connect with college and high school friends, current and former co-workers, extra-curricular sports club members, and other people in your social circle.

Even more importantly, reach out to your professors, instructors, coaches, and even high school teachers and administrators. Internship supervisors and present/former employers and supervisors are absolutely the "quality connections" who can add immeasurable value to your job search.

> **PRO TIP: Do not use LinkedIn's "Easy Connect" feature.** Rather, take the time to write a short, personal note to each individual you are inviting to connect. Here's the process:
>
> - *Don't* simply click "Connect" when LinkedIn recommends "people you may know." Rather, navigate to each person's profile.
> - Then hit the blue "Connect" button (below the name and headline), and a pop-up will tell you, "Your invitation is almost on its way. You can add a note to personalize your invitation to NAME."
> - Click the "Add a Note" button and add your personal message before sending.
>
> Similar to your message when accepting a connection, your outreach to people should be brief and friendly. Feel free to add a comment that explains your reason for reaching out—"I'm about to graduate and getting my professional image in order!" Or, "As I start my post-graduation job search, I'd love to learn how you're using LinkedIn professionally." Or, "Let's catch up soon. I'd love to hear how you're navigating the work world since you graduated."

Your **third** method of building your network is connecting with people you *don't yet know.*

How to do it? Start by checking out who is connected to people who are already in your network. Use LinkedIn's search function to find individuals who work at your target companies, and follow the connection to see how they link to you. You can then ask *your* contact for an introduction.

In our experience these second- and even third-degree connections are often the most productive contacts you will make.

For now, put that idea on hold. We'll go into much more detail in the Networking section, and you'll also see scripting for how to write the important outgoing messages to new contacts.

> **PRO TIP: Strive for 100 to 125 quality connections on LinkedIn.** In our experience, that number will lead to good things happening. You'll have more resources in your target industry, more potential contacts at companies of interest, and more ways to get to the people you want to meet.

3. Find and Apply for Jobs

At last we get to the fun part! LinkedIn is a valuable source for job postings, and you will find recommendations for you under the "Jobs" tab at the top of your profile.

You can fine-tune these recommendations a bit by adding your job preferences to your profile. At the top of your profile page, under the blue Connect button, click "Get Started" in the left-hand box ("Show recruiters you're open to work"). The pop-up will let you enter job titles and work preferences. Note that "Internships" is one of the options.

The final option in the pop-up is labeled "Choose who sees you're open." We recommend that you choose *recruiters only*, not all of your contacts on LinkedIn. Why? If you choose "all," a big green "open to work" frame will surround your photo. We think it looks a bit desperate, and it does not make you more findable—recruiters and others continue to search using keywords.

Okay, you're ready—but don't apply just yet. Read on to learn the best way to respond to posted openings from all sources to give yourself the very best possible chance of being selected as a candidate.

Career Centers Say …

"Don't limit yourself! A lot of students don't think they're qualified and they don't apply. Sometimes the beginning of the process involves a pep talk! You *are* qualified.

"Be proactive instead of reactive. It's not all about applying to online positions; there should be an equal importance on networking and being proactive in search of networking partners—rather than sitting around and waiting to hear back.

"Even in a hotshot market, networking is still super critical—not only to have more success, but to find out if the culture is a good fit. Go beyond the website."

— *Career Center Staff, Western Washington University*

Launching Your Job Search

You've completed your prep—created your activity-tracking system, identified your target jobs and companies, built your online profile on LinkedIn and Handshake, and familiarized yourself with the features of those and other apps and tools you'll encounter in your job search.

It's time, at last, to launch your search. Remember those four methods for "How to Find a Job" from the beginning of this chapter? Let's go through them one by one.

Method #1: Apply to Posted Openings

You'll find job postings on countless sites and platforms, including:

- **Job Aggregators**—Sites that compile postings from many different sources and promise a one-stop platform for managing your search. The most popular aggregators are Indeed, SimplyHired, Careerbuilder, and Monster.
- **LinkedIn** is also a job aggregator and will recommend opportunities to you based on your preferences and profile contents.
- **Handshake** posts job and internship openings for which you may have an advantage through your university affiliation.

- **Specialty Job Aggregators** are focused on a specific industry, profession, or other factor that will help weed out less-relevant postings. Good examples are DiversityJobs, FlexJobs (for remote and flexible opportunities), Dice (for jobs in technology), HealthECareers, NationalNonprofits, and eFinancialCareers. You can do a Google search to find special sites for your niche.
- **Social Media:** It's a good practice to follow companies and influencers related to your career targets. You may gain early notice of job openings as well as info that will be helpful during interviews.
- **Facebook Groups:** If you are targeting smaller companies in a specific geography, an insider tip is to join Facebook Groups for that area. You'll often find local postings that are not advertised elsewhere.
- **Company Websites:** Company career pages post openings and also provide information regarding the company culture, mission, locations, and other helpful information.

Yes, job postings are easy to find, and you are likely to be overwhelmed. Here's a process for managing the flood, responding for best results, and keeping track of everything.

First, narrow your sights. Run a few test searches on various sites to see which yield the best results. You can search by a number of criteria—job title, skills, company name, location, and other factors. Keep track of search terms you use that yield the best results (a pen and pad of paper is easiest!).

Many college students and new grads find it helpful to add "entry level" or "intern" to the field of interest.

We suggest starting a search broadly, then narrowing down. For instance, a LinkedIn search for "entry-level analyst" produced 11,000+ jobs in the US. When adding a geographic parameter of Chicago, the number decreased to just under 800. Adding "financial" to entry-level analyst increased opportunities in Chicago to nearly 4,000. Substituting "business" for "financial" analyst cut the number of jobs to under 2,000.

Experiment with descriptors for the role you want to target. Again, keep track of the terms that are producing the best results.

Career Centers Say …

"Think of the job search as a research project. I recommend the Rule of Three: Follow three news sources relevant to your field of choice, identify three organizations of interest, then three people to speak with. Repeat.

"Students understand the concept of a research project and the need to gather data … done right, serendipity will take over and lead to an opportunity."

— *Sharon Belden Castonguay, EdD, Executive Director, Gordon Career Center, Wesleyan University*

As your search progresses, you will naturally gravitate to a few favorite sites. You might spend a few minutes now and then on an alternate site, but chances are you're going to see plenty of opportunities (and less repetition) if you choose just a few for regular visits.

Select your targets. Now, as you visit your favorite sites, use your best-performing descriptors to collect postings for jobs of interest. As you identify each, do a deep dive into the job description and the company information presented to learn as much as possible about the opportunity. If you're definitely interested ... **wait!** Don't apply just yet.

We strongly recommend that you invest just a little time and effort to gain a definite advantage for your candidacy. That means avoiding—at least for now—the instant "Apply" feature found on every job board.

Instead, follow these steps for every job that interests you.

1) See who in your network might be connected in some way to the company. Perhaps a relative or a friend of the family ... a LinkedIn connection ... an alumnus you can reach through Handshake.

2) Reach out to that person to see if they can make a personal introduction or just provide the name of the hiring manager for you to contact directly.

3) At the same time as you are doing step 2, ready your resume and cover letter, tailoring as much as possible to the specific opportunity.

4) If your contact provides a referral, great! Reach out immediately to that person, and be certain to mention your contact's name up front. (See section on Handling Referrals, beginning on page 93, for details and scripts.)

5) If your network connection doesn't respond within about 24 hours, move forward to apply so that you don't lose the potential opportunity.

6) Go first to the company's own website to see if you can find the specific posting. If so, follow directions to apply on the company site. As we discussed in Chapter 3, if there is a place to include a cover letter, be sure to do so even if it is not required.

7) If you can't find the specific position on the company website, and if your contacts haven't responded, go back to the original posting site and follow the steps to apply. Again, always include a cover letter if you are able to do so.

8) Always print or otherwise save a copy of every posting to which you apply. Otherwise, you may not be able to locate the posting online by the time interviewing starts, and your preparation for interviews will not be as thorough as it should be.

9) Record all of this activity in your spreadsheet or CRM app—job title and company name, when you responded and to whom, referral source if any, version of resume and letter you used, when you plan to follow up (if that's possible—typically only if you have been referred), and other details that will help you keep track of your many applications.

Career Centers Say ...

"Especially with recent alums ... find the trifecta: Find the position, look on LI for an alumni network for a contact, connect for an informational interview, figure out what they're looking for—and THEN apply. Make a personal connection. There's much more bang for your buck when you use a networking approach."

— *Kate Chroust, Senior Director of Career Services, and Helen Eaton,*
Associate Director of Career Services, Endicott College

PRO TIP: Referrals matter—a lot. Why invest the extra time and energy it takes to get a referral? It's simple. Studies show that **100% of referred candidates who have the qualifications will get an interview.**

On the other hand, when you are one of dozens or perhaps hundreds of candidates coming through the mass-application portal, you have to be a nearly perfect fit to score an interview—in the top **3% to perhaps 10%.** It's simply a matter of math. The company is going to hire one person and interview only a handful.

Given the numbers, your investment in seeking a referral will provide a big payback.

That leads to the conclusion that the more people you have in your network, the better your chances of getting that referral. And *that* conclusion leads us to our next topic: Networking.

Career Centers Say ...

"Don't rely only on job postings ... many of the most interesting jobs are never posted! Thus, the emphasis on networking one's way into a company. Especially in business schools with strong alumni networks, networking really is the #1 strategy.

"In building a list of target companies or industries, it is very useful to use LinkedIn to identify internal advocates who can introduce students to the right people and even potentially support their candidacy for a specific role. I often hear, 'I don't know anybody' and I'll say, 'Well, let's think about that ... who might there be within that company who knows someone you know—or is that person an alumni?' LinkedIn can be especially valuable in searching for alumni contacts.

"An exercise I use that's particularly effective is have students reach out to an alumnus via email to ask, 'May I have some of your time?' And I say to those students, 'Yes, I actually want you to do that.' My experience is that at least 90% of alumni are more than happy to help. Keep in mind that someone helped *them* when they were a student. This is an opportunity for them to give back. What students should use that 15 minutes of time for is learning about the career trajectory of the alum, learning more about what the company does, and exploring a career path ... and *not* asking for a job or internship."

— *Carla Coury, Interim Executive Director, Career Management Center, A.B. Freeman School of Business, Tulane University*

Let's Talk About Networking

Networking gets a bad rap. Many job seekers—whether new college graduates or very successful senior-level executives—dislike the term because of their perception of what it means.

You might have had some of these negative thoughts about networking:

- It means asking people for a favor.
- It means reaching out to people I don't know (especially uncomfortable for introverts).
- It feels manipulative.
- It requires me to "schmooze" in an artificial way.
- It means asking people for a job.

With all of that negativity, no wonder the idea of networking strikes fear in many hearts and can even immobilize you before you begin your job search.

That doesn't have to be the case. Try substituting some of the following words and phrases for "networking":

- Idea exchange
- Collaboration
- Exploratory discussion
- Talking (yes, simply talking—in other words, having a casual conversation)

This shift in your thinking is important because—you've heard it many times, and it's absolutely true—**networking is your #1 success strategy in finding a job.** When you network—when you make human, one-to-one connections with people who are tuned in to companies, jobs, and other people who can help you—you gain many advantages:

- You separate yourself from the crowd of applicants for many positions.
- You gain insights into careers, companies, and work environments.
- You can become a referred (and preferred!) candidate for highly competitive jobs.
- You are likely to learn about opportunities that are off the radar—not posted for general applications.
- You build confidence in talking to others on a professional level about careers in general and yourself in particular—very helpful when you begin formal interviews.

Networking is a core component in every one of the four job-search methods we've mentioned. Read on for detailed guidance and tips that will make networking seem as easy as … finding a film on Netflix.

Career Centers Say …

"Networking is the most effective strategy for your job search. It entails building relationships with people in your industry of interest. Most jobs are attained in the hidden market, and networking allows you to break into that market, increasing your odds of earning a quality role now and in the future. Network with professors/instructors, professionals in your industry, friends, family, and classmates. Consider requesting 15- to 30-minute informational interviews (career conversations) with professionals in your industry of interest to learn more about their role and to seek their advice."

— *Micall Searles, Career Coach, University of Montana*

Networking

The next two methods in "How to Find a Job" are closely related:

Method #2: Talk to People You Know
Method #3: Meet New People
That's what networking is all about: Talking to people about your future career, telling them about your search, asking for their help if appropriate, and finding new people to connect with.

Start with people you know, using a direct approach by phone, text, email, or in-person contact.

> ### *Career Centers Say …*
>
> "Use connections to help you secure introductions to people in *their* networks. Try to use connections to garner informational interviews. Networking can help to get past the gatekeepers *and* avoid the slush pile."
>
> — *Chaim Shapiro, Director of the Office for Student Success, Touro University*

The cardinal rule of networking is never to ask for something your contact can't give you. In most cases, they can't give you a job! So while of course you are *looking* for a job, don't start by *asking* about a job. Instead, ask for something your contact can give—and is probably very happy to share: advice, ideas, feedback on your resume, insight into their industry, and why they made certain career choices.

Your relationship will dictate the formality of your approach and how much help you ask for, but here are some ideas for scripts you might use when you reach out to ask for a meeting:

"Name, can I ask for a few minutes of your time? I'd love to get your advice and ideas regarding my job search. I can come to you, or we can FaceTime if that's more convenient."

"Name, I hope you're well and still enjoying your job at Big Bank. I was hoping you'd be willing to spend 15 or 20 minutes helping me get my job search off the ground. I'd really appreciate getting your advice and learning about your experience after graduation."

"Name, I know I've been out of touch—senior year has been really challenging—but I'm about ready to graduate and I'm looking for some wisdom about getting my first job! Can I buy you a cup of coffee and ask you a bunch of questions about your career?"

After your contact agrees to a meeting, send an email confirming the date, time, and other details and attach your resume. You can bring a paper copy to an in-person meeting, but a PDF will be most useful for your contacts to share with others.

Your goal for the meeting is a "talk shop" conversation—a discussion around professional ideas of common interest. It might also be referred to as a career conversation or an informational interview. While every conversation will take different paths, here's an outline that will help you structure the meeting in a professional manner and so that you get helpful information.

- Thank your contact for sharing some time with you.
- Offer a brief explanation of what you're interested in doing and why. This is your "elevator pitch," a short message whose name derived from the concept that you can deliver it in the 30–60 seconds it takes to ride to the top of a skyscraper with a senior executive. Your pitch should be a brief, clear overview of your career interests and key qualifications. Prepare it and practice it, because you'll be using it often!
- Share the names of your target companies.

- Ask open-ended questions that encourage your contact to share insights and experiences. For example:
    - "Why did you choose your line of work?"
    - "What was the hardest thing about starting your career?"
    - "What do you love most about your job, and what aspects do you dislike?"
    - "Where do you think our industry is headed, and what kind of skills will be needed in the future?"
- Ask for something **specific.** You can ask for more than one thing if it feels appropriate during your conversation.
    - "I saw on LinkedIn that you are connected to David Rodriguez at Lumen Technologies, a company I'm exploring. Would you be willing to introduce me to him?"
    - "Do you have a contact at PriceWaterhouse that you can introduce me to?"
    - "Given my career interests, what other companies do you recommend I look into? Can you refer me to someone there?"
    - "What advice would you give me as I start my career, based on your own experience?"
- Keep it brief—15 minutes or so by phone or Zoom, perhaps a bit longer in person.
- Thank the person for their time, ideas, and assistance. Ask if you can get in touch in the future if a follow-up question arises. Promise to keep them apprised of your progress.
- End by asking if there's anything you can do for them. Networking is a two-way street, and if you approach it in the spirit of giving as well as receiving, you'll be welcomed if you reach out to that same contact later in your search.
- Within 24 hours, send a quick email to thank your contact, follow up on any items you discussed, and, if you haven't already, share a PDF copy of your resume and cover letter that they can use when introducing you to others or advocating for your candidacy. You'll see a sample of these communications near the end of this chapter.

Finally, be sure to enter details from each conversation into your activity tracker.

Career Centers Say …

"Job search is something you do every day as every connection you make may be 'THE' connection. See each professor as someone who can connect you to alumni working in interesting roles. Career development and job search happen in and out of the classroom, in internships or the laboratory, or while volunteering or participating in club activities.

"Be curious about the paths your faculty, boss, and parents took to their careers, the pitfalls and the successes. Ask them what they would do differently if they could do college all over again. What did they do that was helpful for their career or personal growth and what did they NOT do that was detrimental to their career or personal growth.

"Document hard skills you gained from each opportunity, especially from class. For instance, from 'History' you learned to analyze policy and data, conduct research, write reports, make public presentations, forecast historic trends, curate artifacts, think critically, write persuasively, etc."

— *Cheryl Minnick, EdD, Career Success Director, College of Humanities & Sciences, University of Montana*

Meet New People

During your meetings, you are likely to gather additional names of people to contact. As well, you may want to reach out "cold" to people you are able to identify who work at your target companies or who are in the same line of work.

Using LinkedIn and/or Handshake, you may also find affinity groups such as alumni from your school, fraternity/sorority members, or members of a professional organization for your industry.

First, reach out to connect with these new people:

> "Name, I was referred to you by Jack Mullaney, who was my internship supervisor at Croyden Chemical. I'm looking to broaden my network in the industry and hope you're willing to connect."

> "Hello. As I enter my final year as a Mechanical Engineering major at RPI, I'm broadening my network. Given your background, I would very much like to connect here on LinkedIn. Thanks!"

> "Good afternoon. I enjoyed reading about your background as an analyst with EY. As this is my intended career path after I graduate from Villanova, I wanted to reach out to connect. Thank you."

> "Good morning. I see we are both members of Beta Tau Sigma. I'd love to connect on LinkedIn!"

After connecting, you can ask to set up a meeting, following the same procedure described above.

At the beginning of your search, you can focus your questions on general industry and career information as well as requesting referrals to others who might be able to help you. As you move into a more active phase, use your network to gather insights about specific companies you are interviewing with and people who work there.

Remember to always ask for things that your contacts can give you. (Most people love to give advice!) Don't ask for a job and don't act entitled. Be polite and appreciative. And keep in mind that you are building a network for today *and* tomorrow. You will use these techniques and tap into these contacts many times throughout your career.

Handling Referrals and Introductions

In all of your networking conversations, do your best to get names of additional people you can connect with. Some of these might be general contacts—people to add to your network and perhaps have a "talk shop" conversation with. For them, simply follow the "Meet New People" guidelines above.

Sometimes you'll be referred to a person who can be extremely influential—perhaps an inside contact at a company with a job posting of interest. In these cases, you should reach out immediately. Be sure to mention your referral source, then express your interest in the role and ask for their advice and guidance around submitting your application.

Here are a few ideas for how you might approach these referrals.

"I understand from my folks that you might be in a position to introduce me to the hiring manager in Customer Experience at your company. As you may be aware, I'll be graduating in May and am actively exploring opportunities …"

"Angela Watts, my career advisor at Ohio State, suggested that I reach out to you as we share a common background and career interests. I will graduate this spring with a degree in Visual Communications and I'm very interested in careers in U/X Design. Since you've been so successful in that field, would you be willing to share some advice with me, and perhaps refer me to the hiring manager for a couple of posted openings at TechStars?"

"My favorite professor at Rice University, Dr. Salah Ahmed, strongly suggested that I reach out to you. I'm about to graduate with a degree in Mechanical Engineering and I'm pursuing opportunities in the aerospace industry. Dr. Ahmed told me of your success at AeroDyne and thought you could point me in the right direction for opportunities there."

The insider info that you glean from these contacts can help you in several ways:

- You may gain valuable information about the company or the job that you can include in your cover letter.
- You'll gain some insights about company culture and what it's like to work there.
- Ideally, you'll get a direct referral to the hiring manager for that particular job.
- You might learn about specific problems or challenges affecting the job, the department, or the company and can then frame your interview answers to show you have the skills to handle those problems.

Following the meeting, send a thank-you/follow-up note to your new contact *and* a brief thank-you to your referral source, letting them know how valuable their assistance has been.

In still other cases, your contact may offer to make a personal introduction to someone influential. You want to make it as easy as possible for them to do so—and with the right kind of information so that your new contact is prepared to help you. Here's an example of a message you might send.

Dear Mr. Thomasetti:

I enjoyed talking with you at the alumni basketball game over spring break. I appreciate your willingness to help me in my job search. Thanks for offering to introduce me to the Director of Operations at Alpha Technologies, Ms. Jasmine Delacorte.

To assist you in making the introduction, I've attached not only my resume, but a cover letter that explains the types of opportunities I'm interested in exploring and brief information about my background.

I will certainly keep you posted and sincerely thank you once again.

Best regards,
Jonathan McCarthy

As the email notes, you would attach a PDF of your resume *and* a PDF of a cover letter of introduction—formatted as a proper business letter with a heading that matches your resume and including a date and an inside address.

Use the letters provided in Chapter 3 as inspiration. Essentially, you take your cover letter and customize the opening and closing paragraphs to reference any details you have learned about the company and/or the specific opportunity.

"What if I don't hear back from someone I've been referred to?"

You've received a valuable lead to an influential person in the business community. You reached out with an invitation to connect on LinkedIn, mentioning your referral source. Or you've directly sent an e-note and your resume at the recommendation of a trusted referral source. A few days go by without a reply. What should you do?

We recommend that you wait at least a week before following up. Then it's certainly appropriate to send a follow-up message. You can preface the same message (slightly edited) that you sent originally with, "I just wanted to follow up to my original message—I'm reaching out to you at the recommendation of Dr. James Leachman ..."

One additional follow up a week or two later is acceptable and can sometimes prompt a reply (many people have extremely busy email boxes!). If you hear nothing after your initial inquiry and two follow ups, you can move the contact to the bottom of your list.

Method #4: Follow Companies and Influencers on Social Media

The reasoning behind this strategy is to surround yourself with people and resources relevant to your career interests. Our two top recommendations for career-relevant social/professional platforms currently are Twitter and LinkedIn. Keep an eye on developments in social media to be sure you're in the right places where your target people and companies are active.

On **Twitter,** you can follow companies and individuals. Search for people affiliated with your target companies and industries. Keep an eye out for industry news and—especially—references to job openings.

As with all social media, keep your tweets and comments professional. It's fine to have fun and let your personality come out, but always remember that potential employers often search social media to evaluate candidates. You want to continue to make a good impression.

On **LinkedIn,** the last section on your profile, labeled "Interests," allows you to choose Individuals, Companies, and Schools to follow. You can also join Groups. Posts from these sources will then populate your daily news feed and provide opportunities to identify and connect with more people.

LinkedIn **Groups**, in particular, can be extremely valuable. Explore Groups related to your target field or industry. Try to identify those that are active and have sufficient membership numbers and ongoing activity—but not so huge that you can't keep up with it or have a chance of making connections.

Most Groups will require you to reach out to seek approval to join. Lurk before you leap. Visit regularly, watch the conversations, then decide where you might participate. Asking questions is always a good plan, once you've taken the time to ensure that the platform is the appropriate place for doing so.

Consider tapping into the broader knowledge of a group: "What recommendations do you have for newer graduates seeking to contribute to this field?" "If you were to think back on the best steps you took when building your career, what comes to mind?" "Any top takeaways you'd be willing to suggest to a newbie in this industry?"

Just as in your networking meetings, don't ask (at least not initially) about whether someone is hiring or knows of specific job openings. Save these types of "asks" until you have made a connection with someone using LinkedIn's messaging feature and are in direct communication.

Don't Put All Your Eggs in One Basket …
and Don't Count Your Chickens Until They're Hatched

You may have heard these timeworn poultry expressions from a family member. They are quite applicable to job search and interviewing. No matter how perfect an opportunity appears—and how confident you are of receiving an offer—don't halt your job search.

Be relentless in continuing all of your networking activities, job applications, and interviews until you have received and negotiated an offer and had it formally accepted.

Then, when you start your new job, it's time to celebrate, post your new position on LinkedIn, and thank all of your friends, family, and network contacts for their support. They'll be thrilled for you and proud that they helped.

CHAPTER 5:
Ace Every Interview

Wonderful work: You've landed an interview! Your networking, resume, introductions, LinkedIn, and every other action you used to get through the door succeeded, and you have taken a big step forward in your career journey.

In this chapter we'll discuss different interview methods you might encounter—telephone prescreening, in-person (individual or group), Zoom/Teams, robot recruiter/AI interview/chatbot—and how you can best communicate your skills and value in every interview.

But first, you'll need to do some prep.

Cover the Basics

When your interview is being set up, be sure to clarify the names and job titles of the people with whom you'll be speaking.

Verify the meeting details—the location if it's an on-site interview, log-in or call-in details for a virtual or phone meeting. Confirm the time and, if possible, determine how long the interview is likely to last. Make sure you have contact details, ideally both email and phone, so that you can get in touch in case you need to reschedule or something (a true emergency) prevents you from keeping the appointment.

Know Your Interviewer
Research the background of the person or team members who will be conducting your interviews. Google each interviewer to obtain background information. Check to see if their bio appears on the company website. Go onto LinkedIn to try to find each person and learn more about their experience and work with the company.

Don't worry that you'll be considered a stalker—it's professional to learn about the identity of your interviewer and the company. As you scroll through details on LinkedIn, you may find useful information that you can reference in your interview—for instance, a connection in common, a membership in a shared organization or fraternity/sorority, or college background or major.

Create an Agenda

An important part of interview prep is determining the key points that you want to cover during the interview—your agenda. We are not suggesting that you write out a personal agenda and share it with your interviewer! Rather, for your own purposes we recommend that you take time to define the top four to six points you want to be sure to communicate. These points should relate to what you know about the job, the company, and the industry.

Think of it this way: If you are hired, what problems are you going to help the company solve? What tasks will you perform, and how will your work support the goals of the organization? What special skills, knowledge, or experience do you have that will be useful and valuable?

Here are two examples.

JOB TITLE: Entry-Level Financial Analyst, Glass & Associates (a Financial Management Service provider for Architectural, Engineering, and Legal firms)
My Agenda—Key points I want to convey

1. My top skill is data mining and data analysis—using data to tell a story that influences strategy and decision-making.
2. I have strong communication and presentation skills and am comfortable expressing an opinion in group settings.
3. I am very good at data visualization—I can transform stats and numbers into visuals that communicate quickly.
4. I'm a good project manager, able to keep an eye on details and schedules.
5. I recently earned my BS in Economics and earned "A" grades in both of my senior-year projects.

JOB TITLE: Entry-level Sales Associate, Precision Solar (provider of solar energy systems to homeowners)
My Agenda—Key points I want to convey

1. Sales experience (internship and 2 part-time jobs)
2. Highly competitive and driven to succeed (NCAA Division I athlete)
3. Passionate about renewable energy (senior marketing project)
4. Good communicator with people of all ages (kids and their parents, coaches, bosses, professors, college activities, etc.)

Your interview agenda is likely to be very similar from job to job, but you should review it carefully beforehand and adjust as needed to fit the specifics of each individual position.

Now that you've created your agenda, it's time to think about how you'll respond to interview questions and how you can work *your* agenda items into the interviewer's program.

Practice Your CAR Stories

In an interview, when you can share a specific example—a story—about how you used a skill or completed an important task, you accomplish several essential things:

- You set yourself apart from other candidates who don't have examples.

- You make yourself more memorable.

- You provide evidence of the skills and knowledge needed for the job.

Your stories—in CAR format—are exactly what you need to share during interviews.

The good news is that you've already developed a number of CAR stories (as discussed in Chapter 1) and used them to write accomplishment statements for your resume, cover letter, and LinkedIn. Now, review those stories, adapt them as needed, and practice telling them in the specific Challenge-Action-Result format.

For each item on your agenda, think of two to four examples—CAR stories—that support the point you are making. For instance, the aspiring Sales Associate whose agenda we just viewed can tell the interviewer that she has sales experience, then reinforce that message with two or three examples of sales challenges she faced and how she handled them.

Keep in mind, the purpose of interviewing is for the hiring manager to select *one* person from a field of many. Every candidate interviewed will meet the basic requirements for the job. Everyone will be able to say, "I have sales experience" or "I am very good at data visualization." The candidate who can back up those claims with specific examples is the one who will stand out, be believed, and be remembered.

> **PRO TIP: Look for every opportunity to go beyond the general and into the specific.** After answering an interview question in a general way, you might say "Let me give you an example" and then share your CAR story—one that you've practiced, that is concise, and that has a logical flow from start to finish. This kind of preparation will give you an edge over every other candidate who has not taken the time to prepare stories and match examples to skills and qualifications.

Prepare for Typical Interview Questions

From our years of extensive interview coaching, feedback from many college graduates, and input from Career Centers, we've assembled a number of questions you should anticipate in preparing for your interviews.

Of course, every interviewer is free to ask the questions that matter most to them. You are bound to get some questions that you haven't prepared for. Simply answer the question, being honest and authentic while also conveying what you bring to the position and the company. For really tough questions, see our advice on page 105 regarding Challenging Questions.

> **PRO TIP: Keep in mind that an interview is a conversation**—an opportunity for you to learn about the company, the job, and the interviewer as he/she learns about you. It gives you a chance to begin to know the culture and assess fit. Of course, this cuts both ways as the company determines if *you* are the right fit for their organization.

"Tell Me About Yourself"

The typical interview opener that you can count on in nearly every job search—now, as a college intern or graduate, and every time you change jobs over the course of your career—is: "Tell me something about yourself." Since you can expect this question, there is no excuse for not being prepared to answer it.

The interviewer is not looking for your entire life story (no matter how fascinating it is!). You want to have thought through a concise response that captures some of what highlights your strengths, shares a little of your relevant studies and/or experience, and embeds what it is about the job opportunity and company that most appeals to you and why you want to contribute and be hired.

Here are two examples.

"I'm about to graduate from Wellesley with a degree in English. One reason I chose that major is because I knew I wanted to work in the field of communications—I've always been fascinated by how people communicate, whether in writing, speaking, or visually. I thought Advertising might be a perfect fit, and I was able to confirm that during two internships with ad agencies—the first a traditional Madison Avenue firm, the second a cutting-edge digital marketing agency. I learned the power of short-form storytelling and how to adapt stories for different media. But I wanted my career to be about more than selling shoes or snack foods. So when I saw your posting for an associate to work on advertising for your nonprofit clients, I jumped at the opportunity! I'm really excited about using my skills to influence people to do good. I believe I have the skills you need and a genuine passion for the work, and I'm eager to learn more."

*　*　*　*　*

"Well, like a lot of kids I played many different sports throughout my childhood. And I loved every one and learned important life lessons about hard work and preparation, winning and losing, teamwork, and good sportsmanship. I was on the varsity teams for football and track and field all four years of high school. So I was pretty good—but not professional-level. So when it came time to think about my career, I knew that I wouldn't be playing in the NFL or on Team USA. But I knew that somehow I wanted to incorporate sports into my career. The way I look at it, people should feel passionate about their work so that they can give it their best.

"My degree in Business Administration qualifies me to work in many areas of different kinds of businesses. I had a very broad education that covered all the fundamentals—marketing and sales, finance, supply chain and operations, human resources, information technology, and general management. I really excelled in the HR and management components, and I focused my senior year capstone project on how to align human resources programs with overall business goals.

"Now I want to apply that broad education in the area I love the most—sports. I may not play for the NFL, but I can work to become a management executive in a sports organization. Starting on the ground floor at Pro Sports Associates is an ideal first step for me, as it exposes me to the professional operation of many different sports. I've heard really great things about your management training program from friends who graduated a year or two ago and from the career center at Michigan State. I'm excited to learn more about it."

How Long Should Your Interview Responses Be?

Generally, aim to speak for around a minute, maybe 90 seconds. Your response to the opening question might go a bit longer—up to 2 minutes. And if you are asked a detailed question about an internship project, for example, you might need several minutes. You can always ask at the end of your reply, "Would you like me to share more details?" Try to carefully read body language (if in person or via Zoom).

How to Prepare

As discussed, create your agenda and practice your CAR stories. From that point, the ideal way to prepare is to have someone ask you questions so that you can practice. If you'd rather do it yourself, be in a space without interruption or noise—and then answer your questions aloud.

Whether working alone or with a helper, we recommend that you record your responses, using Voice Memos on your phone or something similar, so that you can experience the cringe-worthy opportunity of hearing yourself. Seriously, though, recording and listening to your answers will help you hone your responses and become more confident.

The goal is always to feel comfortable telling your stories and responding to anticipated questions. The objective is *not* to memorize your responses. Rather, you want to be so well prepared that the replies you offer are articulate and natural. We'll share tips shortly on what to do in situations where you are stumped or go blank or are asked an especially challenging question.

A few things to keep in mind as you prepare your responses:

- Quantify statements as much as possible—if you have numbers or percentages to describe what you did or the results, use them.
- Understate, don't overstate. In other words, "I raised more than $4,000 during the fall fundraising campaign for Delta Sigma Pi's community pantry"—instead of saying $5,000.
- Tell more about *how* you did something rather than just *what* you did.
- Show, don't tell—establish your credibility by using examples.
- Toot—don't blow—your own horn; there is a subtle difference. Take credit for what you did, and differentiate between what *you* did and what you did as part of a team.

Also practice how to segue smoothly from your response back to the interview situation. A few phrases you might use, as appropriate:

- And that's the kind of challenge I'd really enjoy here at XYZ Corp.
- That's one of the reasons I was so excited about this job—it felt like my internship experience would be really valuable here.
- Does that answer your question? I'd be happy to provide more details.

Typical Questions You Can Expect

Here, then, are top questions to consider in your interview preparation. Most apply to internships and co-ops as well as full-time jobs, although the wording may be a bit different.

You'll see some similarities with the CAR story prep you did for your resume in Chapter 1, so do look back on that material for some additional food-for-thought prompts to inspire you.

We've provided some ideas to get you thinking of your responses. In every case, see if you can come up with at least one CAR story that would be appropriate to add. You won't want to add a CAR story to *every* answer during the interview, but the more you develop, prepare, and practice, the better equipped you'll be to make a strong, positive, and indelible impression during every interview.

- What do you consider to be three key strengths?
  Think of such modifiers as hard working, caring, detail oriented, "no quit," determined, and so forth—and then know the examples you'd share further to demonstrate these strengths.

- Alternatively, what is a weakness?
  Be truthful but not painfully open. Don't cite a weakness that is a major requirement for the job! Whenever possible, describe steps you've taken to improve. For example … maybe in your first year or two as an undergrad, time management was a challenge, but you found several techniques to better manage your schedule, plan for long-term assignments, fit in extracurriculars, and so forth.

- How did you select your major?
  If you are like more than 50% of undergraduates, your initial major probably changed prior to senior year. Talk about what caused that change and why. Or, if you stayed true to your original major, talk about where your early interest came from and what you love about it.

- What do you hope to be able to do in your first job after graduation?
  Try to strike a balance between having an opportunity to collaborate with peers and contribute as well as learn and strengthen your skills in a way that brings value to an organization.

- Tell me about your internship experiences.
  Select those most relevant to your career direction and/or that illustrate transferable skills: perhaps examples of leadership, training a new intern, documenting best practices, and so forth.

- What was the favorite thing you did in your internship—and why?
  Be honest, enthusiastic, and authentic. Interviewers love when they see true energy and passion in a candidate. Ideally, link your response to an agenda item to reinforce your fit for this particular job.

- What would your internship supervisors or employers say about you and your performance?
  Reflect candidly on the top traits and contributions you made in your roles and what was actually said about you—of course emphasizing the positive!

- What do people say about you that "rings true"—those key characteristics about you that truly resonate and define you?
  After you've described those characteristics, it's a great time to add an example. "From the time I was in kindergarten, I've been described as competitive. My internship manager last spring made that comment as well. I always want to do my best and be my best. One good example is when I …"

- What about your work experience? What highlights can you describe about the jobs you have held?
  Remember to tell your stories quickly and briefly, showcasing the experiences you think help you to stand out, especially those elements that might be transferable to the job for which you are being interviewed.

- Were there ways you went above and beyond your job description?
  Of course, be honest and don't exaggerate—but if you can show where you did more than what was asked or expected and that it was recognized and brought value, do tell the story.

- What problems did you solve?
  This is the perfect opportunity to inject a CAR story.

- What impact did your work have on the team, organization, and/or customers?
  This is where you talk about results and/or outcomes of work that you did on your own or with teammates.

- How was success measured in your role?
  While it is sometimes not possible to know long-term effect or success, in most cases you'll have a sense of how well you performed from feedback you receive from your supervisor or coordinator.

- In what ways did you contribute to the team?
  Think of how others have described your contributions and efforts. What was recognized and praised? Was anything stated in writing that you can reference—a review or letter of recommendation at the end of an internship? And, incidentally, it is never too late to go back to a former supervisor or internship manager and respectfully ask for a letter of recommendation—we strongly suggest doing this.

- What would fall apart at your job if you weren't there? How would it impact the organization?
  In other words, what would not have been accomplished if you hadn't been there? This is another opening for a CAR story.

- Looking back at your XYZ position/internship, what are you most proud of accomplishing?
  This question can also get at what you most appreciated having had the opportunity to learn—perhaps a new skill or new software.

- What did you learn about yourself through that experience? Anything that you didn't expect to learn when you started?
  Think of any challenge you may have faced in performing your work—did working through this help to demonstrate your resourcefulness? Tenacity? Perseverance? Ability to overcome a barrier?

- What two or three things would you want to tell a prospective employer about you for "the perfect job" that would convince them to hire you?
  Be certain these characteristics link to your agenda and to accomplishments or experiences you can share in a CAR story.

- What do you do in your free time, outside of school?
  You could share that you created an Instagram account with 1,500 followers about your favorite books or retailers or social influencers … all the better if you can link an interest or hobby to your career pursuit or field of interest.

- What would people be surprised to know about you?
  Share an item that might be a little different from your peers—i.e., that you are a volunteer firefighter or EMT, that you always win "best costume" at Halloween parties, that you taught yourself to play guitar.

- Do you have any questions for us?
  Yes! Always come prepared with questions. Read on to learn more about this important aspect of interviewing.

> **PRO TIP: Always have questions.** When you are asked "Do you have any questions for us?," please *don't* say, "no, I think you've answered everything." Instead, go into every interview (in-person or remote) with at least three or four prepared questions.

Here are a few ideas for questions you might ask. You can add others based on what the job description says about skills, challenges, company culture, and other factors.

- What are you seeking in the ideally qualified candidate?

- Where do you see this role adding to the organization's bench strength?

- Based on my review of the job posting, and our discussion today, it seems that my skills and experience are a great fit for this job. Would you agree?

- Is there anything else about my experience you'd like to know?

- If I'm chosen for this role, what would you like to see accomplished in the first six months?

- Does the company have a formal mentoring program for entry-level candidates? I'm interested in learning and growing on the job and would definitely take advantage of that.

- What do you enjoy most about working here?

It is fine to write your questions down and have them available to consult during an interview. When asked, you can say, "Yes, I have a few questions I'd noted that I would like to ask."

As well, you can have your agenda handy. Then, when asked if you have any questions, you can quickly review to see if you forgot to bring up any of your key points. You might say, "Yes, I do have a question. We haven't talked about *[item that you wanted to convey]*, and I understood that was a key element of the position. Can you tell me about that?"

You can also jot down questions that arise during the interview—add them to your list of prepared questions as they occur to you.

Be sure *not* to ask a question that was already answered in the interview. Also, do *not* ask about compensation, benefits, time off, or other perks of the job. See pages 112–113 for when and how to address these issues.

Finally, make sure that you know what to expect following the interview. You don't want to be in limbo, waiting to hear and uncertain about following up. But ask any of the following questions only *after* you've asked several other job-related questions and are nearing the end of the interview.

- What are the next steps in the process?

- When do you hope to make a decision?
- When can I expect to hear back from you? … If I don't hear back within [*timeframe stated by interviewer*], is it okay if I follow up with you?

Career Centers Say …

"Be real … because you can't fake genuine. People will respond!"

— *Chaim Shapiro, Director of the Office for Student Success, Touro University*

Tips for Challenging Questions (or when you go blank)

You don't have to immediately go into a rapid-fire response on every question. It is good to stop and think for a few seconds before responding.

Things you can say:

- "That's a great question, Mr. Lopez."
- "I'm glad you asked me that, Ms. Williams."
- "I want to be sure I completely understand what you are asking me—could you please rephrase that?"
- "You know, I'd really need a little more time to think through how I might approach that situation." (If you think you can formulate a response, just quietly consider your words for a few seconds and then speak. If you really are stumped, you can add: "I promise to give very careful thought to that and respond later today in an email.")

If you've been asked a multi-part question, after you've responded to the first and maybe second parts, don't worry if you've forgotten the third item. Simply ask: "Now, what was the third thing you'd asked me?"

Always respond honestly to all questions. If you don't know something, be candid about it.

If your GPA is not high and not shown on your resume, you may be asked about it. As discussed earlier, if your GPA is higher in your major, use that number. Don't be apologetic in discussing a low GPA. Keep it short and matter-of-fact. Possible explanations (if true) could include:

- "I challenged myself with a more difficult course load and learned a great deal."
- "I was balancing studies along with being a Division III athlete and it took me until my sophomore year to figure out the best study strategies for me."
- "To be honest, I didn't take school seriously at first. I had always coasted through high school with good grades, but that didn't work in college. But I finally grew up and took responsibility for my grades and my education. My GPA my senior year was nearly 4.0."

Curveballs present an opportunity for you to really think about your reply. Again, it is okay to pause when you are interviewing—you don't have to immediately jump back with a response. You might be surprised at how much thinking you can do in 10 or 20 seconds!

Interview Etiquette

Whether in person, via Zoom, or over the phone, there is no excuse for being late to an interview. Double-check the address and directions and arrive early—but don't enter the office until about 15 minutes before the interview. For Zoom, make sure that the battery on your phone or laptop is fully charged and the meeting link is readily accessible so that you can enter at least five minutes before the scheduled start time.

Other things to keep in mind:

- For an in-person interview, prepare for a handshake or not (since Covid, many people have stopped shaking hands). Take your cue from the interviewer, but be prepared to extend your right hand for a firm handshake.

- Have your resume ready—bring print copies to in-person interviews and have a copy on your desk for easy reference during Zoom or phone interviews.

- Be fully engaged throughout the interview. Excellent eye contact is important and essential. Practice a Zoom meeting with a friend who can tell you when your eye contact is best—you might need to look at the camera eye rather than directly at the interviewer.

- Turn off all email indicators on your laptop and phone, and be absolutely certain to completely silence your phone—including the vibration feature, which can typically be heard.

> **PRO TIP: Prepare your references before you interview.** You will need at least three references and may be asked to provide them during or shortly after an interview. Select people who will say great things about you from different perspectives—perhaps an internship supervisor, a professor, a long-time family friend who works in your target industry, a boss from your part-time job, a college or high school athletic coach.
>
> Be certain your references have a clear idea of what you're seeking. Provide them with a copy of your resume and ask if they are willing to serve as a reference. Assuming yes, get their current title, place of employment, and best email address and phone number. Using the header format from your resume or cover letter, prepare your reference list on a single page.

Types of Interviews

During your job search you can expect to encounter a variety of interview methods. Here is an overview with relevant tips for each type.

> **PRO TIP: Make good use of voicemail.** Before beginning your search, record a professional voicemail message, stating your name and phone number so that callers know they have reached the right person. Once you begin applying for jobs and getting interviews, it's a good strategy to allow calls to go to voicemail to give you an opportunity to review and prepare before returning the call. You can check the application or email you sent and remember details about the job and the company. Do *not* let prescheduled interview calls go to voicemail. You are expecting these and should answer immediately.

Prescreening Interview

You can anticipate a prescreening phone call, often from someone in Human Resources/Talent Acquisition, as the first step after you have been selected as a candidate. To prepare, review the job description and practice describing the skills and experience you have that most closely match the job requirements.

At the conclusion of the call be certain to ask the next steps. Also obtain the email address for the prescreener (if you don't already know it) so that you can write a thank-you letter. See pages 108–111 for discussion on these important post-interview messages.

Candidate Assessment Test

You may be asked to complete one or more assessment tests as part of the prescreening process. Larger companies frequently use exams that assess aptitude, personality, problem-solving skills, and other measures—and these tests often precede the regular interviews. They are generally timed and completed online, often with a webcam component.

The tests will typically propose situations and ask you to describe how you would handle them. As you will do in any type of interview, be focused, authentic, and candid in responding to questions.

Zoom/Teams/Video Interview

Beyond preparing for your responses to interview questions, use the following strategies to make the best possible presentation.

- Be aware of your surroundings. Make sure your lighting is good and doesn't cast shadows. Be certain your background is neutral and professional and doesn't look as if you are in a bedroom or kitchen space.
- Try to ensure a quiet environment. Fully silence your phone and any notifications on your computer.
- "Dress all of you" professionally—not just the upper half!
- Have a bottle or glass of water at hand.
- Print your resume so that you can refer to it discreetly if desired.
- Use Post-it notes to highlight keywords and points you want to remember. You can attach them to the perimeter of your laptop/monitor. Use tape so that the notes don't accidentally flutter down in front of the camera during an interview.
- Fully charge your laptop.
- Verify the technology that will be used in advance of the interview—and have the link readily available so that you are not scurrying around at the last minute trying to find it. Also be sure you have verified the time zone for your scheduled interview.
- Consider posting a notice or two at your home or dorm room advising family/roommates that you are interviewing and to please be quiet and not knock or ring a doorbell.

Phone Interview

- Ahead of time, double-check the details regarding interview time, time zone, and who's calling whom. Be certain you have the name and job title of your interviewer.
- Conduct the phone interview in an area where you have excellent cell coverage.
- Try to ensure a quiet background and minimize distractions.

- Review tips provided for other interview methods.
- As with a Zoom interview, post a notice that you are interviewing and would appreciate not being interrupted with noise.

Robot Recruiter/Artificial Intelligence (AI)/Chatbot Interview

Use of AI technology—such as Headstart, VidCruiter, Scoutible, and myInterview—is increasing, and you may very well be interviewing with a robot. Some software will allow you to practice first. In certain cases, you'll have an opportunity to retake your answers. Most challenging will be trying to establish good eye contact with the camera on your laptop as if it were a real person.

In-person Interview

As with all methods of interviewing, be sure to complete your prep and practice well in advance of the interview. Additionally:

- Scout the location, travel time, parking, and actual office for your interview in advance.
- Arrive early.
- Dress professionally. Pay attention to the culture of the company and gear your attire accordingly. Especially for very casual workplaces, we recommend that you dress one step up from what you would as an employee.
- Bring extra copies of your resume.
- Be sure to silence your phone.

For ALL Interviews

The minute your interview is over, quickly debrief, capturing notes about key points you want to reinforce in your thank-you letter or issues you wish to do over using the "mulligan" strategy discussed on page 109.

After the Interview

The interview is over, but the process is not yet complete! Here's what you need to do, and what you can expect, as follow-up to every interview.

Thank-you Notes

Thank-you notes are essential. Not only do they convey good manners, they can actually give you an edge over other candidates.

Career Centers Say ...

"Thank-you notes might seem like an optional step for students and recent graduates, but I have heard many stories where an employer was down to two final candidates and went with the candidate who took time to send a nice thank-you email. The email does not have to be lengthy. Express gratitude, note something you appreciated learning more about during the time together, and indicate that you welcome the next steps in the hiring process."

— *Amanda Schagane, Associate Director of Alumni Career Services, University of Kentucky*

A few key points:

- Send your thank-you notes by email. You might hear advice to send a handwritten thank-you note or card, or to send a formal letter by regular mail. We prefer email because it is immediate and can make a difference as employers quickly whittle down a candidate pool to semi-finalists and then finalists.

- Try to write your thank-you emails the same day as the interview—next morning at the latest.

- Write a separate email to each person with whom you met or spoke. If you don't have email addresses for everyone, reach out to the person who coordinated the interview(s) and ask.

- If you are writing to multiple interview panel members, don't use the exact same message in every email. You can express similar thoughts in slightly different language. And, whenever possible, in each note express something that is particular to that individual—a common interest you discovered, an issue or question that seemed of particular concern, or another topic that shows you were listening and learning during the interview.

- Keep the message relatively brief—two or three short paragraphs.

- Reflect on key points about the job and how your background is a fit.

- If there were any points you believe you didn't address or did not convey clearly, use the thank-you to reiterate and strengthen your message (see "Mulligan" section immediately below).

Career Centers Say …

"Thank-you messages are a critical component to a successful interview process. I encourage students to send a thank-you to their interviewer(s) within 24 hours of the interview. This provides an opportunity to thank the interviewer(s) for their time and offer a brief, final pitch highlighting their fit for the position."

— *Micall Searles, Career Coach, University of Montana*

Don't Be Afraid to Call a Mulligan

A mulligan is a super-effective strategy we recommend for interviewing, borrowed from the game of golf. Very simply, it's a do-over. For whatever *did* or *did not happen* in the interview that you'd like another shot at, the mulligan is what you can and should do in your follow-up thank-you letter immediately after the interview.

It is the rare job seeker at any age who completes an interview and doesn't think, "How could I have forgotten to talk about xxx, or why didn't I bring up yyy when they asked me about zzz?" The mulligan thank-you gives you that chance.

In addition to what you say in your typical thank-you, you can address things you wish you had an opportunity to talk about and either weren't asked or forgot. You can also add a few applicable details to points that you did discuss.

Here are two examples.

"When you asked me about my project management experience, I neglected to mention that I had worked with the customer care team to develop and document a set of best practices for all of the firm's care associates. I helped to implement the new practices that were credited with boosting customer engagement scores in the very next month."

*   *   *   *   *

"In considering our discussion about handling conflict, I also wanted to share that I was able to use effective problem-solving skills in one of my assignments with the Mattson Company. I was asked to shadow an experienced member of the data analytics team and offer my assistance. However, on the first day, it was obvious that this person had not been informed that he would have a shadow. He was clearly not happy to have someone at his side asking questions and offering to help. At our midmorning break, I respectfully asked if I could speak with him about figuring a way that I wouldn't be intrusive but could offer assistance and meet the requirements of my internship manager. I openly explained that it wasn't my intent to get in the way of his doing his job but, rather, to try to learn from him as a very experienced and respected employee. This helped to smooth communications and resolved the awkwardness."

Career Centers Say ...

"I do strongly encourage people to send thank-you notes when they feel as if they need to clarify or emphasize a certain point from their interview or to show enthusiasm for the position. Some employers love thank-you notes, and I have met employers for whom sending one is positively dispositive as to a candidate's success. Many other employers are not swayed one way or another by them.

"I know that many career coaches advocate a handwritten thank-you note. I think for some positions, that is a great idea. However, in this day and age, when many people are working remotely and don't retrieve their mail from the office or are working in fast-paced high-tech, sending a snail-mail envelope might mean the intended recipient will not receive it; and if they do receive it, it could reflect that the candidate is a bit out of touch with the industry."

— *Cara Mitnick, Director of Professional Development, University of Rhode Island*

Thank-you Samples

Dear Mr. Lee:

Thank you for meeting with me yesterday to discuss the opportunity to join Brentley Corporation. I am confident that I will come up to speed very quickly as a member of your User Experience team and contribute to the efforts of an already high-performing organization.

I look forward to the next steps in the hiring process, which I understand will include a panel interview next week. I will be flexible and available to meet and look forward to this opportunity.

Please reach out if you have any questions in the meantime. Thank you, again, for your consideration.

Sincerely,
John Crandall
john.crandall@mail.com • 555-781-9109 • LinkedIn.com/in/john-crandall

* * * * *

Dear Ms. Santiago:

I sincerely appreciated the opportunity to meet with you to discuss joining TM's Retail Banking Team. Your questions were insightful, and I believe they showcased the value I can bring to TM if offered an opportunity as a manager trainee.

When we discussed examples of initiative taking, I didn't mention that in my internship with Avis Corporate Finance, I recommended to my supervisor a streamlined method of capturing a monthly statistic that had proven elusive; my idea was accepted and I was able to implement the positive change before my internship concluded.

I have a reputation for always trying to optimize procedures and protocols—and you can count on me to bring this same level of energy to TM. I look forward to hearing from you and participating in the next steps in the candidate selection process.

Sincerely,
Taylor Pastrnak | 555-823-1810 | taylor.pastrnak@gmail.com

Career Centers Say …

"We teach students that thank-you letters are mandatory and should be completed as soon as possible, within 24 hours of the interview. They should express gratitude and professionalism, as well as highlight any truly important points that they feel they didn't get to cover during the interview."

— *Gretchen Heaton, Dean of Career Development, Bay Path University*

Job Offers and Negotiations

Receiving a job offer is extremely gratifying! Your hard work in school and in the job search has paid off, and you are achieving an important goal as you secure an internship/co-op job or begin your professional career.

Job offers for new graduates are frequently for entry-level positions and there is typically little room for negotiation in the compensation. However, that doesn't mean you should just accept an offer without a conversation.

Before you begin that conversation (negotiation), make sure you are clear on the details of the job. Ask for a written job offer, if one has not been provided to you. If the company does not provide written offers, write down all the details of what they're offering and reiterate them verbally to the interviewer: "I understand you're making me an offer for the job of [Job Title] at an annual salary of $xx with the following benefits: …"

You can, of course, accept the offer immediately. But we recommend that you pause, just a bit, to think carefully before making such an important decision.

> **PRO TIP: Be enthusiastic!** Even if you are not accepting the offer right away, express appreciation and enthusiasm. You want them to know that you're truly excited about the job, the company, and the overall career opportunity. Here's some language you might use.
>
> "Thank you! I'm really excited and honored. I'd like to give everything careful consideration and get back to you with my decision within 48 hours—is that timeline okay for you?"
>
> The maximum time you should request is one week, although shorter is better. Use that time wisely to do all of the research, outreach, and reflection you need to be certain you're making the right decision. Get back to the employer when promised (if not sooner) either to accept the offer or to discuss additional questions or requests.

Negotiating Your Offer

As mentioned, you may have little wiggle room in negotiating compensation for an entry-level job. But you should consider *all* of the aspects of the job and perhaps request additional information or benefits. Here's how you should proceed.

- Compare the salary offer with information you've gathered throughout your job search. Use Glassdoor, Salary.com, Payscale, and other sites to expand on what you've discovered on your own.

- Review the benefits and make certain that features important to you (Hybrid or remote work? Reimbursement for continuing education/master's degree?) are specifically mentioned. If not, you can ask about these during your follow-up discussion.

- Think carefully about what you learned in the interview process. The job may not be *perfect* (few things are!), but it should be a good fit for your skills and interests. You should feel excited about going to work at the company and in the environment they offer.

- Consider other jobs you are pursuing. Are you expecting an offer from any of them very soon? Does another position seem much more desirable to you? (See discussion on multiple offers on page 113.)

Assuming that you decide to accept the job offer, get back in touch with your company contact. Indicate that you're excited to accept the offer and have just a few questions. Try to schedule an in-person follow-up meeting; if that's impractical, you can meet via Zoom or phone. As a last resort, you can hold your discussion over email, although this is least desirable because it's too easy for misunderstandings to occur.

When you meet, reiterate your enthusiasm for the job and appreciation for the offer. "I'm really excited to get started! I have just a few questions about the offer details that I'd like to iron out."

Then, one by one, bring up your questions/issues/requests and try to come to agreement on each. You never want to come across as greedy or grasping, so keep your conversation calm and businesslike. Use language like, "My research shows that entry-level salaries in this industry are $XX to $XX. Can you do something in this range?" Or, "One of the things I'm most excited about is continuing to learn more about accounting and auditing. If I decide to take a CPA review course, would the company cover the tuition?"

Your "asks" should be for things that are really important to you. Mix up your requests with questions for clarification about other issues. For example, will the company provide you with a phone and laptop, or will you be using your own? This discussion is often a good time to ask about the company's customary performance review process (every six months? once annually?) and how increases to salary are handled.

As you come to agreement on each point—some the employer may agree to, others not—jot it down and move on to the next. At the conclusion of your meeting, recap what you agreed to and ask if the written offer will be revised to reflect this information (assuming some things have changed).

Once satisfied with the outcome, tell them that you accept the offer and look forward to starting. If some items remain up in the air, state that you look forward to starting as soon as these last few items are resolved. Above all, continue to express enthusiasm for the opportunity and excitement about the job.

> **PRO TIP: Employers expect candidates to negotiate.** When you negotiate, you are not being "pushy" or "greedy." You are holding a civil business discussion about terms of employment and asking for things that will make you a better, more satisfied employee. The negotiation should not be confrontational. It's simply an ironing out of details. Go into it with confidence and a businesslike aspect, and you'll do fine—and likely emerge with more than you began with.

Multiple Offers and Counteroffers

Particularly in some fields, there is keen competition for top talent and you may find yourself with multiple offers. If it happens that you receive competitive offers simultaneously, you'll want to weigh a number of factors, the most important of which is where you believe you'll be happiest, learn the most, perform successfully, and have the greatest opportunity for advancement.

If you receive, negotiate, and accept an offer and then receive a subsequent (perhaps better) offer from another company, you have a decision to make: Should you stick with the old offer or go with the new?

Carefully weigh the two different positions—the work you would be doing, opportunity for growth, long-range potential, compensation, benefits comparison, and other tangible and intangible aspects of both jobs.

Should you determine that you prefer the second offer, you will need to resign from the job you accepted. Do this both verbally, to your direct manager, and in writing. Provide a two-week notice—but recognize that your new employer might accept the resignation on the spot, and you might be asked to leave immediately.

Language for the resignation memo is very short and straightforward. Date the memo, direct it to your manager, and consider using the following:

"It is with regret that I resign my role as *[your job title]* with *[company name]* effective *[date, two weeks out]*. Thank you for this opportunity."

Sign the printed copy and present it in person when you verbally give your notice. You do not need to explain your reason for leaving in the memo. You might express verbally that another opportunity was presented to you that aligns more closely with your long-range career goals. You can identify the new employer and job.

Onboarding

Congratulations! You've done it—landed your job! How can you optimize your first days and weeks in your new position?

You'll likely participate in orientation activities to onboard with your new company. The larger the company, the more formalized the onboarding process is likely to be. This is an opportunity to meet key people within your department or company as well as make a great first impression.

Be sure to ask your HR representative for basic information: hours for your workday, parking details, break room, "dress code"/work culture, and so forth. You'll obtain your company email address, phone number, office or cubicle location (if not working remotely), and any company-issued computer equipment.

In learning about your new role, be strategic in taking good notes, following through on action items and assignments, and demonstrating initiative wherever possible. Ask questions freely. As you complete assignments and/or projects, always seek additional work or projects you can do to add value.

Over the course of the first few weeks in your new position, check in periodically with your manager to learn expectations around how often you will have status meetings. You will find that you will assimilate fairly quickly to your new company and role. And, before you know it, you'll be updating your resume and LinkedIn to incorporate your new professional experience.

We wish you much success as you launch your career!

Resumes for College Students and New Graduates

What's the value in looking at other people's resumes? We don't want you to copy, of course—your resume must be your own story. But seeing many different samples will help you in numerous ways.

- You'll get ideas for design and layout. What catches your attention, and why? Can you do something similar with your own material?

- You can peruse the content to get into the flow of "resume style." It's a bit different than regular writing and may feel choppy at first, but it's designed to convey information succinctly and quickly.

- You can compare your draft with resumes you really like. Does yours look as good, read as smoothly, contain ample keywords, and get key messages across as quickly?

- You're likely to see something—a graphic, a layout, a phrase, a special section—that sparks your creativity for your own resume.

- You'll see how to handle circumstances similar to yours. Lots of projects, little experience? Return-to-school graduate with significant work history? Mediocre grades but a great deal of campus involvement?

These stories and circumstances, and many more, can be found in the portfolio that follows.

Below each resume you will see several important bits of information.

First is the name and contact information of the professional resume writer who created that resume. We are proud to feature the excellent work of nearly three dozen career professionals. If you are looking for help with your own, please reach out to a writer whose work you admire.

Next, you'll see the college major and current career target. That information will help you understand the strategy that went into creating the resume and identify samples that match your own story.

Finally, there's a short comment on "Notable" features of each resume.

The sample resumes, combined with the advice and examples we shared in the first five chapters of this book, are designed to inspire, educate, and prepare you to create a resume that reflects your value in the workplace, your uniqueness as an individual, and the preparations you have made for your career.

We congratulate you on your accomplishments thus far and cheer you on as you begin your professional career.

Kristin Wells

555-781-4435 | kristin.wells@gmail.com
Seattle, WA 98112

Immediate Goal

Sales and/or Marketing Internship, Summer 2023

Career Interests

Medical Device or Pharmaceutical Sales—drawing on business education, people skills, work ethic, and deep interest in medical fields gained through sports and sports injuries.

Education

University of Washington   Seattle, WA
BS BUSINESS ADMINISTRATION—Marketing Concentration   Anticipated May 2024

- *Academic Performance:* GPA 3.51 | Dean's List
- *Marketing Class Project:* Worked with 2 teammates to create and market a seasonal salad in support of Breast Cancer Awareness Month. One of 5 groups chosen to present to the owners of Salads-n-More; received second place.
- *Distinction:* Accepted into UW's first-of-its-kind "Future Focus" program for 2023–2024. The year-long program, a deep dive into a specific industry, exposes high-achieving undergraduates to senior executives and business school experts who will share insights and strategies to prepare students for career success.
- *Athletic Recognition:* Recruited to NCAA Division 1 Soccer Team as full-scholarship athlete.
- *Work Ethic & Academic Performance:* Fulfilled demanding athletic schedule (20+ hours per week) while maintaining a high GPA.

Experience

Footy Fun   Seattle, WA
COACH (Young athletes ages 4–8)   March 2022–Present

- Designed training sessions to develop skills while keeping sessions fun and engaging.
- Learned to interact with and motivate players with different personalities and behaviors.

Angelo's   Tacoma, WA
HOSTESS   May 2022–January 2023

- Managed greeting and reservation desk of busy restaurant. Maintained a well-organized reservation system, served guests in a timely fashion, and resolved customer complaints.
- *Notable:* Promoted from part-time to full-time role within weeks of hire based on quick learning, people skills, and teamwork orientation.

Stansfield School   Seattle, WA
TUTOR AND MENTOR (Volunteer)   September 2021–May 2022

- Tutored elementary through high school students, assisted with difficult assignments, and became a trusted advisor to help students solve problems.

Hard working and competitive | Organized and efficient | People oriented
Dedicated to top performance—both individually and as a teammate

Louise Kursmark, MRW, CPRW, JCTC, CEIP, CCM | Best Impression Career Services | louisekursmark.com
Major: Business Administration/Marketing | **Goal:** Sales or marketing internship
Notable: The Education section highlights Kristin's distinction in several areas—academics, athletics, intangible character assets, and selection for a special program. Soft skills, positioned as a footnote, close the resume on a unique and positive note.

ZANDER OWENS

zanderowens@gmail.com
555-673-8902

Candidate: Internship with Mylan Pharmaceuticals

SALES — MARKETING — CUSTOMER RELATIONSHIP MANAGEMENT

PROFESSIONAL SKILLS SUMMARY

Product Pricing	Contract Negotiations & Transactions
Financial/Economic Analysis	Customer & Business Communications
Project Planning & Execution	Team Building & Leadership
Time & Schedule Management	Customer Relationship Building

Proficient in MS Office Suite (including advanced Excel) and marketing via social media.

EDUCATION

Pursuing BS Degree in Marketing—to be conferred December 2023
FLORIDA STATE UNIVERSITY, Tallahassee, FL

- Coursework in Marketing, Economics, Business Management, Accounting, and Statistics
- Member, Sigma Chi Fraternity—focus on teamwork, community outreach, and philanthropy

WORK EXPERIENCE

Sales Associate, Coastal Motors, Sarasota, FL (May 2022–Present)

Top-producing sales associate in one of the region's largest automotive dealerships.

- Demonstrate superior skills and performance in product pricing, contract negotiations, customer relationship management, product delivery, and product quality.
- Consistently achieve/surpass all sales goals and objectives.

Auto Detailer, Owens Auto Care, Sarasota, FL (Summers 2018–2021)

Built from startup to steady summer revenue and retained 100% of customers over 4 years.

- Launched entrepreneurial venture that combines personal interest in exclusive automobiles with the ability to instantly build customer rapport, relationships, and repeat business.
- Used social media to build visibility in local market. Created and maintained website, Instagram feed, and Twitter account.

Sales Associate, Best Buy, Orlando, FL (November 2016–May 2018)

Averaged 130% of monthly sales quota.

- One of only 4 seasonal employees hired permanently based on strong sales performance. Consistently ranked as a top producer.

Bat Boy, FCL Orioles (Baltimore Orioles Rookie Team), Sarasota, FL (Summers 2015–2016)

Promoted to Head Bat Boy after first year based on dependability, reliability, and leadership.

Wendy Enelow, MRW, CPRW, JCTC, CCM | Enelow Enterprises | wendyenelow.com
Major: Marketing | **Goal:** Internship with a pharmaceutical company
Notable: The Professional Skills Summary groups relevant keywords right at the top of the resume. Sales and other performance highlights are noted in a shaded box below each job title.

STEPHEN JENKINS

972.999.4646 | stephenjenkins@gmail.com | www.linkedin.com/in/stephen-jenkins-sj

ACCOMPLISHED MULTILINGUAL INTERN CANDIDATE

Seeking an internship in Engineering, Bioscience, Medical Research, or Data Science.

Highly focused with a tireless work ethic and determination to excel. Quick to take on new responsibilities and leadership roles. Proven ability to manage full class load and professional activities. Strong in data analysis, testing methods, and medical research.

Fluent in Spanish. Read and write Japanese.

EDUCATION & HONORS

UNIVERSITY OF OKLAHOMA | NORMAN, OK   **EXPECTED GRADUATION MAY 2026**
Major: General Engineering + Pre-Med; *actively pursuing Chemical Engineering*

- Accepted into Engineering to Medicine (E2M) Early Assurance Program
- Accepted into the University Honors Program
- Accepted into the Davis Engineering Honors Program
- Recipient of President's Endowed Scholar Award

LOS LAGOS HIGH SCHOOL | DENTON, TX   **GRADUATED MAY 2022**

- National Merit Scholar Recipient
- National Honor Society (3 years)
- Weighted GP: 5.32/6; Unweighted GPA: 3.96/4

ACADEMIC PROJECTS
Research ★ Computer Science ★ Healthcare

AP RESEARCH PROJECT | DENTON, TX   **10/2021 TO 04/2022**

- Conducted research to determine if a correlation exists between technology and neck posture issues in different age groups.
- Employed a cross-sectional study on x-rays analyzed for signs of cervical lordosis or excessively inward curvature of the neck using the Cobb method.
- Utilized Python to perform multilinear regression analysis, co-variance tests, normality tests, and a Random Forest Regression analysis to determine correlation.

COMPUTER SCIENCE PROJECT | DENTON, TX   **SUMMER 2020**

- Created a dataset from Spotify and its music features on favorite songs from K-Pop artists.
- Performed normality test, co-variance test, linear regression, and multi-linear regression.
- Results indicated that music features did not affect popularity of songs, but rather the group popularity.

HEALTHCARE APPLICATION PROJECT | DENTON, TX   **SUMMER 2020**

- Created app using R-language for medical offices to assess patient COVID symptoms.
- App still used by staff at two office locations.

Kristi Meenan, CPRW | We Write It Now | wewriteitnow.com
Major: Engineering | **Goal:** Internship in engineering, bioscience, medical research, or data science
Notable: This resume includes projects and activities from high school, appropriate for this internship-seeking college student. Impressive academic honors are highlighted.

STEPHEN JENKINS, CONTINUED

WORK HISTORY

PEDIATRIC ASSOCIATES OF DENTON | DENTON, TX   04/2021 TO 04/2022
Medical Aide (Part Time)

- Created intake forms for patients to complete before appointments.
- Answered incoming calls, scheduled appointments, and provided support to staff.
- Prepped patient rooms prior to appointments.
- Shadowed doctors, observing daily responsibilities and patient interactions.
- Monitored supplies in patient rooms; restocked when needed.

KNOWLEDGE LEARNING CENTER | DENTON, TX   07/2021 TO 03/2022
Teacher Aide (Part Time)

- Assisted teachers with preparing class materials and grading assignments.
- Tutored students on math and reading comprehension.
- Provided additional support to center director, when needed.

TECHNICAL KNOWLEDGE

GENERAL: Microsoft Office Suite | Google Drive | Python | Java | R Studio

CERTIFICATIONS: Certified Entry Level Python Programmer | Python Institute | Summer 2022

HIGH SCHOOL LEADERSHIP & EXTRACURRICULARS

HOBY Leadership Seminar, 2020
Renaissance Leadership Conference, 2019

National Honor Society, 3 Years
Academic Integrity Co-Chair, 2 Years

Student Ambassador, 3 Years

K-Pop Club, 3 Years
Vice President, 1 Year; Secretary, 1 Year

Gifted & Talented Humanities Program, 1 Year

COMMUNITY SERVICE

Summer 2022: Brighten-a-Day Foundation
Summer 2020: National Breast Cancer Foundation

LUPITA SANDERS

555-789-9812 | Boston, MA 02110 | lupita-sanders@mail.com

Internship Candidate | Hospitality Industry   *Bilingual Spanish / English*

Well-traveled and well-educated college junior with strong planning, organizational, communication, and interpersonal skills. A true multi-tasker with combination of work experience and academic training in:

- Special Events Planning & Coordination
- Guest Relations & Public Relations
- Exclusive Restaurant & Club Operations
- Marketing & Business Development

- Conference & Meeting Planning
- Hospitality Industry & Hotel Management
- Business Communications
- Personnel Training & Leadership

Education

B.S. Candidate—Hospitality Administration (to be conferred May 2024)
BOSTON UNIVERSITY, Boston, MA
- Major GPA 3.7 | Overall GPA 3.6 | Eta Sigma Delta Honor Society
- Spanish Language & Culture Studies, Universidad de Alicante, Alicante, Spain (Summer 2022)
- Gamma Phi Beta Sorority: Pi Chi Counselor for new recruits (2022-2023); PACE Chairperson planning and orchestrating special events and educational programs (2021–2022).

Experience

Hospitality Server & Golf Shop Attendant | U.S. OPEN TOURNAMENT, Brookline, MA (June 2022)
- Privileged to work at one of golf's most prestigious tournaments. Served VIPs and other guests in hospitality tent, assisted customers with golf shop purchases, responded to special requests, and provided general information about on-site events.

Hostess & Banquet Server | THE COUNTRY CLUB, Brookline, MA (Summers 2020–2022)
- Managed outside seating area and designed seating charts to accommodate guests and special event programs. Collaborated with kitchen and wait staffs for planning and managing on-site events, weddings, and celebrations for up to 400 guests.

Hostess | NORTH END TRATTORIA, Boston, MA (Summer 2019)
- Greeted and seated incoming guests, assisted wait staff with guest relations, and coordinated customer pick-up orders.

Lacrosse & Tennis Coach | THE FESSENDEN SCHOOL, Newton, MA (Summers 2017–2019)
- Coached players and assisted with competitive sporting events.

International Experiences

Spent summers with family in **Mexico** ages 4–12. Traveled extensively throughout **Latin and South America.** Visited 6 **European** capitals during 3-week high school trip. Completed an international exchange program during junior year of high school, living with a family in **Copenhagen** and hosting a Danish student in return.

Wendy Enelow, MRW, CPRW, JCTC, CCM | Enelow Enterprises | wendyenelow.com
Major: Hospitality Administration | **Goal:** Internship in the hospitality industry
Notable: The resume describes Lupita as "well traveled" in the opening paragraph and documents that travel experience in the final section. Relevant experience is highlighted, along with college activities.

John McIntyre

So. Salem, NY 10590 | 917.555.1234 | jmcintyre@sunybinghamton.edu

Applicant: MS Accounting Program, New York University

Dedicated to Academic Excellence | Highly Collaborative | Poised to Excel
Known for diplomatic leadership, cooperative disposition, authentic interpersonal skills, and stellar work ethic.

✓ Ranked among top 5% of applicants selected for Binghamton School of Management Honors Program.
— Enriched leadership proficiency through Honors Program personalized development, mentor-guided curriculum.
✓ Hired by Ernst & Young for Summer 2022 Internship.
— Gained expert training and experience in evidence-based auditing and internal controls practices and procedures.

Personal Values
Sincerity, Responsibility, Respect, Collaboration, Trust, Optimism, Positivity

Professional Attributes
Situationally Perceptive| Culturally and Socially Poised | Decisive
Sound Judgment | Emotional Stability and Maturity
Team-Inspired Group Leader | Analytical Thinker | Attentive Listener | Collegial Partner

EDUCATION

Bachelor of Science, Business Administration, Binghamton University, The State University of New York
Major – Accounting
GPA – 3.7 | *Dean's List:* Spring and Fall 2021, Spring and Fall 2022
Graduating – May 2023 | Anticipate satisfying the 150-hour CPA requirement by June 2024

School of Management Honors Program (Spring 2021–Spring 2023)
Only 5% of students are invited to apply and 25 are selected to participate in a development plan customized for each individual to strengthen leadership skills and intensify classroom learning through tailored coaching by a faculty mentor.

TECHNOLOGY PROFILE

Microsoft Office: Word, PowerPoint, Excel (advanced proficiency) | Google Docs | Tableau | Salesforce

ACADEMIC PROJECTS

WANTEDLY – International Business Project (Spring 2023–In Progress)
Target
Raise awareness of company's value proposition to stand out from the competition. Create a distinctively branded strategy for Singapore market, positioning the company's hiring platform as the #1 choice for employers.

Results
Member of 5-person team that conducted SWOT analysis, industry analysis, competitor analysis, and customer analysis. Developed strategic focus and crafted go-to-market plans of action positioning Wantedly as the superior choice.

STUDY ABROAD – Consulting Project with Farm in Costa Rica (Spring 2022) **Grade: A-**
Target
Create robust digital marketing strategy for Costa Rica farm and promote the company's All-Natural, organic pesticide seedlings.
Results
Researched local culture and conducted SWOT analysis of Costa Rica's international market. Created digital marketing strategy using FB Marketplace, YouTube, Instagram, and WhatsApp with ready-to-go weekly and seasonal posts, recipes using vegetables grown from their own seeds, and a customer feedback survey with smart goals to monitor success.

Cheryl Milmoe, NCOPE, CARW, ACRW, CDBS, CCLP | Cardinal Expert Resumes | cardinalexpertresumes.com
Major: Business Administration | **Goal:** Admission to graduate school (MS Accounting)
Notable: The Personal Values statement reflects John's character and offers immediate branding. The Academic Projects section details relevant studies—and results.

John McIntyre

So. Salem, NY 10590 | 917.555.1234 | jmcintyre@sunybinghamton.edu

ACADEMIC PROJECTS, continued

GEICO (Fall 2022) **Grade: 93**

Target

Led team of 5 to address retention issues of minority client populations in New Jersey. Selected as GEICO team representative.

Results

Collaborated with Regional Underwriting Manager to explore and develop retention strategies. Enhanced customer experience using Artificial Intelligence to identify strategic locations for kiosks to assist with claims, and cultivated new business opportunities by earning their trust through personalized relationship building.

PAPER-BASED ACCOUNTING PROJECT (Spring 2022) **Grade: 85**

Target

Learn concepts of invoice preparation, mock checks, journal entries, and financial accounting procedures.

Results

Acquired aptitude for recording business activity results, accounting systems, flowcharts, internal control concepts, documentation, flow and control of financial information, auditing, and financial accounting.

MASTER BUDGETING PROJECT (Fall 2021) **Grade: 97**

Target

Assume role as CFO of a product company overseeing the accounting and finance functions and prepare the 2021 Master Budget and Budgeted Income Statement.

Results

Applied advanced Excel skills to prepare detailed performance for each quarter and yearly totals.

VOLUNTEER/COMMUNITY SERVICE

September 2022: Participated in *Tunnel to Towers Annual Run* to raise funds for 9/11 survivors and First Responders. Served as mentor and event leader for special needs children in community sports and fitness activities.

MEMBERSHIP

Binghamton University Accounting Association, Social Committee member.

EMPLOYMENT

At Your Service Catering & Event Planning – *Waiter*　　　　　　　　　　　Summers 2022, 2020, 2018, 2017
Clients Included: Hampton Classic, Michael Bloomberg, LLC, American Express, Morgan Stanley, Capital One, Jaguar
Organized event partners into teams to plan, promote, and deliver top-tier service and an outstanding client experience.

Quogue Shop – *Cashier/Salesperson*　　　　　　　　　　　　　　　　　Summer 2020
Led team of 3 and managed day-to-day operations. Created and implemented social media marketing campaign.

PERSONAL INTERESTS

Golf, Bruce Springsteen, U2, Chess, NY Jets, NY Yankees, Reading

Jess Tomlinson

jess.tomlinson@mac.com • 617-345-7821

Applicant to Cleveland Clinic School of Medicine

Education

NORTHEASTERN UNIVERSITY, Boston, MA
B.S. Behavioral Neuroscience, anticipated 5/2023
Honors Program—Dean's List all semesters—GPA 3.96

Pre-Med Coursework: Biology, Chemistry, Analytical Chemistry, Organic Chemistry, Physics, Calculus, Neurobiology, Genetics, Anatomy & Physiology, Biochemistry

Psychology Coursework: Statistics; Abnormal Psychology; Social Psychology; Learning & Motivation; Lab in Personality; Behavior Modification; Psychobiology; Psychopharmacology; Sensation & Perception

Honors and Activities:
— President's Award, Spring 2010—One of the top 10 students in the Class of 2023 at NU
— The Academy of Arts and Sciences—Northeastern University Honor Society
— The National Society of Collegiate Scholars
— Phi Kappa Phi Honor Society—elected as a junior, representing top 7.5% of class across all disciplines
— NUAMSA—Northeastern University American Medical Student Association

Experience

Medical Assistant • CHILDREN'S HOSPITAL, Boston, MA   6/22–12/22
- Worked directly with chronically ill children at the hospital's Center for Ambulatory Treatment and Clinical Research. Formed close relationships with children while assisting during their recurring visits.
- Checked patients in; took vital signs throughout IV infusions; removed IV lines; drew blood; stocked supplies; interacted with patients and families; assisted nurses as needed in a wide range of activities.
- Worked full-time June–December and invited to remain on a part-time basis during winter/spring semester.

Medical Assistant • CATHERINE DORVIL, M.D., Boston, MA   6/21–12/21
- Quickly learned and performed full range of medical assisting duties—interviewing patients, taking vital signs, drawing blood, observing and assisting doctor, and managing the patient visit.
- Scheduled appointments and surgeries, checked patients in, and performed other administrative tasks.
- Interacted extensively with patients, in person during office visits and answering questions by phone.

Health Care Assistant • CROSS-CULTURAL SOLUTIONS, Lima, Peru   12/19–2/20
- Supported staff members and tended children at an orphanage for children with HIV/AIDS.
- Developed close personal relationships with children through intensive 5-days-weekly contact.
- Assisted staff with severely disabled children in Mother Teresa's Hospital and conducted home visits to impoverished senior citizens.
- Communicated primarily in Spanish.

Clinical Research Coordinator • CHILDREN'S HOSPITAL MEDICAL CENTER, Cincinnati, OH   3/19–9/19
- Performed research and administrative tasks for the Cincinnati Asthma Prevention (CAP) Study.
- Telephoned families, assessed eligibility, and conducted follow-up interviews.
- Entered data and verified correctness of scanned information to ensure the integrity of study data.
- Attended lectures on diverse medical topics and observed rounds, procedures, and patient visits.

Community Receptionist • NORTHEASTERN UNIVERSITY, Boston, MA   10–15 hours weekly, 2020–Present
Emergency Department Volunteer • NEW ENGLAND MEDICAL CENTER, Boston, MA   2018–2019
Pediatric Volunteer • CHILDREN'S HOSPITAL MEDICAL CENTER, Cincinnati, OH   Summers 2017–2018

Skills
- **Technical:** MS Word, PowerPoint, Excel • Data entry
- **Medical:** Phlebotomy, vital signs measurement, CPR certified
- **Language:** Conversant in Spanish

Louise Kursmark, MRW, CPRW, JCTC, CEIP, CCM | Best Impression Career Services | louisekursmark.com
Major: Behavioral Neuroscience | **Goal:** Admission to medical school
Notable: The resume highlights extensive experience—from high school and international volunteer positions to college co-ops—to demonstrate long-standing interest in a medical career.

JUSTIN MARSHALL

Justinzmarsh@amherst.edu ▪ 863.789.0121 ▪ LinkedIn Profile

2023 HONORS GRADUATE/ACADEMIC SCHOLARSHIP RECIPIENT/PROVEN LEADERSHIP SKILLS
—Seeking entry to top-ranked graduate school to advance education in international trade and law—

Laser-focused and intellectually curious professional who is passionate about improving the way global cultures and business intersect, and leveraging commerce and law to transform underserved cultures and economies. Consistently praised by employers, professors, and peers for impeccable work ethic, altruistic nature, and cultural awareness.

- **Leadership & Service**—Elected youngest-ever President in 150-year history of International Students Council. Transformed poorly perceived council into one of the college's most admired organized student groups.

- **Academic Honors & Awards**—Recipient of full academic scholarship to Amherst College; achieved 4.0 GPA every semester. Earned multiple prestigious academic achievement awards.

- **Communication & Negotiation Skills**—Naturally diplomatic and respectful of others' perspectives but not afraid to negotiate for desired outcomes. Able to diffuse contentious situations and repair fractured relations.

- **Language & Technical Proficiencies**—Fluent in Spanish and Russian, basic knowledge of Mandarin. Computer skills include Word and PowerPoint and working knowledge of Excel and Photoshop.

EDUCATION

AMHERST COLLEGE ▪ Amherst, MA ▪ **BS, International Relations, minor in Spanish,** expected May 2023 ▪ 4.0 GPA

Highlights of Relevant Courses

- **International Relations**—Researched and analyzed political theories and their flaws; honed ability to rapidly analyze complex issues and identify potential solutions. Presented *"The Opportunities and Downfalls of Globalism"* to full board of professors from economics, international relations, and political science departments.

- **Economics of Contemporary Issues**—Learned to analyze forms of healthcare and other contemporary monetary issues to identify strengths and weaknesses within both developed and developing countries.

- **Middle East Culture**—Examined this culture through traditions of all religions and ethnicities. Studied politics and economics from ancient era to modern times.

- **Economics**—Gained a comprehensive understanding of micro and macro monetary systems. Learned societal and economic influence of migratory workers on an economy. Studied historical development of economic systems.

- **You Are What You Speak**—Analyzed the use of language in the business world and implications of colloquialisms and other elements of the English language to determine the most effective ways to communicate in business.

EXPERIENCE

AMHERST COLLEGE ▪ Amherst, MA ▪ **Program Manager—Office of International Programs**   Summer 2022

Selected to lead a Spanish summer program, *Grande Español*, based on prior successful internship and knowledge of Spanish culture and language. Oversaw all aspects of program: Screened candidates for selection, developed cultural immersion programs, and coordinated itineraries for two summer trips.

EN ESTE LUGAR ▪ Madrid, Spain ▪ **Intern**   Summer 2021

One of four out of 70 candidates chosen for internship with European trade fair organizaiton. Communicated exclusively in Spanish with high-profile clients regarding logistics, upcoming events, and invoicing. Attracted new clients and helped expand brand awareness of the organization. Offered full-time opportunity at conclusion of internship.

LEADERSHIP and COLLEGIATE ACTIVITIES

AMHERST COLLEGE ▪ Amherst, MA ▪ **President, International Students Council (ISC)**   2020 – 2022

Elected to represent 400-member organization in this paid role. Led 5-member board and managed $14K budget. Revamped recruiting strategies. Served on Student Equity and Inclusion Council and Five College Consortium board.

- Fostered a culture of goodwill, community, and collaboration, uniting polarized and diverse cultural groups.
- Revamped the new member process to better integrate and welcome inductees and attract potential recruits. Used the latest technologies to manage most processes virtually in response to global pandemic.
- Introduced changes that helped students with academic performance and assimilation to college and campus life.

Member, Law Review and Big Brothers, Big Sisters   2020 – 2022
Tutor (paid position)   August 2019 – December 2019

Jill Grindle, CPRW | Pinnacle Resumes, LLC | pinnacleresumes.com
Major: International Relations | **Goal:** Graduate school admission
Notable: In addition to academic highlights, the resume includes detailed work experience along with leadership and collegiate activities to paint the portrait of a high achiever with clear career goals.

Jason Friesen

905 555 5555 | jasonfriesen@gmail.com | LinkedIn | Hamilton, ON & Ready to Relocate

PILOT

Focused, Friendly & Committed to Safety

A determined aviation enthusiast on track for a career in the commercial airline industry. Aviation college graduate with flight experience, business education, and leadership skills. Known for commanding knowledge of technology and engaging personality.

AIRPLANE LICENSES & PILOT QUALIFICATIONS

TRANSPORT CANADA

- Class IV Instructor Rating (2022)
- Commercial Pilot License (2022)
- Commercial Multi-Engine Rating (2022)
- Certified Written Exam Invigilator (2022)
- Group 1 Instrument Flight Rules (2023)

FEDERAL AVIATION ADMINISTRATION

- Private Pilot License (2019)

HOURS

- Total flight hours: 750+
- As pilot in command hours: 225+
- Night hours: 75+

MULTI-ENGINE AIRCRAFT

- PA-44
- C 172/50
- SMEL Rated

EXPERIENCE

First Class Air Services & Training Ltd. Cambridge, ON   2020–Present

Flight Instructor (2022–Present) **Flight Dispatcher** (2020–Present)

Assist in multiple operational areas of a commercial flight school. Provide private pilot and ground school instruction, fuel and clean aircraft, perform administrative duties, and update website and social media.

- Planned and delivered pilot training lessons for students aged 16–60 with safety as priority.
- Performed basic aircraft maintenance under authorized personnel and established my reputation as a quick learner and valuable contributor.
- Selected to become company's sole Authorized Exam Invigilator and became the youngest of 4 exam invigilators in the company.
- Transformed multipage aircraft checklist into a single sheet and improved efficiency. Commended by owner for initiative and praised by students for ease of use.
- Developed a strategy that expedited student ability to land an aircraft.

Superior Aviation Services. Hamilton, ON   March 2022–December 2022

Ramp Services Agent

Provided ground-handling services to multiple commercial airlines, meeting company safety, efficiency, courtesy, and performance standards. Pushed back aircraft from parking positions using specialized ground vehicle, loaded baggage compartments, and serviced lavatories.

Barb Penney, MCRS, CWS, CPHR | Winning Resumes Career Solutions | winningresumes.ca
Major: Business/Aviation | **Goal:** Position as commercial pilot
Notable: Experience is placed before Education to highlight several years of work in the aviation industry. An appropriate engine graphic adds visual interest in the header. Airplane "bullets" are fun and distinctive.

Jason Friesen

905 555 5555 | jasonfriesen@gmail.com | LinkedIn

Superior Aviation Services. Ramp Services Agent (cont'd)

- Played a leadership role and trained 4 new employees.
- Resolved passenger lost-baggage complaints.
- Developed a hand-signal system that overcame jet engine noise and increased worker safety.

Mel's Air Service. Ancaster, ON   July 2021–September 2021

Ramp Agent
Worked 12-hour shifts for aerial agriculture business providing aerial application, agronomy, seed, and chemical sales in this seasonal role.

- Ensured smooth operation for the crop-dusting season as a chemical loader, aircraft fueler, and cleaner.
- Traveled to various airports and provided on-site services.

Bernie Morelli Recreation Centre. Hamilton, ON   April 2018–August 2019

Guest Services Representative / Recreation Facility Monitor
Hired as the youngest employee on team. Monitored facility patrons and addressed safety and behaviour concerns. Received customer service training modelled on Disney Institute Customer Service program.

EDUCATION

Business Management, Aviation Major   University of Waterloo
Diploma 2023   Waterloo, ON

Associate of Applied Science Flight Technology Degree   Lane Community College
Graduated 2020   Eugene, OR

Business Administration   University of Oregon
Courses in 2019–2020   Eugene, OR

PERSONAL LEADERSHIP

- Selected as **Captain for Junior Olympics Canada Roller Hockey Team** and won gold. Learned leadership lessons of accountability, inclusion, selflessness, and more.
- Played university-level hockey and developed strong team skills.
- Served as a volunteer and paid referee for Ontario Hockey Federation for 3+ years.

Jana Clark

Chicago, IL 48183 | (555) 555-5555 | janaclark@gmail.com

Career Target: Paralegal

Logical, detail-oriented critical thinker, writer, and communicator who leads with confidence and gets the job done. Excellent relationship skills built through service-oriented jobs with high-end clientele.

Eager, fast learner with the confidence to work independently while contributing as a team player.

Education

DePaul University, Chicago, IL | BA English (concentration in Public Policy), May 2022

- Pace Chair | Alpha Chi Omega, Beta Chapter. Conducted PR for the sorority. Managed social media posts and follows (Instagram, Facebook, Twitter); publicized events across campus; stepped in to address and resolve a claim of social media "plagiarism" by another sorority.
- Relevant coursework: Marketing/SEO, Health Communications

Work Experience

Service Member | AmeriCorps   August 2022–April 2023
An independent agency of the US government focused on community-based acts of service.

Hired to set groundwork for, coordinate, and facilitate creation of a service dog training and education club/program on DePaul's campus, with aim to service surrounding lower-income townships by providing access to disability services that would normally be out of reach. Working independently and on a team, strategized and handled the logistics of having a club on campus, including interfacing Student Life Office and Director of Student Development for Extracurricular Activities.

- Advocated for club establishment and funding by creating a Google Slide presentation stating how the club would benefit the campus and community, what was needed to set it up, and what updates to the Campus Handbook would be warranted.
- Researched bylaws of comparable organizations to compile first bylaws for DePaul chapter.
- Overcame delays due to the pandemic, including challenges with sick coworkers and meeting as a cohort, to finalize a solid plan of how to introduce the club and program to DePaul University.
- Identified qualified candidates who continue to perform this leadership role and other positions.

Phone Surveyor | Chicago Clinical Research Institute and *The Chicago Tribune*   Sep 2021–Apr 2022
Invited to participate in a nationwide survey of Americans and their reactions to the ever-evolving political climate. Surveys were later analyzed and presented in *The Chicago Tribune*.

- Worked phone/computer programs for cold-calling regions across the United States with the intent to survey random citizens on topics related to the 2022 presidential election.
- Provided research for *Politico* during time of high political tension in America.

Property Manager | Hales Property Management   May 2020–Aug 2020, Jan 2021

- Served many high-end clients. Executed background checks and managed the signing of NDAs.
- Performed home and boat upkeep and management; trained new hires on company processes.
- Recommended to manager that she hire a personal assistant, which decreased her workload.

Skills & Interests

Technical Skills: Microsoft Office – Word, Outlook, PowerPoint | Google – Docs, Slides
Interests: Tennis, Sailing, Baking
Languages: Basic comprehension of French

Brenda Bernstein, CMRW, CERM, CARW | The Essay Expert | theessayexpert.com
Major: English | **Goal:** Position as paralegal
Notable: Without formal paralegal training, this candidate focused her resume on work (including a post-graduate stint with AmeriCorps) and college experiences that demonstrated the skills needed.

JADA WILLIAMS

(555) 565-6555 ◆ Jada.williams@gmail.com ◆ linkedin.com/in/jadawilliams ◆ New York, NY 11014

HUMAN RESOURCES ADMINISTRATOR

Collaborative, organized human resources professional with administrative experience across HR Functions, including data tracking and reporting, recruiting, learning management systems, and payroll.

Professional Skills & Attributes

HR Administration • Compensation & Benefits • HR Software (HRIS) • Talent Management Systems
Recruiting & Onboarding • Confidentiality • Payroll Administration • Data Entry & Analysis • Team Building
Employee Relations • Event Planning • Project Management • Communications • Diversity & Inclusion

EDUCATION & HONORS

A.S. in Business Administration—MANHATTAN COMMUNITY COLLEGE—New York, NY—*Expected May 2023*

Business Education Program—Information Technology Concentration—YEARUP—2021
Selected for competitive national program of 6 months of intensive business training and 6-month internship.
Relevant Coursework: HR Management, Project Management, MS Excel, Communications, Business Policies

Excellence in Community Service Award—JACK AND JILL OF AMERICA FOUNDATION—Rockland County, NY
Recognized for 100+ service hours presenting at K-8 schools and supporting homelessness solutions

PROFESSIONAL EXPERIENCE

LINKEDIN CORPORATION

Human Resources Intern—*New York, NY*   **Apr 2022—Present**

Administer human resources generalist and recruiting processes for HR team supporting 10,000+ employees throughout the U.S. for the world's largest professional social network of 740M members across 200 countries.

- Screened 900+ resumes and recommended qualified candidates to HR manager, resulting in 6 new hires.
- Increased HRIS employee profile accuracy and completeness 20% by updating 2,000+ incomplete staff profiles.
- Met 100% of payroll deadlines in processing biweekly compensation for 500+ per diem third-party contractors.
- Improved candidate 6-month retention rate by researching, presenting, and integrating 2 new recruiting practices.

STATE FARM INSURANCE COMPANY

Customer Representative—*Rockaway, NY*   **Jun 2021—Apr 2022**

Facilitated online payment processing, data tracking, and client inquiry resolution for region's largest insurance firm.

- Updated payment records to complete 50 incomplete profiles and reconciled 100+ client accounts per month.
- Selected to handle client phone inquiries after demonstrating active listening and effective communication skills.

HOME CARE SOLUTIONS

Caregiving Service Provider—*Brooklyn, NY*   **Jun 2020—Jun 2021**

Created and implemented home care plans for national provider of trusted in-home senior care for 40+ years.

- Established enduring relationships with 4 seniors and their families to foster trust and continuity of care.
- Ensured 100% accuracy, utilizing Health Monitor App to track and report medication administration and vital signs.

COMMUNITY SERVICE

JACK AND JILL OF AMERICA FOUNDATION—Corresponding Secretary & Outreach Presenter   **2018—2020**

Promoted public health and housing by facilitating fundraising meetings, presenting at schools, communicating with partners, and participating in conference. Created award-winning mural depicting African-American heritage.

Julie Wyckoff, MEd, Certified Career Transition Coach, YouMap Coach | Custom Career Solutions | customcareersolutions.com
Major: Business Administration | **Goal:** HR administrator role
Notable: Highlights of this resume are the prestigious YearUp program (mentioned under Education) and a relevant internship. Valuable skills are "mined" from work experience that is not directly related.

Keisha Browne

New York, NY 10030 | 646-215-1133 | keishabrowne@gmail.com | https://www.linkedin.com/in/keishabrowne

ASPIRING HUMAN RESOURCES PROFESSIONAL

Solutions-driven professional with experience supporting new hire onboarding process, managing Human Resources database, and handling confidential information with care. Detail-oriented team member with keen ability to organize data and meet aggressive deadlines in fast-paced environments. Customer-focused individual who enjoys interacting with clients, responding to inquiries, and resolving issues, while maintaining 100% customer satisfaction.

Communication | Applicant Screening | Recruitment | Critical Thinking | Organization | Data Entry | Recordkeeping | FMLA
Conflict Resolution | Time Management | Relationship Building | Diversity & Inclusion | Staffing | Employee Relations
Marketing | Customer Service | Regulatory Compliance | Talent Acquisition

Software: Microsoft Office (Word, Excel, and PowerPoint); Workday; ADP; PeopleSoft; Workforce Management

EDUCATION

Bachelor of Arts: Economics | *CUNY City College* | New York, NY   Expected Graduation May 2023

Associate of Arts: Philosophy | *CUNY Kingsborough Community College* | Brooklyn, NY   June 2022

RELATED PROFESSIONAL EXPERIENCE

Human Resources College Assistant | *CUNY City College* | Brooklyn, NY   August 2019–Present

▸ Streamline communication between leadership team and employees through internal HR database.

▸ Collaborate with Time and Leave Specialist to process medical leave requests and confirm employee eligibility according to New York State Family and Medical Leave Act (FMLA).

▸ Maintain accurate records of employee annual time-off usage, direct deposit forms, contact information, and tax documents in City University Personnel System.

▸ Respond to employee inquiries by answering phone calls and emails, providing top-quality customer service.

▸ Assist with new hire onboarding process by creating presentations on department policies, guidelines, and resources for orientation workshops.

Human Resources Intern | *Harlem Heights* | New York, NY   June 2019–August 2019

▸ Screened 100+ resumes to identify potential candidates based on eligibility requirements.

▸ Monitored recruitment calendar and scheduled interview appointments with prospective candidates.

▸ Navigated ADP and PeopleSoft database to update new employee information, including W-4 forms.

▸ Attended monthly diversity and inclusion trainings to learn how to create an inclusive hiring process and work environment for employees.

ADDITIONAL WORK EXPERIENCE

Seasonal Sales Associate | *Bath, Bed, and Beyond* | New York, NY   September 2020–January 2021

▸ Delivered exceptional customer service by answering questions and assisting customers through checkout. Handled cash and credit-card transactions.

▸ Ensured customer safety by staying abreast of COVID-19 protocols and enforcing store policies.

Communications Intern | *Museum of Art* | New York, NY   June 2016–August 2016

▸ Collaborated with Communications team to develop innovative strategies to improve marketing and increase museum attendance.

▸ Devised engaging weekly emails to build community with subscribers and promote upcoming events.

Kaljah Adams, ACRW | The Career Advising Hub | careeradvisinghub.org
Major: Economics | **Goal:** Human resources generalist
Notable: The beefiest section of this resume is "Related Professional Experience," highlighting two roles that clearly demonstrate this candidate's skills and qualifications related to her target jobs.

Paris Schumer

Los Angeles, CA 55555 • 555.555.5555 • parisschumer@gmail.com • LinkedIn

TRILINGUAL GRADUATE TARGETING ENTRY-LEVEL DIVERSITY POSITION

⊙ Detailed and creative graduate with track record of championing diversity to facilitate inclusive organizations that attract top global talent. Fluent in German and French with conversational knowledge of Farsi. Long-term tutor of English as second language to students in both French and German.

⊙ Dynamic researcher and project manager with experience balancing multiple priorities for complex projects and ability to thrive in interdisciplinary teams and unstructured environments.

⊙ Adept collaborator and relationship-builder who provides responsive client service that drives business.

CORE STUDIES & EMERGING SKILLS

Cultural Diversity • Inclusion & Diversity Programs • Internal & External Communications • Research
Project Management • Inclusion Strategy • Data Review & Analysis • Calendar Management

EDUCATION

BS, MANAGERIAL ECONOMICS/MINOR, COMMUNICATION — *California State University* 2023; Los Angeles, CA
Select Projects:

- **Gender Wage Gap Regression Analysis** — Partnered with classmate to examine data from U.S. Bureau of Labor Statistics. Identified previously unidentified gender-based wage gap causes, such as post-parental leave job market re-entry. When adding additional variables, found additional factors such as varying impact on women of different races.
- **Marketing Plan** — Collaborated with classmate to develop marketing plan for hypothetical new protein bar. Plan components included objectives, situational analysis, strategy, marketing tactics, product benefits/selling points, customer growth tracking, and marketing evaluation metrics.

RELEVANT EXPERIENCE

ARTS & CULTURE WRITER — *The California Chronicle* 2021–2023; Los Angeles, CA
Wrote articles for newspaper focusing on arts, entertainment, and diversity. Covered local events, shows, and movie reviews. Proposed topics, gathered sources, researched data, and created original journalism.
Select Articles:

- A more equitable film festival.
- Seven movies from the seven countries targeted by President Trump's Muslim ban.
- English professors recall books that left lasting impressions.

MARKETING INTERN – *Computer Industry, Inc,* January–June 2021; Sunnyvale, CA
Supported marketing team in executing daily tasks related to advertising, promotions, presentations, social media, direct mail, and website content. Distributed marketing materials and co-organized marketing events.
Select Accomplishment:

- Established process for creating instructional collateral for product marketing managers. Nearly eliminated previous high rejection levels from legal and PR due to lack of formalized process. Completed project within three months.

ADDITIONAL EXPERIENCE

SERVER — *Olive Garden* 2019–Present; Glendale, CA
SPECIALIST — *Apple, Inc.* 2018–2019; Pleasanton, CA

Andrea Adamski, CPRW | Write For You Resumes | writeforyouresumes.com
Major: Managerial Economics | **Goal:** Position in HR/diversity
Notable: Highlighted college projects and work experience focus on her greatest area of interest—diversity, equity, and inclusion. Note "Core Studies & Emerging Skills" headline for keyword section.

KENDRA DAVIS, MSW

Aurora, IL | kendra@gmail.com | 630-473-5934

SOCIAL WORKER

Leading with Patience, Understanding, and Thorough Communication

Empathic Social Worker committed to providing equitable care for the most vulnerable populations.

Adept at serving as the bridge between patients and the complexities of the healthcare system.

Trusted to guide patients towards achieving ultimate wellness and peak independence.

KEY COMPETENCIES

Case Management | Crisis Intervention | Documentation | Integrative Care | Geriatric Healthcare | Nursing Facilities
Long- & Short-Term Care | Palliative Care | Hospice | Admission/Intake | Discharge Planning
Care/Treatment Planning | Rehabilitation | PointClickCare (PCC) | Medicare/Medicaid

EDUCATION

Master of Social Work | Aurora University | 2023

Bachelor of Social Work | Aurora University | 2022

PROFESSIONAL EXPERIENCE

Sunrise Transitional Care | Social Worker Assistant | Richardson, TX   **5/2022 – Present**

▸ Balance caseload of ~15 while guiding patients through admission/intake, assessment, care planning, and discharge.

▸ Enable seamless discharges by answering patient inquiries, ordering necessary equipment, and recommending referrals.

▸ Demystify complex insurance, Medicare, and treatment planning scenarios, ensuring patients are well informed.

▸ Build relationships with families of hospice patients to offer emotional support and assist in counseling sessions.

▸ Accelerate rehabilitation for geriatric patients by coordinating therapeutic services—physical, speech/language, and occupational—bringing patients back to baseline and prioritizing ADLs (activities of daily living).

Chicago Hospital | Social Worker Intern | Houston, TX   **Summer 2021**

▸ Performed initial assessments and weekly progress notes for patients at luxury nursing home and rehabilitation center.

▸ Cared for geriatric patients in need of long-term palliative care and hospice services.

▸ Pioneered partnerships with hospice, hospital, and home health facilities.

Testimonial: "Kendra is **loved by patients and the nursing team alike**. Her **contributions to the team are invaluable**, her **positive personality is contagious**, and her **passion is a breath of fresh air**." —Portia Edgers, RN at Chicago Hospital

Chelsey Opare-Addo | Not Your Mother's Resume | notyourmothersresume.com
Major: Social Worker | **Goal:** Social work
Notable: Both soft skills and professional competencies are highlighted in this resume, which ends with a strong endorsement. Graphics are clean, attractive, and attention-getting in all the right ways.

ROBERT NOLAN

(555) 555-5555 • robertnolan@gmail.com • www.linkedin.com/in/robnolan • New York, NY 10001

| COMMUNITY OUTREACH • PROGRAM MANAGEMENT • FUNDRAISING AND EVENTS |

PROGRAM MANAGER

Collaborative, results-driven program manager leading innovative community initiatives, outreach, events, and fundraisers to enhance intellectual, economic, physical, social, and emotional well-being.

Program Development • Team Leadership • Community Outreach • Fundraising • Public Speaking • Mentoring
Education Enrichment • Event Planning • Communications • Corporate Partnerships • Social Media Campaigns

| PROFESSIONAL EXPERIENCE |

NYC TEACHING FELLOWS—Educator and Curriculum Developer—*Bronx, NY*   **Jun 2021—Present**

Create differentiated course content and teach 5 US and World History classes in an integrated co-teaching environment for general and special education Exploration High School students while earning MS degree.

- Individualized instruction to engage Special Education and English as a Second Language students.
- Selected by administration after 1st year to create curriculum as a content specialist certified in all subjects.
- Stepped up in first year to fulfill need to teach US and World History in addition to English.
- Employ Collaborative and Proactive Solutions behavior model that enables students to focus on learning.
- Received rare "Highly Effective" review for a new teacher from NYS Classroom Quality Review observation.
- Appointed to serve on faculty activities and culture advisory teams promoting social and emotional health.
- Contributed to maintaining school's 85% graduation rate and helping student prepare to pass NY Regents.

TENNIS TITANS—Program Director – *Harlem, NY*   **Sep 2020—Jun 2021**

Promoted to lead programming, administration, case management, and events for non-profit providing at-risk urban youth with academic enrichment, tennis training, mentoring, service learning, and college preparation.

- Improved student attendance, engagement, and outcomes by building rapport and defining expectations.
- Planned and executed matches and tournaments. Made travel accommodations and provided supervision.
- Created Young Leadership Committee and planned and executed YLC fundraising and events.
- Mentored junior Tennis Program Coordinator, approved program plans, and coached elite summer camps.
- Completed crisis management and communications training and crafted weekly social media content.

TENNIS TITANS—Program Coordinator – *Harlem, NY*   **Sep 2019—Sep 2020**

Developed and taught tennis programs for urban at-risk youth competing in 25+ Northeast matches.

- Coached team to achieve 1st tournament win over teams with superior funding and facilities.
- Led Brick City Cup Tournament fundraising team, raising $15K through email and social media solicitation.

STEIN & LEIBOWITZ—Intern Program Manager – *Wyndham, NY*   **Summer 2017, 2018**

Led corporate law firm's participation in NJ LEEP, a non-profit program exposing urban youth to legal careers.

- Supervised 7 interns, screened full-time candidates, and managed databases, documents, and proceedings.

| EDUCATION |

MS in Education, Certification Students with Disabilities – NEW YORK UNIVERSITY – 5/2023—**3.97 GPA**
Bachelor of Arts in English (BA) – DARTMOUTH COLLEGE – 2019
Varsity Men's Tennis Captain for Top 15 US Collegiate Team — **Study Abroad** in **Rome**

Julie Wyckoff, MEd, Certified Career Transition Coach, YouMap Coach | Custom Career Solutions | customcareersolutions.com
Major: Education (Students with Disabilities) | **Goal:** Position in nonprofit program management
Notable: This candidate has quite a bit of relevant experience, so it is positioned most prominently on the resume. He hopes to integrate his expertise in both education and athletics in his next role.

RENEA J. CUNNINGHAM

Lansing, MI 48917 | 517-333-1234 | rjcunningham@gmail.com | linkedin.com/in/reneacunningham

CAREER TARGET: VOLUNTEER RECRUITMENT MANAGER FOR THE TREVOR PROJECT

Operational Support | Client Advocacy | Workshop and Group Facilitation | Customer Service | Team Leadership

Resourceful and socially aware professional with profound ability to drive initiatives that promote collaborative, educational, and supportive environments. Advocate for developing products that positively influence and impact consumers while addressing social issues.

 Collaborative Team Player: Enthusiastic and energetic facilitator dedicated to guiding meaningful conversations that spark inspiration, motivation, and creativity among students, peers, and colleagues.

 Passionate and Innovative: Known for taking initiative to create and streamline processes to enhance customer (student) experiences. Adept at designing educational lesson plans and presentations that increase engagement.

 Continuous Learner: Dedicated to expanding personal growth through diving into immersive experiences (U.S. and international), participating in relevant trainings and workshops, as well as offering value and perspective in a variety of group settings.

EDUCATION

Bachelor of Arts in Business Management | Minor: Public Relations| 2023
Michigan State University | East Lansing, MI

PROFESSIONAL EXPERIENCE

Michigan State University| East Lansing, MI   September 2019—May 2023

Co-founder and Vice President: WE RISE

Instrumental in the development and launch of the We Rise Organization. Created the strategic vision and implemented programs and processes to reach outreach goals. Carried out planning and execution of major campus events to increase membership, recruit volunteers, gain university recognition, and receive $50K+ in alumni donations.

➤ Spearheaded the development of campus organization to increase LGBTQIA and BIPOC student engagement and create safe spaces for dialogue, networking, and support.
➤ Grew membership to 300+ students and spread awareness through large campus events, including the award-winning "You're Included" showcase that drew 500+ attendees.

Peer Mentor

Collaborated with first-year students to develop strategic and feasible plans to meet their professional and academic goals. Served as an advocate and on-call resource for students to address concerns, navigate grounds, and become accumulated to campus life. Planned and co-facilitated first-year experience seminar with Athletic Director.

COMMUNITY INVOLVEMENT AND RECOGNITION

Recipient of the 2020, 2021, and 2022 Class Award for Outstanding University Engagement
Recipient of the first annual 2023 Peer Mentor of the Year Award
Michigan State University | East Lansing, MI

Volunteer | Home Restoration, Client Relations, Resource Coordinator
Habitat for Humanity | East Lansing, MI

Chelsea Wiltse, NCRW, NCOPE, CPRW, CPCC | Seasoned and Growing LLC | seasonedandgrowing.com
Major: Business Management | **Goal:** Volunteer recruitment manager for a specific nonprofit organization
Notable: The target is specifically stated in the headline, sending the message that the resume was created for this particular job. Appropriate graphics in the summary call attention to key soft skills.

Adam Okeno

555-229-1217 | New York, NY 10011 | adam.okeno@mail.com | LinkedIn.com/in/adam-okeno

Program Manager | Learning Specialist
Nonprofit Organizations • Education Mission • Measurable Impact

Educator—Certified teacher, currently pursuing MPA, with 3+ years' teaching/tutoring experience serving diverse students (K–12) and supporting academic achievement, standardized test success, and college and career planning.

Leader—Innovative problem solver who repeatedly stepped up to manage programs and ensure the achievement of program goals and student objectives. Effective communicator, empathetic listener, team collaborator.

Data Geek—Analytical thinker with foundation in data analysis and informatics, committed to data-driven solutions.

Education

Master of Public Administration | NEW YORK UNIVERSITY, New York, NY   Anticipated 2023
Current coursework emphasis: Geographical Sciences, Urban Informatics, Economics, Data Analysis

BS Education | FORDHAM UNIVERSITY, New York, NY   2019
Certification: 4-Year Resident Educator Middle Childhood (Grades 4–9) | *GPA:* 3.8

Professional Experience

Tutor — EDUCATION, INC. | STUDYPOINT | MATHNASIUM — New York, NY   2020–2021

Provided individualized tutoring to diverse K–12 students, accommodating special needs and circumstances to bring specialized support to each student. Worked up to 30 hours per week while attending school full time.

- *Education, Inc.:* Assisted students in maintaining grade-level knowledge while undergoing treatment at New York-Presbyterian Children's Hospital. Adapted flexibly to capabilities and stamina levels that varied with children's health and medical treatments.
- *StudyPoint:* Provided in-home, one-on-one tutoring to prepare high school students for the standardized ACT test. Created study roadmaps and customized lesson plans based on preliminary and interim test results.
- *Mathnasium:* Supported students attending after-school tutoring centers that built math skills. Provided group and individual support for both low achievers striving for grade-level performance and high achievers seeking admittance to AP classes.

Notable: With only 2 days' training, assumed role of Lead Tutor at Children's Hospital. Created schedules, on-boarded students, and opened lines of communication to ensure student/parent satisfaction and quick resolution of any issues.

AmeriCorps New York College Guide — QUEENS YOUTH COLLABORATIVE — New York, NY   2019–2020

Selected through competitive interview process for year-long AmeriCorps program, joining team working within New York Public Schools to assist students in planning for post-secondary education and careers.

- Launched College Guide program into Queens Career Technical High School and, within 1 month, enrolled a full caseload of 120 students, grades 7–12.
- Worked individually with 10–12 students daily. Assisted with college applications, research, and essay writing.
- Presented more than 2 dozen informational sessions and programs to introduce students and parents to higher education and inspire students' passion to further their education.
- Planned and executed 6 group service projects, collaborating with teams, school staff, and community stakeholders.

Notable: Acted as de facto Program Manager for first 6 months when PM left unexpectedly. Took the lead in communicating with team members, tracking data and deliverables, and ensuring that 100% of program tasks and goals were completed on schedule.

Student Teacher — BOOKER T. WASHINGTON MIDDLE SCHOOL — New York, NY   2018

Key Skills

SPSS | Microsoft Office Suite | ArcGIS | Mathematics | Data Analysis
Additional: Competitive soccer player (6 years) | Avid traveler interested in diverse cultures

Louise Kursmark, MRW, CPRW, JCTC, CEIP, CCM | Best Impression Career Services | louisekursmark.com
Major: Public Administration | **Goal:** Role in nonprofit program management
Notable: Each position is highlighted with a shaded box describing a "Notable" achievement for this master's degree candidate. Both hard and soft skills are described in the summary/profile.

Ellen Wong

Philadelphia, PA 19103 ♦ 555-345-1182 ♦ ellenwong@mail.com

CAREER TARGET: PUBLIC RELATIONS

Sales — Recruitment — Client Retention — Event Planning — Promotions — Community Partnerships
Program Development — Writing and Editing — Supervision and Training — Relationship Building — Presentations

EDUCATION

THE OHIO STATE UNIVERSITY, Columbus, OH   June 2023
Bachelor of Arts in Journalism, emphasis in Public Relations

ACTIVITIES
- ♦ **ORDER OF OMEGA, GREEK HONORARY**   Initiated May 2021
- ♦ **DELTA PSI EPSILON SORORITY**   Initiated September 2019
- ♦ **ALPHA LAMBDA DELTA/PHI ETA SIGMA HONORARIA**   Initiated Fall 2018

EXPERIENCE

MULTI-CAMPUS HILLEL, Philadelphia, PA   August 2020 to present
Jewish Campus Service Corps Fellow
THE LANTERN NEWSPAPER, The Ohio State University, Columbus, OH   September 2018 to June 2020
Recruitment Editor, Minority Affairs Reporter, Copy Editor & Free Lance Writer
THE COLUMBUS JEWISH FEDERATION, Bexley, OH   Summer of 2018
Campaign & Fundraising and Community Relations Intern

SKILLS AND ACCOMPLISHMENTS

RECRUITMENT/SALES
- Devised 13 on-site strategies to effectively meet and recruit 750+ Hillel members in 18 months.
- Met with students individually to create focused programming and develop meaningful relationships.
- Developed regional campaign and supervised staff in the location and recruitment of Jewish students for the Birthright Israel program. The organization sponsored a nationally recognized free trip to Israel for qualified college students.
- Recruited and mentored Journalism students with story ideas, news articles, and writing techniques.

EVENT PLANNING
- Spearheaded two region-wide events, each with three student committees from seven different colleges.
- Coordinated 27 cutting-edge, innovative social, cultural, and educational events designed to create exciting opportunities for students.
- Served as an advisor and aided in the organization of five event-focused student committees.

WRITING/GRAPHIC DESIGN
- Designed two informational pamphlets and four one-page handouts to explain Jewish holidays and rituals.
- Aided in design of six company newsletters that promoted events on 11 campuses to 2,000 students.
- Compiled data and wrote 10 full-page campaign theme articles for Columbus Jewish newspaper.
- Wrote 20 articles in 10 weeks, covering abortion, minority affairs tension, and motivational speakers.

COMMUNITY BUILDING
- Designed and presented seven different workshops to college students and community members throughout Tri-State area.
- Educated campus communities and advocated on behalf of students regarding antisemitic issues.
- Partnered with university officials within academic and student affairs departments to increase student life on campus.

Beverly Baskin, EdS, LPC, MCC, CPRW | BBCS Counseling Services | bbcscounseling.com
Major: Journalism/Public Relations | **Goal:** Entry-level public relations position
Notable: The "Skills and Accomplishments" section is the richest on this resume, presented in the style of a functional resume that groups all related skills and activities into a single section.

NICKI BROWN

630.222.4023 | nicki@gmail.com | Aurora, IL 60506 | LinkedIn

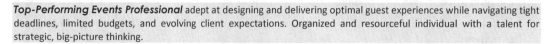

EVENTS COORDINATION

Top-Performing Events Professional adept at designing and delivering optimal guest experiences while navigating tight deadlines, limited budgets, and evolving client expectations. Organized and resourceful individual with a talent for strategic, big-picture thinking.

| End-to-End Event Planning | 100+ Attendees | $45K+ Budget |

EDUCATION & CERTIFICATIONS

Bachelor of Hospitality & Tourism Management, Minor in Business | Aurora University | 2023

Associate of Arts, Hospitality | College of DuPage | 2020

Google Project Management: Professional Certificate | 2023

KEY COMPETENCIES

- Full Cycle Event Planning
- Client Relations
- Day-of Event Management
- Budget Management
- Vendor Management
- Project Coordination
- Stakeholder Engagement
- Social Media Management
- MS Office Suite

PROFESSIONAL EXPERIENCE

Events Coordinator   2021–Present

Nicki Brown, LLC

- Launched consultancy and supported 7 small business owners with full-cycle event planning.
- Generated $100K—5X higher than $20K goal—in managing fundraising event for philanthropic organization.
- Surpassed attendance goal 10%—attracting 65 attendees within short notice—by promoting college event on social media.
- Earned 5-star rating on Google & Yelp through 14 positive reviews from clients and event guests noting best-in-class service.
- Drove end-to-end planning for 36 events with up to $45K budgets and 100+ attendees, overseeing budget management, procurement/purchasing, vendor relations, catering, staffing, transportation and accommodations, and all other details.

Project & Events Coordinator   2019–2020

Aurora University

- Selected for high-visibility work-study position coordinating projects and events to drive alumni engagement.
- Generated $5K in donations by planning and executing fundraising event that garnered 90 attendees.
- Grew social media following 50%—from 500 to 750 Instagram followers—by creating original content to promote events.

Chelsey Opare-Addo | Not Your Mother's Resume | notyourmothersresume.com
Major: Hospitality & Tourism Management | **Goal:** Events management position
Notable: This candidate's Professional Experience includes running her own events management business while attending school. The resume design is fresh, attractive, and easy to read.

MOLLIE BISHOP

817-555-5555
mollie-bishop@gmail.com | LinkedIn

ELEMENTARY TEACHER
Creating culture of learning — challenging tomorrow's leaders.

Certified First-Year Elementary Teacher dedicated to providing children foundational skills for school and life success. Caring educator who creates supportive and engaging learning environments for developing social and emotional skills and academic excellence. Eager to begin full-time teaching career in Dallas-Fort Worth Metroplex.

Core Subjects (Grades EC-6) – 391: Capturing Kids' Hearts Certificate Program | Science of Teaching Reading 293 Pedagogy & Professional Responsibilities EC-12 | Supplemental (Grades NA) 154 | English as Second Language

EDUCATION & CERTIFICATION
Teaching (EC-6) Certification | TEACHWORTHY | San Antonio, TX | 2023
Bachelor of Science, Communication | BAYLOR UNIVERSITY | Waco, TX | 2023
Associate in Arts, Communication Studies | DALLAS COLLEGE | Dallas, TX | 2019

SKILLS AND COMPETENCIES

Curriculum Development	Creative Learning Strategies	Parent-Teacher Relationship
Classroom Management	Experiential Learning	Standardized Testing
Self-Managing Classroom	EXCEL Teaching Model	Test Preparation
Classroom Technology / MS Office	SMART Board Aptitude	Record Keeping

EDUCATION-RELATED EXPERIENCE

INSTRUCTIONAL ASSISTANT | HOPE ACADEMY | Dallas, TX   2018 – 2019

Provided instructional support for **22 third-grade students**. Assisted teacher in classroom activities based on Common Core curriculum for constructive and imaginative learning. Worked 1:1 and in small groups.

- **Emergency Teaching Assignment.** Volunteered and approved for one-day emergency teaching assignment. Established clear objectives and taught students without pre-prepared lesson plans.
- **Classroom Technology.** Used alternative lesson delivery strategies including **SMART Board** technology.
- **Student Management.** Monitored student progress and graded papers. Organized and prepared supplies and learning materials for lessons.
- **Standardize Testing.** Assisted in administering and monitoring ability and achievement tests.

PRIVATE NANNY | MULTIPLE FAMILIES   2011 – 2020

Gillespie Private Nanny | Full Time | Dallas, TX (1 child from ages 4 to 8)   2016 – 2020
- **Creative Learning.** Planned activities for developing independence and self-accountability.
- **Life Skills.** Promoted activities for learning positive reinforcement and family responsibilities.
- **Field Trips.** Organized museum visits for interactive multisensory play, creativity, and inspiration.

Christianson Private Nanny | Part Time | Dallas, TX (2 children ages 6 months and 5 years)   2014 – 2015
- **Creative Learning.** Assisted with activities in helping infant reach developmental milestones.
- **Life Skills.** Created chore reward system for 5-year-old to learn responsibilities and self-reliance.

Timothy Private Nanny | Full-Time Live-In | Dallas, TX (4 children ages 7 to 12 years)   2011 – 2013
- **Creative Learning.** Created positive learning environment while tutoring children in reading, math, and science.
- **Life Skills.** Taught importance of contributing to family and bonding with siblings doing chores.

OTHER WORK EXPERIENCE

OFFICE ASSISTANT II	CITY OF DALLAS MUNICIPAL COURT	Dallas, TX	2015 – 2016
ACCOUNTS PAYABLE CLERK	AEROTEK	Dallas, TX	2013 – 2014

AFFILIATIONS
Association of Supervision and Curriculum Development (ASCD)
American Federation of Teachers (AFT) | National Education Association (NEA)

Roshael Hanna, CPRW | Resumes 4 Results USA | resumes4resultsusa.com
Major: Communication | **Goal:** Role as elementary teacher
Notable: Although this new graduate had limited classroom experience, her related experience as a nanny provided high-value content for the resume.

BRUCE R. THOMAS
DEDICATED TEACHER AND COACH

Keyport, NJ 07735
555-567-8910
bruce.thomas@email.com

EARLY CHILDHOOD/SPECIAL EDUCATION/ TEACHER OF SOCIAL STUDIES CERTIFICATIONS

QUALIFICATIONS PROFILE

Familiar with All Grades
Teaching & Inspiring Students
Coaching
Lesson Planning
Classroom Management
Classroom Organization
Unit Planning
Diverse Student Populations
Patience and Understanding
Enthusiastic & Energetic
Personable & Positive Attitude
Proficient in Spanish

- **Enthusiastic, committed educator with innate ability to motivate children**. Focus on creating age-appropriate curriculum to challenge and academically prepare students to develop into independent learners. Proficient in Spanish.

- **Coaching experience with youngsters and adolescents; home and traveling venues.**

- **Create a cooperative community in the classroom**. Serve as a role model for students, fostering the importance of mutual respect and cooperation among all community members.

- **Finely honed communication skills.** Equally effective with students, parents, colleagues, and administrators.

- **Teaching Experience.** Worked with special education students, differentiated groups, and various state-of-the-art programs in Math and Reading.

- **Hands-on experience and knowledge working with** McGraw-Hill My Math ConnectEd – Math K-8; Houghton Common Core K-5 – Pearson Language Arts Common Core Edition Grades 6-8; Achieve 3000; IXL – Math (among others).

EDUCATION AND CERTIFICATIONS

SKIDMORE COLLEGE, Bachelor of Arts in History, Dec 2022, Dean's List
- Collegiate Division II Baseball

NEW PATHWAYS TO TEACHING, Brookdale College through New Jersey City University, Graduate-Level Class
MONMOUTH UNIVERSITY, Early Childhood Education Program

Certifications: Social Studies K-1 | Early Childhood Education | Teacher of Students with Disabilities

EXPERIENCE

Teaching | Old Bridge School District | Old Bridge, NJ, Jan 2023–Present
Work as a Daily Substitute Teacher Pre-K to 12 and as a Home Instructor. Carry out lesson plans five days per week, teaching a variety of subjects for all grades. Enjoy working in teams and starting up new programs. Known for my professionalism throughout the district.

- Scored in top 15% on Praxis (Social Studies Content Knowledge) ETS Recognition of Excellence.
- Know all 700+ students in the Old Bridge Central School and many High School students by name.
- Provided Home Instruction Services for an 8th Grade student.

Coaching
Served as the Head Coach, Jones Construction Baseball Team: High School Showcase Team, 2020, 2021.

Beverly Baskin, EdS, LPC, MCC, CPRW | BBCS Counseling Services | bbcscounseling.com
Major: History | **Goal:** Early childhood/special education teacher and sports team coach
Notable: The headline and subheading immediately identify both target roles (teacher and coach), and the Profile conveys a wide range of skills and character traits needed for success in the classroom.

Patient Advocacy · Patient-Centered Care · Holistic Care

LACEY M. JOHNSON

Indianapolis, IN 46077 | 219-333-1104 | laceymjohnson@gmail.com | linkedin.com/in/laceymjohnson

CAREER TARGET: CHILD THERAPIST | SCHOOL SOCIAL WORKER

Case Management | Mental Health Assessments | Client Advocacy | Community Collaboration | Conflict Resolution

Compassionate and solution-focused social work graduate primed to build an impactful career in social services. Natural advocate dedicated to bridging communication gaps, increasing access to resources, and providing safe spaces for clients throughout Indiana.

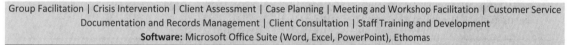

- **Engaging facilitator** with 3+ years' combined experience leading social-emotional workshops and group interventions for parents and teens.
- **Solutions-oriented advocate** committed to empowering individuals by providing the tools and programs they need to thrive.
- **Changemaker** adept at creating respectful, welcoming, and collaborative environments.

Group Facilitation | Crisis Intervention | Client Assessment | Case Planning | Meeting and Workshop Facilitation | Customer Service
Documentation and Records Management | Client Consultation | Staff Training and Development
Software: Microsoft Office Suite (Word, Excel, PowerPoint), Ethomas

EDUCATION

Master of Social Work (M.S.W), 2023
Indiana University | Bloomington, IN

Bachelor of Science in Behavioral Science (Social Work Concentration), 2021
Indiana University | Bloomington, IN

PROFESSIONAL EXPERIENCE

CARE of Southeastern Indiana | South Bend, IN   August 2022—Present
SUBSTANCE USE PREVENTION INTERN

Provide care and support to clients by co-facilitating group interventions for parents and teens. Create safe spaces for community and transparency among participants during meetings. Collaborate cross-functionally with staff to develop a comprehensive training program for new social service staff.

➢ Created and implemented step-by-step training manual and presentations for the Employee Assistant Program.
➢ Co-facilitated internal substance abuse prevention group sessions.
➢ Analyzed and improved processes and tools related to SASS Assessment to increase effectiveness.

Winans Middle School | South Bend, IN   August 2021—June 2022
SCHOOL SOCIAL WORKER INTERN

Led interactive and engaging classroom-based social emotional workshops for students. Conducted one-on-one crisis interventions. Provided updates regarding student goals and progress to parents. Worked alongside school social workers to create IEP goals and updated records as needed.

➢ Co-developed solutions to improve behavior plans for emotionally impaired students.

Mt. Hope Trauma Services | Gary, IN   January 2020—August 2021
TRAUMA SERVICES INTERN COORDINATOR

Managed and maintained sensitive data for clients and providers. Utilized internal database to record and update intakes, progress, assessments, and diagnosis. Shadowed mental health professionals and observed best practices in initial intakes, counseling sessions, and record keeping.

Chelsea Wiltse, NCRW, NCOPE, CPRW, CPCC | Seasoned and Growing LLC | seasonedandgrowing.com
Major: Master of Social Work | **Goal:** School social worker/child therapist
Notable: Three relevant internships highlight this resume, which opens with a strong profile and an attention-getting graphic that emphasizes a compassionate and empathetic approach to her work.

Susan Chen
Boston, MA 02110   susan.chen@gmail.com | 555-345-1234

Health & Wellness Professional

Food & Nutrition graduate with experience in a large corporate wellness department (Procter & Gamble), a genetics-based weight management company (LiveLong), and the nutrition and athletic departments of a major university.

Value Offered:

✓ **Initiative:** Identified opportunity with P&G, created detailed proposal, and became the *first* Boston University Nutrition student to intern in a Corporate Health and Wellness setting. Created a model for future corporate internships and sparked a great deal of interest among students and faculty.

✓ **Professional Skills:** Demonstrated ability to manage multiple concurrent tasks, see projects through to completion, present findings and ideas to senior staff, and tailor programs to meet the needs of different audiences and individuals. Years of practical experience with MS Office applications.

✓ **Work Ethic:** Worked full-time (summers) and part time (school year) while participating as an elite college athlete and maintaining Honor Roll and Dean's List status.

Education

Bachelor of Science, Food & Nutrition | BOSTON UNIVERSITY | Boston, MA   May 2023

- Dean's List Honors 2021, 2022, 2023 | Academic Honor Roll 2020, 2021, 2022, 2023
- Northeast Division Rowing Championship Team 2021, 2022

Professional Experience

Marketing Intern | LIVELONG | Remote   8/2022–12/2022

- **Professional Skills:** Managed multiple tasks and projects supporting the company's diversified marketing and communication efforts. Tailored programs to meet the needs of different audiences and individuals. Gained considerable practical experience with all Microsoft Office applications, Adobe InDesign, and Adobe Photoshop.

- **Social Media Management**: Set up, maintained, and managed social media activities. Broadcast announcements and facilitated daily dialogue on LiveLong blog, Facebook, Twitter, LinkedIn, and Instagram.

- **Tradeshow Activities:**
  - ✓ Anticipated the make-up of tradeshow attendees and created relevant sales and marketing brochures.
  - ✓ Contacted prospective clients before tradeshow and scheduled meetings. Greeted walk-ins at the booth and described how LiveLong can assist them to improve health, wellness, and lifestyle.

- **Sales and Marketing Support:** Created artwork and messaging that stimulated viewers' interest in nutrition, health and wellness, and lifestyle change.

- **Application Development:** Assisted in creating an interactive app that helps healthcare professionals manage their practice and plan patient meals and workout routines based on genetic analysis.

Corporate Health & Wellness Intern | PROCTER & GAMBLE | Cincinnati, OH   Summer 2021

- Gained broad understanding of the Corporate Health and Wellness operation and the benefits of the program to the company, its employees, and their families.
- Shadowed Health and Wellness Director and staff members and participated in meetings with the Medical Director and other MDs.
- Initiated and completed several special projects, including:
  - ✓ **Employee Survey:** Conceived and executed a survey to gauge employee opinions of the Corporate Health and Wellness department. Received highly favorable feedback.

Louise Kursmark, MRW, CPRW, JCTC, CEIP, CCM | Best Impression Career Services | louisekursmark.com
Major: Food & Nutrition | **Goal:** Role in corporate health and wellness
Notable: Following a summary that highlights "value offered," internship and part-time positions are presented in detail to showcase a wide variety of activities and several notable accomplishments.

Susan Chen   susan.chen@gmail.com | 555-345-1234

Corporate Health & Wellness Intern | PROCTER & GAMBLE, continued

- ✓ **Wellness Research:** In response to health concerns for manufacturing workers, researched and wrote article on the effect of sports drinks in the workplace. Recommended changes to improve employee health and fitness. Article chosen by Medical Director for publication in the biannual company newsletter.
- ✓ **Nutrition Education:** Created nutritional pamphlets to educate 2 groups of P&G employees on healthy eating.

- Delivered PowerPoint presentations sharing health and wellness information with diverse audiences.
    - ✓ **Dehydration in the Workplace,** presented to P&G Health and Wellness team.
    - ✓ **Importance of Lean Protein in a Healthy Diet,** presented to P&G Health and Wellness team.
    - ✓ **Internship Summary,** presented to 80+ students and faculty of BU Nutrition Department.

Nutrition Department Student Assistant | BOSTON UNIVERSITY | Boston, MA   3/2020–5/2021

- Worked full-time summers and 10 hours per week during school year, assisting BU's football and hockey teams with nutrition information, education, and support.
- Created custom nutrition programs to help individual athletes reach specific goals such as weight loss or energy increase.
- Educated athletes on portion size, healthy snacks, and nutrition supplements.

Additional Information

- **Competitive Athlete:** As a rower with BU's regional and national championship team, performed at my best through healthy eating, regular conditioning, hard work, discipline, and personal drive.
- **Volunteer:** Prepared healthy "backpack" meals for children through the Greater Boston Food Bank. Worked in the Horace Mann School and St. Francis soup kitchen. Participated in a Habitat for Humanity summer project.

CHARLI A. POTTER

Ann Arbor, MI 48103 | 313-886-4321 | cpotter@gmail.com | linkedin.com/in/charlipotter

CAREER TARGETS: BEHAVIORAL HEALTH SPECIALIST | YOUTH AND FAMILY SERVICES COORDINATOR

Case Management| Crisis Management and Intervention | Program Coordination | Community Engagement

Purpose-driven and community-oriented graduate primed to build an impactful career in social services. Dedicated to limiting barriers and increasing access to essential resources for underserved communities and populations.

➤ **Natural problem solver:** adept at quickly identifying client needs and making connections to available resources.
➤ **Adaptable and proactive project catalyst:** accustomed to working in fast-paced and high-pressure environments.
➤ **Servant leader:** passionate about training staff on industry best practices in customer service.

Staff Hiring, Training, and Mentoring | Customer Service | ASIST Methodology | Community Relations | Budget Management
Meeting Facilitation | Client Advocacy | Process and Program Implementation | Social Services
Software: Microsoft Office Suite (Word, Excel, PowerPoint, Outlook), Adobe Creative Suite (Photoshop, Premiere, Final Cut Pro), Dropbox, Zoom, Canva, Social Media Platforms (Instagram, Twitter, YouTube)

EDUCATION

Master of Social Work (MSW) | University of Michigan | Ann Arbor, MI | 2023

Bachelor of Arts in Psychology | University of Michigan | Ann Arbor, MI | 2020

PROFESSIONAL EXPERIENCE

Eisenman Center | Ann Arbor, MI   May 2020—Present
RECOVERY ADVOCATE

Monitor and promptly respond to incoming crisis calls from across the U.S. Identify appropriate resources for individuals based on current needs. Collaborate cross-functionally with internal and external community partners (case management teams, law enforcement, behavioral health professionals) to track current availability of services and enrollment processes. Conduct follow-up with callers to check progress and ensure needs are met.

➤ Trained and mentored staff on crisis intervention methods and community and partner resources.
➤ Co-developed schedules to improve rotation and time off for staff.
➤ Showcased leadership team's knowledge on mental health and substance abuse by coordinating topic schedule and creating content for weekly webinars to inform staff and public about current trends and status.

University of Michigan| Ann Arbor, MI   May 2019—May 2020
MANAGER OF SOCIAL SERVICES AND EDUCATION

Partnered with President and Dean to lead and oversee efforts related to raising awareness of organization and improving on-campus experience. Participated in committee meetings and provided advocacy on topics such as financial aid, scholarships, and housing. Facilitated financial meetings with student-led groups to discuss travel arrangements, grants, and future projects. Coordinated and hosted events for 10K+ students. Fostered community of acceptance and transparency throughout campus regarding individual barriers.

➤ Managed $50K+ budget (travel fund, club dues, and university funding).
➤ Bridged communication gap between students and advisors by creating appointments and one-on-one opportunities through internal portal (Blackboard) to address commonly asked questions regarding courses, professors, and graduation.
➤ Decreased food insecurity rate by providing additional access and resources to the food pantry on campus.

Chelsea Wiltse, NCRW, NCOPE, CPRW, CPCC | Seasoned and Growing LLC | seasonedandgrowing.com
Major: Social Work (MSW), Psychology (BA) | **Goal:** Career in social services
Notable: Career targets are explicitly spelled out in the headline, followed by a strong summary that combines hard and soft skills. Relevant experience is spelled out in appropriate detail.

NAYTE **HERNANDEZ**

📞(555) 555-5555 | ✉ nhernandez@uofa.edu | 🔗 LinkedIn | 📍Los Angeles, CA

🌐Bilingual Global Health Research Coordinator – *Rallying key stakeholders behind a united cause.*

EDUCATION

Bachelor of Arts, Global Health | Minor, Psychology | University of Arizona | Expected Graduation: December 2023
Study Abroad Program: Adventures in Culture, Health, Sustainability, & Environment in Kuaka, New Zealand, Summer 2022
- Face-to-face experience learning about indigenous Māori culture of New Zealand.
- Spent a night in the rainforest with the Māori people and documented sacred practices. (Itinerary on LinkedIn.)

SKILLS & TRAINING

Advanced Excel	Community Outreach	Event Planning and Management
Research & Reporting	Interviewing	Marketing Communications
HIPAA Training (UCLA)	Presentations	Workshops and Training

EXPERIENCE

Global Impact Collaboratory Research Apprentice | University of Arizona | Tucson, AZ | August 2022–May 2023
- One of only 3 students selected to participate in international research project studying the influence that gang violence, police brutality, and corruption in Latin American countries have in undermining the justice system.
- Conducted virtual, open-question interviews in Spanish and presented findings to principal investigator.
- Organized high-profile, virtual, and in-person events for monthly faculty seminar series and biannual community fundraisers, reaching 200+ attendees per event.
- Translated 20+ brochures and reports into Spanish for participating international partners.
- Recruited participants and led 2 workshops per week for students, faculty, funders, and community leaders.

Culture, Health, and Environment Lab Research Apprentice | University of Arizona | Tucson, AZ | May 2022–May 2023
- One of 25 students selected to participate in international research studying the natural disaster preparedness of citizens in New Zealand, Australia, and Latin America.
- Synthesized and presented complex data from interviews and research gathered during study abroad programs.

UCLA Health Summer Intern – International Services Department | Los Angeles, CA | June–August 2022
- Reporting to Director of International Strategy in department responsible for 20% of hospital's funding, provided international patients with concierge services, including language translation, doctor/surgeon selection, hospitality, and financial arrangements.
- Initiated idea and redesigned department's neglected 10-year-old website.
- Designed and authored 3 patient, community, and clinician marketing newsletters, vital to department support.

UCLA Health Summer Intern – International Services Department | Los Angeles, CA | June–July 2021
- Improved redundant communications among UCLA school of medicine, Center for Global Health, and international services department by evaluating effectiveness of internal platforms and making recommendations that are still used today.
- Published 10+ articles concerning UCLA Health's international activity on UCLA Health public websites.

ORGANIZATIONS & VOLUNTEERING

Global Health Student Association Vice President | University of Arizona | Tucson, AZ | July 2022–July 2023
- Re-established defunct student association after all previous club officers abandoned their responsibilities.
- Rebuilt and reconstructed GHSA mission, revamped membership recruitment, and initiated marketing/networking activities to include monthly community service events, industry guest speaker series, and freshman orientation.
- Increased membership 200% over previous year.

Red Cross | Disaster Preparedness Training and Workshop Volunteer | Tucson, AZ | August 2020–Present
Assist with school district disaster preparedness workshops and teacher training regarding fire, monsoon, and lightning safety.

Lucie Yeomans, NCOPE, CEIC, CGRA, OPNS | Your Career Ally | yourcareerally.com
Major: Global Health | **Goal:** Role in global health focused on event management and public education
Notable: Nayte's resume is full of examples of how he made a difference, specifically related to his career interests in educating people about global health issues and inspiring action.

Kelly Crawford

kcrawford@email.com | (555) 555-1234 | LinkedIn

Recent Medical Physics master's degree graduate. Strong interest in applying education and work experience to help treat people with cancer. Hands-on experience with dosimetry machines in hospital. Committed to continuous learning and development.

Work Experience

IMRT QA Technician

Springfield Hospital • Springfield, RI —————————————————— December 2021 – Present

- Perform clinical patient dosimetry, verifying precise prescribed dose is received.
- Troubleshoot issues with failed plan files independently and efficiently, reporting findings to head physicist for correction so that patient treatment plans proceed on schedule.
- Operate LINAC under supervision of Radiation Oncology Physicists.
- Contribute to physics-related aspects of research projects by setting up equipment, taking measurements, and recording data.
- Run automated and manual QA checks on machine.

Classroom Media Assistant, IT Tech Team Leader

University of Rhode Island • Kingston, RI —————————————————— September 2017 – May 2022

- Supervised five student technicians in multiple campus locations; reported weekly to manager.
- Go-to contact when team members encountered roadblocks and could not solve the issue.
- Enabled professors to address technical problems over the phone by walking through troubleshooting steps without using technical jargon.
- Tackled unfamiliar media issues by employing problem-solving skills.
- Set up, maintained, updated, and managed media systems, including projectors and computers.

Teaching Assistant

University of Rhode Island • Kingston, RI —————————————————— September 2020 – May 2022

- Guided labs, explained material, and enjoyed "seeing it click" for students.
- Reinforced own understanding of physics fundamentals.

Research

Research Assistant

University of Rhode Island • Kingston, RI —————————————————— September 2021 – May 2022

- Contributed to HA-pHLIP and pHLIP-STINGa immunotherapy research.
- Dissected mice for blood, lung, and tumor samples; created spheroids of collected tumor cells.
- Used varying wavelength to compare the ratio of treated cancer cells to untreated.

Education

University of Rhode Island • Kingston, RI • *CAMPEP Accredited*

THE UNIVERSITY OF RHODE ISLAND

Medical Physics • Master of Science ———————————— May 2022

Applied Mathematics and Physics • Bachelor of Science ———————————— May 2020

Additional Skills

C++ | Java | R | Python | AutoCAD | SQL (elementary knowledge) | Microsoft Office Suite

Teresa Hutton, CPRW | Best Resume Forward | bestresumeforward.com
Major: Medical Physics (MS), Mathematics and Physics (BS) | **Goal:** Position in medical physics related to cancer treatment
Notable: Experience and research are placed up front because they are very relevant to career goals. A recent prestigious university accreditation is brought to readers' attention by the placement of the university logo.

Ebony D. Samuels

New York, NY 10013 | 513.555.6543 | ebony.samuels@nyu.edu

Nutrition | Dietetics | Wellness
~ Bringing a high "sincerity factor" to the team climate ~

Highly motivated and innovative new professional poised for a career in nutrition services, integrated nutrition therapy, or community-based nutrition education and program support.

People-oriented and verbally fluent with innate empathic listening style. Easily talk with people of all ages, backgrounds, and levels of an organization to build both trust and credibility.

Offer the following technical knowledge, job skills and experiences:

- **Academic and field experience,** leading to broad understanding of basic sciences and theoretical/applied aspects of nutrition and dietetics.

- **Strong research skills backed by natural curiosity;** familiarity with WebMd, MyPlate.gov, and other public information sites.

- **Mastery of basic recipe planning and cooking techniques** and experience facilitating hands-on classes.

- **Proven team leadership and operations management capabilities;** prior summer employment training, supervising, and scheduling foodservice employees, managing concession stand, and serving patrons of all ages.

- **Basic office skills,** including filing, answering phones, social media management, Microsoft Office (Word, Excel, PowerPoint), and customer service.

"When people feel cared for and heard, they are open to new information and ways of thinking... and with this able to implement plans of action to achieve health and nutritional goals"
– Ebony Samuels

Education

Bachelor of Science, Nutrition and Dietetics | **New York University** (New York, NY)   May 2023

- *Didactic Program in Dietetics (DPD) Accredited,* Academy of Nutrition and Dietetics

- *Select Coursework:* Diet Assessment and Planning, Clinical Nutrition Assessment and Intervention, Nutrition Counseling Theory and Practice

- *Professional Affiliation:* Student Member, Academy of Nutrition and Dietetics

- *Candidate for Dietetic Technician Registration Exam*

Relevant Experience

Nutrition Education Volunteer, **The Market Basket** (New York, NY)   Aug. 2022 to Jan. 2023

Completed 60-hour field-class experience, working closely with nutrition department manager and community partners providing nutrition education programming. Wrote and presented final report to professor and classmates.

- Took active role in facilitating and enhancing the *Just Say Yes* program, through research and development of creative nutrition lesson plans and by leading weekly nutrition discussions and activities with groups of ~20 teenagers.

- Helped facilitate *Cooking Matters for Teens* hands-on cooking classes, teaching small group of adolescents (grade 6 and above) how to prepare healthy meals and snacks and make smart food choices.

Summer & High School Employment

Lexington Sports & Social Club (Lexington, KY) | **Assistant Manager, Concession Stand**   Summers 2018 and 2019
South Hill Gallery (Midway, KY) | **Office Assistant/Workshop Assistant**   Aug. 2016 to Dec. 2018

Norine Dagliano, NCRW, NCOPE | EKM Inspirations | ekminspirations.com
Major: Nutrition and Dietetics | **Goal:** Career in nutrition services and education
Notable: An expansive summary provides a solid overview of knowledge, skills, and experience along with evidence of this candidate's passion for her chosen field—enhanced by a quote and heart graphic.

TIARIA H. BOOME

New York, NY 10030 | 646-234-7930 | thboome@gmail.com

LICENSED REGISTERED NURSE
IN THE STATE OF NEW YORK

Versatile Registered Nurse with hands-on experience delivering safe, competent, and quality care to patients in emergency room setting. Establish nurturing environment for patients and family members through patient advocacy, emotional support, and thorough communication. Skillfully conduct intake assessments, identify patient needs, and collaborate with medical staff to ensure patients achieve healthcare goals.

HIPAA • Patient Assessment • Medication Administration • Catheter Placement & Care • IV Fluid Therapy

Venipuncture • Phlebotomy • Tracheostomy Care • Wound Care • Suctioning • Vital Signs • Critical Care

Patient Monitoring • Resuscitation • Blood Transfusions • Records Management

LICENSES & CERTIFICATIONS

Registered Nurse • *New York State Board of Nursing* • Expires 04/2024

Basic Life Support for Healthcare Providers (BLS) • *American Heart* Association • Expires 04/2023

Advanced Cardiac Life Support (ACLS) • *American Heart Association* • Expires 04/2023

RELATED WORK EXPERIENCE

Registered Nurse   06/2023–Present
Harlem Hospital • New York, NY

- Deliver optimal bedside care to patients in a 286-bed emergency room setting by assessing physical health, monitoring vital signs, and treating wounds.
- Facilitate inpatient admissions process, maintaining accurate records of medical condition and current health status.
- Administer medication, both orally and via IV, to patients as prescribed by physician.
- Monitor patient health and adapt plan of care appropriately, while communicating with physicians, healthcare providers, and family members.
- Assist in discharge planning process, connecting patients and families to resources to encourage continuity of care.
- Coordinate with multiple healthcare providers and specialists to provide adequate care and improve patient outcomes.
- Respond to medical emergencies with urgency and care while complying with HIPAA regulations.

ADDITIONAL WORK EXPERIENCE

Veterinarian Technician   12/2019–05/2023
Cornell Weil • New York, NY

- Conducted thorough evaluations of animal research center to maintain compliance with IACUC protocol.
- Assessed, diagnosed, and treated sick animals, while maintaining detailed documentation.
- Monitored procedure rooms and discarded non-controlled substances and supplies appropriately.

Kaljah Adams, ACRW | The Career Advising Hub | careeradvisinghub.org
Major: Nursing (BS), Biology (BS) | **Goal:** Registered nurse
Notable: Landing a nursing job immediately after graduation, this candidate wanted to update her resume to be able to respond quickly to opportunities that arose. Current work experience is shown in detail.

TIARIA H. BOOME Page 2 • 646-234-7930 • <u>thboome@gmail.com</u>

Veterinarian Intake Specialist   02/2018–04/2019
Best Petco Center • New York, NY

- Transcribed medical notes and prescriptions for veterinarians.

- Trained 10 veterinarian specialists on policies, safety protocols, and medical procedures.

- Resolved client concerns by identifying solutions to maintain 100% customer satisfaction.

Veterinarian Technician   01/2016–02/2019
Harlem Pet Hospital • New York, NY

- Restrained dogs, cats, birds, and reptiles.

- Conducted initial examinations, monitored anesthesia, collected blood samples, and inserted catheters, as directed by veterinarian.

- Prepared surgical rooms before and after appointment, adhering to safety regulations.

Veterinarian Assistant   02/2013–01/2016
Brooklyn Pet Hospital • Brooklyn, NY

- Informed clients of Optimum Wellness Plan and the importance of preventative care.

- Organized exam rooms and treatment areas, while adhering to hospital standards of care.

- Trained 30 entry-level associates on safety protocols when preparing exam rooms for operations.

EDUCATION

Bachelor of Science in Nursing; GPA: 3.49   05/2023
The College of Mount Saint Vincent • Riverdale, NY

Bachelor of Science in Biology   05/2017
CUNY Brooklyn College • Brooklyn, NY

ANDRIAN BOSWELL

New York, NY 10030 | 917-230-1209 | aboswell@gmail.com | linkedin.com/in/andrianboswell/

HEALTHCARE ADMINISTRATION MANAGER

Patient-focused professional with experience providing exceptional administrative support to streamline operations, optimize patient experience, and improve staff efficiency at healthcare facilities. Solutions-driven healthcare administrator who analyzes data, identifies gaps, and implements new processes to enhance services for patients.

Administration | Communication | Office Management | HIPAA | Health Insurance Verification | Medical Billing
Organization | Leadership | Staff Training | Data Analysis | Medicaid & Medicare | Staff Scheduling
Operations Management | Quality Assurance | Patient Satisfaction | Telehealth Management

Technology: EClinicalWorks; MS Word, Excel, and PowerPoint

EDUCATION

Master of Healthcare Administration | *New York University,* New York, NY   May 2023
 Related Coursework: Healthcare Leadership; Management of Healthcare Organizations; Financial
 Management of Healthcare Organizations; Communications in Healthcare

Bachelor of Arts: Psychology | *SUNY at Buffalo,* Buffalo, NY   May 2018

WORK EXPERIENCE

Adams Medical Health Center, New York, NY   June 2020–May 2023
Healthcare Administrator Intern (January 2023–May 2023)

- Participated in 5 leadership development trainings to enhance skills in healthcare administration.
- Assisted with interviewing and identifying ideal candidates to deliver quality service to patients.
- Updated 100+ patients' medical records by uploading documents into database in timely manner.

Front Desk Receptionist (June 2020–May 2023)

- Effectively managed daily operations of medical office by scheduling follow-up appointments, updating patient health records and financial information, and processing billing invoices.
- Streamlined intake process and boosted productivity 50%, by implementing virtual telehealth platform.
- Submitted outpatient referrals to appropriate specialists to promote continuity of care among patients.
- Trained 5 new hires on front desk protocol and telehealth system to optimize patient experience.
- Collaborated with medical assistants, physicians, and healthcare administrators to maximize efficiency while adhering to HIPAA regulations.

New York Urgent Care, Bronx, NY   March 2019–May 2020
Patient Care Associate

- Enhanced patient satisfaction by answering questions and resolving issues and concerns.
- Verified insurance, such as Medicaid and Medicare, in advance to minimize claim denials.
- Calculated co-pay collections and produced monthly billing reports for management.

St. Nicholas Parks, New York, NY   March 2017–September 2020
Operations Zone Assistant Manager

- Supervised 300+ employees, enforcing park rules and regulations to ensure customer safety.
- Created and finalized employee schedules based on staff availability and operational needs.

Kaljah Adams, ACRW | The Career Advising Hub | careeradvisinghub.org
Major: Healthcare Administration (MHA), Psychology (BA) | **Goal:** Healthcare administration manager
Notable: After opening with a strong summary and core competency list, this resume showcases three years of experience at the same health center—a part-time job that evolved into an internship.

Marcella Lopez, BSN

555-677-2360 | marcella.lopez@gmail.com

GRADUATE NURSE

Targeting: New RN Residency — Med-Surg Nurse — Oncology Unit Nurse

Newly Qualified Nurse (BSN December 2022) eager to begin professional nursing career.

Nurses' Aide since 2020, with 3 years of front-line service to patients on an oncology unit and a reputation for above-and-beyond assistance to both patients and clinical staff.

Demonstrated Skills

- **Competent, Compassionate Care**—Blending professional skill with kindness and empathy.
- **Critical Thinking**—Demonstrating good judgment and providing solutions to identified problems.
- **Teamwork**—Supporting ultimate goal of patient care by assisting teammates and volunteering for extra duties.
- **Verbal and Written Communication**—Emphasizing clarity and timeliness.
- **Process Efficiency and Effectiveness**—Removing obstacles and saving time to focus on critical care functions.

Registered Nurse status—NCLEX planned for early 2023
Certified Nurse Aide, State of Colorado—2020–Present

EDUCATION

BSN | University of Colorado College of Nursing, Aurora, CO   Dec 2022

- Accepted to 15-month Accelerated Bachelor of Science in Nursing program, combining remote classroom learning with in-person practicum assignments.
- Completed rotations in Medical Surgical, ICU, Cardiac Care, Trauma, Mental Health, Rehabilitation, Pediatrics, and Labor & Delivery.
- Named to Dean's List.

BA Ecology and Evolutionary Biology | University of Colorado, Boulder, CO   Dec 2019

- Member, Environment & Natural Resources Scholars Group. Elected member of the Executive Board.

PROFESSIONAL EXPERIENCE

Nurses' Aide | Foothills Hospital, Boulder, CO   Feb 2020–Present

- Assist patients with activities of daily living.
- Check and monitor vital signs. Draw lab samples and submit for analysis.
- Communicate patient status and any changes to nurses.
- Recognized for stepping up to assist medical staff—taking on additional tasks, volunteering for new assignments, and providing willing assistance whenever and wherever needed.
- Completed training to join the Brief Emotional Support Team (BEST). Learned evidence-based skills for supporting team members in challenging healthcare environments and situations. Serve as on-site BEST representative throughout shifts.

Resident Manager | Smithson Residence Hall, University of Colorado, Boulder, CO   2017–2019

- First undergraduate student chosen as Resident Manager of the university's largest residence hall (1,000+).
- Oversaw administrative functions—scheduling, security, mail, keys, safety.
- Trained and managed 35 team members. Conducted twice-yearly performance evaluations.
- Interacted with university administrators and upper management as chief representative of the residence hall.
- Streamlined processes to improve efficiency and effectiveness of resident services.

Louise Kursmark, MRW, CPRW, JCTC, CEIP, CCM | Best Impression Career Services | louisekursmark.com
Major: Nursing (BSN), Ecology and Evolutionary Biology (BA) | **Goal:** Nursing position
Notable: Soft skills are emphasized in the summary to convey the personal characteristics needed for success in nursing. Experience includes both nursing and a non-nursing leadership role.

SARAH FANDISH

078-455 26 70 | sarah@fandish.se
Relocating to Uppsala

REGISTERED PHARMACIST

Innovative, analytical, and timely, with experience working with sterile cell cultures in clean rooms, analyzing Western blot results, FACS (Fluorescence Activated Cell Sorting), and performing toxicological tests with MTT cytotoxicity assays.

Participated in early phase of drug development, executed toxicological in vitro studies, and experienced how clinical Phase 2 and Phase 3 trials are done.

Good knowledge of GMP. Strong interest in regulatory affairs/pharmacovigilance/quality assurance.

EDUCATION & PROFESSIONAL DEVELOPMENT

MSc in Pharmacy, Uppsala University, Uppsala   2023
Thesis: "Targeting ROR-1 Receptor Tyrosine Kinase by a ROR-1-Tyrosine Kinase Inhibitor in Patients with Chronic Lymphocytic Leukemia." Cancer Center Karolinska (CCK), Karolinska Institutet, Solna, Spring 2022.

Only student (out of 80) to be accepted to international cross-functional cancer research team led by Professor Håkan Sollberg with 5 postdocs + 5 biomedical analytics experts (BMAs). Working language was English.

Preclinical in vitro study proved ROR-1-receptor tyrosine kinase inhibitor (co-developed with biotechnology company Kancera) selectively blocks receptor in chronic lymphatic leukemia and causes leukemic cells to undergo cell death.

☑ Worked with sterile cell cultures. Experienced how Phase 2 and Phase 3 clinical trials are performed.
☑ Tried Ficoll separation. Experienced inspection to ensure regulations were followed.
☑ Planned and organized field trips to Medical Products Agency for 20 MSc Pharmacy Program students.

English for Higher Education Studies, 15 credits, Södertörn University   2016

EXPERIENCE

Pharmacist, Apotek Produktion & Laboratorier AB, (APL), Stockholm   Jun 2023–Present
Leading manufacturer of extemporaneous pharmaceuticals in Europe and Scandinavian life science contract sector.

☑ Work with sterile (lean) manufacturing (extempore manufacturing) of medicines for patients with cystic fibrosis and cancer. Manufacturing often came with short lead times, according to GMP regulations.

Pharmacy Assistant, Lloyds Apotek, St. Eriksplan, Stockholm/Svensk Dos   Sep 2022–Mar 2023
6-month internship in outpatient care pharmacy and Sweden's 2nd largest supplier of multidose packaged drugs.

☑ Advised customers and expedited drugs in occasionally stressful environment. Made clinical preparations.
☑ Performed sustainability checks, completed deviation/adverse event reports. Processed antibiotics.
☑ Shadowed investigation team (on incorrect doses) and learned about production and corrections.

LANGUAGES

Swedish (native), **English** (fluent), **Turkish** (bilingual), **German** (basic knowledge)

IT SKILLS & CERTIFICATE

Very experienced **database** user: PubMed, Toxline, SwePub, SciFinder and (bioinformatics) Human Protein Atlas and NCBI. Good knowledge of **Excel** and MS Office, use **Mac** and **PC**. Proficient in **Photoshop**.

FELASA A certificate for working with laboratory animals, part of 3 hp course at Karolinska Institutet.

SAID ABOUT ME

"You're an ambitious, energetic and goal-oriented woman who will go to great lengths to achieve your goals. You wrote a great master thesis and impressed us with your own illustrations, used in your much-appreciated and educational PowerPoint presentation. The lab protocols you voluntarily wrote will be very useful for future employees and students." *Member of research team at CCK (master thesis).*

Birgitta Moller, ACRW, MRW | Cvhjalpen.nu | cvhjalpen.nu/en/home
Major: Pharmacy | **Goal:** Registered pharmacist
Notable: Shortly after landing a job as a pharmacist after graduation, this candidate needed to update her resume as she was relocating to another city. Unique features are the graphic and the "Said About Me" section.

Natalie Sinclair, MPAS

Denver, CO 80249 • 971.770.1460
n.sinclair@gmail.com • LinkedIn

CAREER TARGET: Physician Assistant (PA)

Dedicated to helping patients transform their health and wellness through patient-centered, team-based medical practice

Trained PA offering a recent **Master's in Physician Assistant Studies** accompanied by 2+ years of combined experience, including clinical rotations in family, emergency, OR, and urgent care settings, and as a lead Medical Assistant. Track record of success working with diverse patient populations and managing routine and complex patient treatment. Posses a broad range of clinical and administrative skills, including taking medical histories, conducting physical exams, prescribing treatments, assisting with surgeries, interpreting lab results, and providing specialty referrals. **PALS, ACLS, BLS certified.**

> *"She is a **fantastic PA** who exhibits all the intangible qualities any medical group would want in a provider. She is compassionate, thoughtful with her approach, well learned, and exhibits a willingness to continue to learn."*

EDUCATION

EMORY & HENRY SCHOOL OF HEALTH SCIENCES, Marion, VA
Master of Physician Assistant Studies (**MPAS**), GPA 3.83/4.00 — Aug 2023

UNIVERSITY OF COLORADO AT BOULDER, Boulder, CO
Bachelor of Arts (**BA**), **Integrative Physiology**, GPA 3.32/4.00 — 2019
Honors: **Dean's List** — Spring 2019
Leadership: Teaching Assistant (**TA**), **Exercise Physiology Lab** — Spring 2019

KEY SKILLS & ATTRIBUTES

Patient History & Examination	Verbal & Written Communication	JCAHO Standards (Patient Safety)
Diagnosis & Treatment Plans	Patient Relationship Management	Infection Control Policies & Protocols
Patient Education & Confidentiality	Clinic Operations Management	Quality Improvement Programs
Laboratory & Imaging Test Results	Medical Staff Support Training	Electronic Medical Records (Athena, Epic)

CLINICAL EXPERIENCE

PA Student • MOUNTAINVIEW MEDICAL ASSOCIATES, Purcellville, VA — Jun 2023 – Jul 2023

Acted as a PA by managing 25–30 patients daily, conducting annual and acute health examinations and maintenance visits. Performed common procedures, including immunizations, skin biopsies, wart removal, pre-cancerous cryotherapy, and medication management. Created the practice's first welcome packet with before, during, and after-visit information.

PA Student • SOUTHWESTERN VIRGINIA MENTAL HEALTH INSTITUTE, Marion, VA — May 2023 – Jun 2023

Challenged to work with acutely psychotic patients and understand how mental health conditions and illnesses present themselves and proper safety methods for treating patients suffering from an episode. Interviewed inpatient psychiatric patients and assisted clinicians with medication management and screening/follow-up labs.

PA Student • ASSOCIATE ORTHOPAEDICS OF KINGSPORT, Kingsport, TN — Apr 2023 – May 2023

Built OR knowledge as the 1st Assistant for common orthopedic surgical procedures, such as total knee and hip arthroplasty, and acute and chronic conditions. Administered corticosteroid injections for knee, shoulder, elbow joint, trochanteric/ischial bursitis, epicondylitis, and carpal tunnel. Learned to take calls, make rounds, and treat walk-ins.

Kate Williamson, MS, CPRW, CRS+ES, CRS+IT, CSBA | Scientech Resumes | scientechresumes.com
Major: Physician Assistant (MPA), Integrative Physiology (BA) | **Goal:** Physician assistant
Notable: A bold, branded headline/subheading and medical symbol instantly announce this candidate's career goal. The resume is loaded with medical keywords highlighting her broad experience.

PA Student • GREENVILLE COMMUNITY EAST ER, Greenville, TN   Feb 2023 – Mar 2023

Triaged and administered treatment for simple and complex ER conditions, including sinus infections, pelvic fractures, strokes, heart attacks, laceration repair, I&Ds, and splinting. Strengthened documentation and procedural skills by conducting detailed patient interviews and obtaining complex patient histories. Ordered and interpreted basic labs.

PA Student • WELLMONT MEDICAL ASSOCIATES HOSPITALISTS, Bristol, TN   Jan 2023 – Feb 2023

Managed own patient load, including performing daily rounds, physical exams, and checkups for an internal medicine clinic. Received ER admissions, documented histories and treatment progress in Epic, and ordered routine and complex lab tests, imaging, and diagnostics. Managed patient medication and treatment plan development activities.

PA Student • BRISTOL SURGICAL ASSOCIATES, Bristol, TN   Nov 2022 – Dec 2022

Served as the 2nd Assistant on many surgical procedures, including hernia repair, lipoma removal, port placement, general procedures, and closing surgical sites in a dynamic OR setting. Shadowed physicians who managed chronic wounds.

PA Student • BLUE RIDGE PHYSICIANS FOR WOMEN, Galax, VA   Sep 2022 – Oct 2022

Acquired surgical/clinical experience in women's health by assisting in operative cesarean sections, performing pap smears, collecting cultures, and measuring fundal height and fetal heart tones. Documented histories and exams in EMR.

PA Student • MOUNTAIN VIEW PEDIATRICS, Marion, VA   Aug 2022 – Sep 2022

Performed annual wellness and physical exams on newborns and children, obtained detailed patient histories, and documented diagnoses and treatment plans for acute and chronic conditions in the EMR. Built rapport with patients, parents, and caregivers by involving them in diagnosis, treatment plans, and immunization discussions.

PROFESSIONAL EXPERIENCE

Medical Assistant • BOULDER VALLEY CENTER FOR DERMATOLOGY, Boulder, CO   May 2019 – Mar 2021

Brought on board to provide daily clinical and administrative operations support to Dermatologists and PAs in a multidisciplinary capacity. Managed triage activities, including scheduling surgeries, biopsies, and follow-ups, sterilizing instruments, wrapping surgical packs, administering anesthesia, scripting and renewing prescriptions, and interpreting pathology lab results. Scribed chart notes, obtained medical histories, assessed vitals, and provided patient education.

- Rapidly advanced to become the **lead Medical Assistant**, oversee the PA's patients, create and organize administrative systems, and onboard and train every new batch of incoming Medical Assistants.
- Played a key role in maintaining OSHA compliance by properly cleaning lab equipment, sharpening tools, and regularly checking expiration dates on medical and laboratory supplies.

VOLUNTEER EXPERIENCE

Student Volunteer • MEL LEAMAN FREE CLINIC, Marion, VA   May 2021 – Present
Work as a Physician Assistant to treat underserved patient populations in Southwest Virginia.

CERTIFICATIONS & LICENSURE

Advanced Cardiovascular Life Support (**ACLS**) • ACLS Provider   Jul 2021 – Present
Pediatric Advanced Life Support (**PALS**) • PALS Provider   Jul 2021 – Present
Medications for Addiction Treatment Waiver Training • American Academy of Addiction Psychiatry   Apr 2022 – Present
Basic Life Support (**BLS**) • American Heart Association   Mar 2021 – Present

PROFESSIONAL AFFILIATIONS

Virginia Academy of Physician Assistants   Jan 2023 – Present
American Academy of Physician Assistants   May 2021 – Present
American Academy of Family Physicians   Mar 2021 – Present

MARK CAMPBELL, MBA

703-222-0009 I Mcampbell@gmail.com
linkedin.com/in/mark-campbell-MBA | Columbus, GA

PROFILE

Healthcare administrative professional with 5+ years' experience in the field. Sharp acumen to prioritize strategic objectives while boosting morale through effective communication, training, recruitment, and retention. Manage day-to-day operations, implement new initiatives for growth and improvement, and handle delicate matters with poise and tact. Recent graduate of MBA program in Healthcare Management.

KEY COMPETENCIES

Customer Service	Relationship Management	Process Improvement
Leadership	Coaching & Mentoring	Microsoft Office, Zoom & Slack
Press Ganey	Medical Terminology	EPIC Electronic Medical Record

HEALTHCARE EXPERIENCE

PIEDMONT COLUMBUS REGIONAL, Columbus, GA   2016–2023
Patient Experience Representative, 2020–2023
- Identified and addressed deficiencies in metrics and advanced initiatives to bridge gaps between multiple departments throughout the medical center focusing on effective communication of front-line staff.
- Interpreted patient survey and statistical data from Press Ganey platform to uncover areas in need of improvement and gathered qualitative data from patients.
- Prepared and delivered data briefings for senior leadership, management, and front-line staff to increase overall awareness of public perception and survey findings.
- Improved Emergency Department scores by 10% consistently within a 15-month period and continued to support efforts that resulted in maintaining a 6-month 99th percentile score for Pediatric Emergency Department.
- Increased customers by 6% above the highest recorded season.

Office Coordinator, 2018–2020
- Maintained department budget of $36K using Excel. Oversaw purchases and accounts payable.
- Greeted an average of 50 patients daily upon arrival. Completed check in and verification procedures.
- Answered all incoming calls from multi-line system and scheduled appointments for separate departments.

Rehabilitation Technician, 2016–2018

OPERATIONS & TRAINING EXPERIENCE

WHITEWATER EXPRESS CHATTAHOOCHEE, Columbus, GA   2021–Present
Operations Manager, 2022–Present
- Actively participate in recruitment of approximately 50 guides plus front-desk associates, focusing on college campus visits as a talent resource.
- Instruct and train 50+ employees in person, delivering curricula on trip management and customer service.
- Coordinate staffing for tours, balance cash drawers, open and close retail area, provide transportation, and manage front office.
- Streamlined communications to improve operations efficiency, resulting in 20% YOY increase in productivity.

Rafting Guide & Trainer, Kayak Instructor, 2021–Present

EDUCATION

MASTER OF BUSINESS ADMINISTRATION, *Healthcare Management,* Western Governors University   2023
BACHELOR OF EXERCISE SCIENCE, Columbus State University   2016

Carolyn Kleiman, CPRW | Kleiman Careers | carolyn.kleimancareers@yahoo.com
Major: Business (MBA), Exercise Science (BS) | **Goal:** Healthcare administration role
Notable: Relevant experience takes center stage, while the recent degree (MBA) is mentioned in the summary and, of course, included in the Education section.

CHANNING A. WILLIAMS

Clinical Research Coordinator | Bioinformatics Specialist

Davenport, FL 33837 | 123.123.1234 | channingwilliams@gmail.com | LinkedIn.com/in/channing-research

Intuitive, analytical healthcare professional and osteopathic medicine graduate with advanced knowledge of research methodologies, clinical documentation, and imaging techniques. Finely tuned investigative strengths and expertise collaborating with multi-disciplinary teams across the care continuum.

CLINICAL RESEARCH PROTOCOLS: Advanced cancer therapy research and increased identification of targets through early mTOR pathway changes by producing image identifying cell markers for common cancers.

BIOMEDICAL IMAGING: Exposed proteins and receptors instrumental in oncology therapies and interventions by leveraging advanced imaging and wet lab techniques.

LAB EXPERIENCE AND DATA ANALYSIS: Developed new method of creating dentifrice and created base slurries, determining lab methods; analyzed material viscosity and rheology and operated 3D printer.

KEY STRENGTHS AND TECHNICAL PROFICIENCIES: MS Office – Word, Excel, PowerPoint; Python; MATLAB; Epic; Skype; Zoom; medical records management, medical terminology, programming, imaging and visualizations, organizational skills, MRI scanning, processing, lab protocol creation, medical history documentation, and accurate data collection.

+ *Leadership*
+ *Medical Research*
+ *Neuroimaging*
+ *Machine Learning*
+ *Data Analysis*
+ *Records Management*
+ *Communication Skills*
+ *Interpersonal Skills*
+ *Research Protocols*
+ *Risk Analysis*
+ *Cross-functional Collaboration*
+ *Problem-solving*
+ *Compliance*

EDUCATION

DOCTOR OF OSTEOPATHIC MEDICINE | Florida University – Orlando, FL | 2023
MASTER OF SCIENCE IN BIOMEDICAL IMAGING | University of Florida – Gainesville, FL | 2020
BACHELOR OF SCIENCE IN MICROCELLULAR BIOLOGY | University of Florida – Gainesville, FL | 2018

EXPERIENCE HIGHLIGHTS

Research Assistant | Dr. Evan Michael's Lab, University of California – San Francisco, CA | 2020

Worked independently, analyzing efficacy of oncological intervention targets using immunofluorescence. Practiced wet lab medical research techniques, including western blotting and PCR. Accomplished seamless prioritization of multiple tasks in quality control, data analysis, neuroimaging, problem-solving, and compliance.

Medical Scribe | Choo Memorial Hospital, Emergency Department – Orlando, FL | 2018 – 2019

Achieved 100% quality and compliance of medical records management. Increased physician availability, improved speed of patient visit, enhanced patient care, and boosted accuracy of recordkeeping, medical charting, and documentation.

Resident Assistant | University of Florida – Gainesville, FL | 2016 – 2018

Accomplished 100% on-time facility rounds, directing university accommodations for 120 students. Demonstrated leadership, interpersonal skills, time management, attention to detail, and written and verbal communication skills, fostering transparency and relationship building for campus residents.

Hospital Volunteer | Christ Hospital – Cincinnati, OH | 2016
Summer Research Intern | Procter and Gamble – Cincinnati, OH | 2016

Launched new formulation approach for 200+ dentifrices, successfully developing new creation method. Collected data and collaborated with field experts, developing lab protocols as part of the Oral Care department.

Jheneal McDuffie, CPRW | The Resume Chic & Co. | theresumechic.com
Major: Osteopathic Medicine (DO), Biomedical Imaging (MS), Microcellular Biology (BS) | **Goal:** Clinical research position
Notable: This newly graduated physician decided to pivot to a career in medical research and, ultimately, healthcare administration. Skills are detailed in the summary, while education is listed only briefly.

Pat Smith

Cambridge, MA

Patsmithchem@gmail.com   978.555.1212   LinkedIn: Pat-Smith-chem

Biophysics Researcher

- Received the MSSM (MIT Scholars in Science and Mathematics) Scholarship—awarded to students demonstrating excellence in fields of mathematics and science.
- Demonstrated and published expertise in Molecular Dynamics, Nuclear Magnetic Resonance, Protein Expression.
- As an undergraduate, chosen as Teaching Assistant for Chemistry classes from Intro to Organic.

Education

Massachusetts Institute of Technology (MIT), Cambridge, MA

B.A. in Chemistry with Physics minor   Expected May 2023

Cumulative GPA: 3.58/4.00

Relevant Coursework: Electron Microscopy; Structural Biochemistry; Thermodynamics and Statistical Mechanics; Capstone in Chemistry Research

Research & Projects

- **Team Lead**—*SH2 Domain* project (2021–Present): Analyze the interaction of the bioactive rich molecules with SH2 using molecular dynamics to simulate each stage of the binding processes.
- **Team Member**—*DNA glycolysis* project: Use molecular dynamics simulations to analyze how the dsRBM domain is impacted by glycolysis; in collaboration with University of Massachusetts, Amherst.
- **Presenter**—Annual Saturn Conference for computational chemistry at William & Mary.   2021–2022
- **Researcher**—Professor D. Sharon, MIT Computational Biophysics Lab.   2020–Present

Publication

Aronson, Baker, Connaught, **Smith**, Jameson-North, and West. "Unbound Bioactive-Rich Signaling Peptide Frequently Samples SH2 Conformations in Gaussian Accelerated Molecular Dynamics Simulations." Front. Mol. Biosci., 15 Sep 2022.

Work Experience

Massachusetts Institute of Technology, Cambridge, MA   Sep 2022–Present

Peer-Led Team Learning Leader—Fundamentals of Chemistry I

Guide student class through Intro Chemistry course; lead Sunday classes through workshops and problems.

MIT, Cambridge, MA   2021–Present

Teaching Assistant—Organic Chemistry

Oversee Organic Chem Lab I students and demo labs; teach students how to perform experiments; hold office hours and meet with professor and students outside of class; proctor exams; grade assignments.

MIT, Cambridge, MA   2021–Present

Teaching Assistant—Physical Chemistry I and II

Manage general cleanliness and organization of the chemistry lab, prepare chemical solutions, and set up equipment for laboratory exercises; demonstrate lab procedures to students.

DISC Behavioral Leadership Assessment

Strengths: Analytical; quick thinker; diplomatic; respect for established systems and organizational protocol.

Natural Traits: Optimistic; ability to help others on team visualize activities necessary to obtain success.

Ed Lawrence, CPRW, NCOPE, CIC; certified to administer MBTI, Strong, DISC, and Skillscan | Get Start-ed | getstart-ed.com
Major: Chemistry | **Goal:** Position in biophysics research
Notable: Research projects and relationships with professors and research teams are the standout features of this resume, along with the DISC assessment characteristics that appear at the bottom.

ANNE MARION

TARGET: ENTRY-LEVEL BIOTECHNOLOGY

San Diego, CA 92014
555.678.9008
anne-marion08@gmail.com

QUALIFICATIONS SUMMARY

Innovative and goal-driven professional seeking entry-level position in the field of biotechnology to utilize knowledge and skills acquired and honed through continuous education, combined with background in program management, activity planning and coordination, and strategic communication. Additional qualifications include:

- Strong attention to detail and accuracy in generating critical data review of clinical, non-clinical, or scientific information; preparing reports; and updating documents related to laboratory work or assays.
- Adeptness in organizing projects and events, from conception to completion, within time and budget constraints.
- Critical thinking and problem-solving skills to provide sound decisions and effective solutions on high-impact, complex problems to drive successful outcomes.
- Ability to build and maintain work relationships with all levels of professionals toward the attainment of common goals; collaborate and work in a team environment; share feedback, exchange insights, and build consensus.
- Fluency in English, with basic knowledge in Hebrew and Spanish languages.

CORE COMPETENCIES

Molecular Biology Laboratory Procedures	Western Blot | SDS-PAGE | Agarose Gel Electrophoresis | Polymerase Chain Reaction (PCR) Amplification | CRISPR-Cas9 Mediated Gene Editing | Cloning and Vector Transformation | Spectrophotometry | Bradford Assay
Interdisciplinary Knowledge	Biochemistry | Molecular Biology | Genetics | Cell Biology | Bioinformatics | Organic Chemistry

EDUCATION

Bachelor of Science in Molecular and Cell Biology, Jun 2023 | University of California San Diego, San Diego, CA
GPA: 3.971 | Graduated summa cum laude | Relevant Coursework: Genetics and Molecular Biology

WORK EXPERIENCE

VONS GROCERY STORE, LA JOLLA, CA
Courtesy Clerk   Jan 2022–May 2022
- Delivered first-rate service and assistance to all customers to ensure a positive shopping experience.
- Maintained positive demeanor in dealing with clients while checking out and bagging items.
- Ensured store cleanliness and sanitation, which involved cleaning up any spills and reorganizing displays.

MIRACOSTA COLLEGE STEM CENTER, OCEANSIDE, CA
Tutor   Aug 2018–May 2020
- Provided help to students to achieve successful testing outcomes. Recommended effective test-taking strategies and study tips and provided guidance for writing formal lab reports.
- Facilitated instruction in Molecular and Cell Biology, Genetics, and Organic Chemistry subjects.

CAMP JCA SHALOM, MALIBU, CA
Program Assistant   Jun 2019–Aug 2019
- Contributed to planning and coordination of camp-wide competition that comprised several athletic and creative events.
- Handled sorting and delivery of mail to over 300 campers throughout the summer.
- Boosted staff morale by working with other supervisors to organize events, including games, icebreakers, and dances.

ACTIVITIES

Former President, University of California San Diego Quidditch Club | **Member,** Hillel | **Volunteer,** Habitat for Humanity

TECHNICAL SKILLS

Microsoft Office Suite (Word, PowerPoint, Excel) | GIMP Graphic Design Tool

Michelle King | Resume Professional Writers | resumeprofessionalwriters.com
Major: Molecular and Cell Biology | **Goal:** Career in biotechnology
Notable: The top half of this resume conveys strong professional and technical skills, while the bottom half shows work ethic, customer focus, and leadership experience.

Chris Vance

(818) 555-1234 | chrisvance@email.com | linkedin.com/in/name

Field Research Assistant

Recent Graduate and Articulate Advocate
Qualified for Positions in Environmental Sciences / Sustainability / Conservation

Biology Graduate with valuable hands-on experience in laboratory and research settings. **Self-starter** who leverages a strong combination of right- and left-brain thinking to provide an out-of-the-box perspective on addressing and solving problems. Meticulously research, organize, and synthesize information with impeccable attention to detail.

Skilled communicator who works well in group settings and as an individual contributor. Build trusting relationships with diverse populations across all ages, interests and professions.

Related Experience / Projects

- ✓ Completed summer internship for genetics research lab of leading healthcare organization.
- ✓ Researched, analyzed, and reported on evolution of salamander sub-species.
- ✓ Produced climate change PSA for university station.
- ✓ Created immersive visual display on global warming for digital art course.
- ✓ Organized groups of students to conduct beach and hiking trail cleanups.

Core Competencies

Research Project Management | Experiment Design and Execution | Lab Equipment Maintenance and Calibration
Oral and Written Communications | Presentations | Public Speaking | Team Leadership | Data Analytics
Basic Lab Knowledge and Experience | Experiment Design and Execution | Organizational Skills | Problem Solving
Interpersonal Skills | Research and Analysis | Project Planning And Management

Education

CALIFORNIA STATE UNIVERSITY, Northridge, CA; May 2023
BA in Biology; Minor in Art; GPA: 3.5
Relevant Coursework: *Biological Sciences and Labs, Microbiology, Ecology, Genetics, Cell Biology, Evolution, Biometry, Plant Anatomy / Physiology, Conservation Biology, Chemistry, Organic Chemistry, Psychology, Psychology of Learning, Mathematics for Science and Engineering*

Related Employment History

PEOPLE'S HEALTHCARE, Los Angeles, CA   Summer 2022
Genomics Lab Research Intern

Gained hands-on experience observing and participating in genetic testing intake and review process. Wrote policy draft regarding insurance coverage guidelines on genetic testing and diagnosis of Beckwith Wiedemann Syndrome.

HOME HAVEN, Los Angeles, CA   (Part Time) Oct 2018 – Sept 2019
Certified Nursing Assistant (CNA)

Additional Seasonal / Part-Time Work

Server—Morrie's Diner, Santa Monica, California; (Part Time) Nov 2020 – Mar 2021
Nanny—Private Residence, Beverly Hills, California; Summer 2017

Professional Development | Certifications | Computer Skills

GIS Certification (in Progress)
Basic Life Support, CPR Certifications

Computer Skills
Microsoft Office (Word, Excel, PowerPoint, Outlook, Access); Adobe Illustrator, Photoshop; RStudio

Vivian Van Lier, CPRW, JCTC, CEIP, CCMC, CPBS, NCOPE | Advantage Resume and Career Services | careerempowermentcoach.com
Major: Biology | **Goal:** Position in field research
Notable: The "Related Experience/Projects" section of the Summary highlights diverse and interesting activities that are bound to be great conversation starters (and CAR story prompts) during interviews.

Katie Smith

Houston, TX 55555 • 555.453.2310 • katiesmith@gmail.com • LinkedIn

PROTECTED SPECIES OBSERVER/OCEANOGRAPHY GRADUATE

⊙ Accurate and detailed Protected Species Observer and Oceanography graduate with hands-on experience collecting, processing, analyzing, interpreting, and reporting data.

⊙ Resourceful problem solver adept at liaising between scientists and clients and translating technical jargon into clear language for general audiences.

⊙ Proficient at prioritizing projects to consistently deliver quality work under tight deadlines. Demonstrate balanced judgment under pressure.

⊙ **Core Competencies:** Metaocean Data Collection • Data Analysis & Interpretation Results Customization • Numerical Model Hindcasts • Statistical Analysis • Report Writing • Project Management Quality Control • Oceanic & Atmospheric Physics • Metaocean Parameter Statistical Analysis • Python • Linux

PROFESSIONAL EXPERIENCE

PROTECTED SPECIES OBSERVER – *Ocean Group*   2023 – Present; Houston, TX

Visually monitor, detect, and identify protected species for Bureau of Ocean Energy Management (BOEM) and Bureau of Safety and Environmental Enforcement (BSEE). Record and report protected species sightings and survey environmental conditions per regulations. Monitor and advise vessel crew on sound source and operations for compliance with environmental requirements for survey plan. Organize and maintain appropriate monitoring schedules.

- Client has incurred zero fines/legal issues related to environmental protocols during tenure to date.
- Developed reputation for submitting accurate reports to *RPS Group*, client and BOEM.

AQUATIC INTERPRETER INTERN – *Texas Aquatic Museum*   2020; Tucson, AZ

Monitored behavior and activity of 18 Cownose Rays. Observed and participated in animal husbandry. Greeted guests and shared information on importance of conservation regarding marine animals and the Sea of Cortez. Encouraged safe interactions between the guests and rays.

EDUCATION

BACHELOR OF SCIENCE, OCEANOGRAPHY – *Texas A&M University, College of Geosciences*   2023; College Station, TX

Emphasis in Ocean Observing Systems & Technology. Select projects include:

- **Time series analysis of hydrographic conditions in Nordic Seas:** Utilized previous cruise data, depth profiles, and PCA plots to analyze water column conditions during summer 1997, 2002 and 2009 in Nordic Seas. Analysis showed phytoplankton abundance and subsequent nutrient depletion are more common earlier in summer and higher dissolved oxygen amounts are typically related to lower temperatures and nutrient availability in water column.
- **Comparison and analysis of results from Galveston Bay:** Collected, processed, and analyzed samples from Galveston Bay research cruise. Data portrayed consistent nutrient concentration in bay with some water condition variances and that Galveston Bay was unaffected by possible chemical influx following major chemical fire.
- **Coding project:** Constructed daily time series of mean sea surface temperature (SST) over specific ocean point. Created loop animation for each monthly SST anomaly in 2020 using time series data.

CERTIFICATIONS AND PROFESSIONAL AFFILIATION

PROTECTED SPECIES OBSERVER TRAINING – *BOEM*	2023
COMPRESSED AIR EMERGENCY BREATHING SYSTEM (CA-EBS) TRAINING – *All Stop*	2023
BASIC OFFSHORE SAFETY INDUCTION & EMERGENCY TRAINING (BOSIET) – *All Stop*	2023
MEMBER – *The Oceanography Society*	2020 – Present

Andrea Adamski, CPRW | Write For You Resumes | writeforyouresumes.com
Major: Oceanography | **Goal:** Entry-level position as an oceanographer
Notable: Highlighted by a graphic showing the intersection of skills needed for her profession, this resume continues with relevant details of education, experience, and proven capabilities.

Bernice Washington

555.679.0246 • bernicewashington@comcast.net

Candidate for Entry-Level Position in

Design / Biomedical Engineering

Biomedical Engineering graduate with a strong educational background in engineering, project management, and computer systems. Skilled in establishing productive working relationships, fostering teamwork, and completing tasks/meeting deadlines under pressure.

Creative self-starter and conscientious employee. Able to perform multiple tasks with attention to detail, information gathering, accuracy, and follow-up.

Accomplished artist, illustrator and technical writer combining creativity and aesthetics with sound engineering knowledge. Adept at grasping complex technical and scientific concepts and presenting them in a simple and easy-to-understand manner.

Competencies

- Troubleshooting
- Presentations/Illustrations
- Technical Writing
- Project Management
- Engineering Design Theory
- Problem Solving
- Research
- Industrial Design

Education

New Jersey Institute of Technology, Newark, NJ
Master of Science in Biomedical Engineering, Spring 2023

New Jersey Institute of Technology, Newark, NJ
Bachelor of Engineering Science, 2019

Awards and Achievements

- Technical paper presented at the 2020 Society for Biomaterials Conference
- NJIT Award, ASME Old Guard Technical Poster Competition, 2017, 2018, 2019
- ASME Student Design Competition, 2017
- Society of Automotive Engineers Mini-Baja Competition, 2017
- Robert Frost Literary Contest: Poetry Competition

Internship

Research Intern • University of Medicine and Dentistry of New Jersey, Newark, NJ   2017

- Part of a team that conducted research trials on various materials that are being considered for use in dental implants, orthodontic devices, and other dental procedures.
- Performed destructive and non-destructive testing on materials using sophisticated analytical instruments. Tested for tensile strength, creep, stress relaxation, and corrosion resistance.
- Collected data and prepared reports that were praised for clarity and accuracy.
- Credited in publication/presentation of the research at 2017 Society for Biomaterials Conference.
- Created numerous medical illustrations for presentations and publications by the research team.

Additional Work Experience While Attending School

Maintenance Assistant • Avon Manner Inn, Avon, NJ   Summers 2014 to 2018
Electrical and carpentry work; computer system maintenance and upgrading.

Freelance Illustrator, Perth Amboy, NJ   2015 to Present
Commercial and residential murals and artwork; industrial product displays and museum exhibits.

Beverly Baskin, EdS, LPC, MCC, CPRW | BBCS Counseling Services | bbcscounseling.com
Major: Biomedical Engineering (MS), Engineering Science (BS) | **Goal:** Biomedical engineering position
Notable: Education, awards, and skill sets are featured at the top of the resume, followed by a relevant internship and other experience that conveys work ethic and diverse talents.

Tyler Edwards

Shepherdsville, KY 40165 | (502) 555-1234 | tyler.edwards@mymail.com | LinkedIn

Mechanical Engineer

Mechanical Engineering master's degree graduate (2023) with strong interest in automotive powertrain. Experience with CAE and product line strategy development. Certified SolidWorks Associate since 2016.

Work Experience

Power Powertrains, Inc. | Troy, MI   2019–2022

Serving automotive industry in design, development, testing, and manufacturing of powertrain systems.

Product Line Engineering Student————————————————*Alternating Semesters 2021–2022*

- ⚙ Worked alongside senior 4WD/AWD product line engineers to develop strategy and execute plan.
- ⚙ Researched data and performed comparative analysis resulting in potential 8% cycle time improvement.
- ⚙ Reported findings and status to senior management in bi-weekly virtual meetings.

CAE Engineering Student————————————————————*Alternating Semesters 2019–2020*

- ⚙ Performed simulations early in design process to thwart failure modes.
- ⚙ Developed and maintained systematic CAE plans.
- ⚙ Communicated status in weekly in-person team meetings.

Screw Machine and CNC Company | Louisville, KY   Summers 2015–2017

Precision turned and machined products manufacturer.

- ⚙ Set up and operated Browne & Sharpe screw machine.
- ⚙ Calibrated automatic Quality Assurance machine.
- ⚙ Operated and serviced CNC machines.
- ⚙ Mentored by retired master machinist.

Education

UNIVERSITY OF LOUISVILLE.
J.B. SPEED SCHOOL OF ENGINEERING

Master of Engineering (MEng) Mechanical Engineering   May 2023
- ☐ Structured Research Project:
  Manufacturing Process Improvement for Automotive Powertrain

Bachelor of Science (BS) Mechanical Engineering   May 2022
- ☐ **GPA** 3.91 / 4.0 | Dean's Scholar List All Semesters

FIRST Robotics

FIRST Robotics Competition (FRC)   2014–2018

Challenging teams of high school students to build industrial-size robots to play a difficult field game.

☐ Dean's List Award Semi-Finalist | Elected Machining Captain | Drove robot in competition matches

FIRST LEGO League (FLL) Robotics Team 2860   2012–2013

Inspiring youth to grow critical thinking, coding, and design skills through hands-on STEM learning and robotics.

Teresa Hutton, CPRW | Best Resume Forward | bestresumeforward.com
Major: Mechanical Engineering (MS and BS) | **Goal:** Engineer in the auto industry
Notable: Auto-industry experience is highlighted before Education because it closely matches Tyler's career interests. Robotics experiences, listed last, illustrate critical thinking and team leadership skills.

AUSTIN THOMAS

734.397.6575 – athomas@umich.edu

Environmental Engineer

PERSONAL PROFILE

Motivated certified Engineer-in-Training seeks to join organization where knowledge and skills in environmental engineering will enhance the company. Known as an honest and inclusive team player, dedicated to meeting and exceeding expectations with the imagination to see what can be.

SKILLS and ABILITIES

- Code in C++ and MATLAB
- Ensure quality and efficiency
- Work well under pressure
- Think critically and analytically
- Speak comfortably in public

- Analyze soil and wastewater samples in lab settings
- Pay close attention to detail
- Communicate effectively orally and in writing
- Set and achieve goals
- Meet deadlines with time to spare

EDUCATION

Bachelor of Science in Engineering, *Environmental Engineering*
UNIVERSITY OF MICHIGAN, Ann Arbor, Michigan, 3.055 GPA, degree conferred 2023

CERTIFICATIONS

- Program in Sustainable Engineering (P.I.S.E)
- Certified Engineer in Training, State of Michigan

PROJECTS

- Created a working water distribution as part of a water supply project, accounting for daily demand and fire flows.
- Participated on Design Team that collaborated with other engineering teams to create a new water treatment and distribution system.
- Consulted in analysis of brewery wastewater and soil, predicting the pathway of an underground pollutant.
- Recalculated pipe flow and recommended changes in pipe size which avoided pipe pressure failure.
- Worked with samples of soil and wastewater to determine air and soil quality and contamination.

HOBBIES and INTERESTS

- Researching current environmental issues, including the Enbridge Line 5 Pipeline and PFAS
- Games and puzzles involving critical thinking skills
- Trivia and historical facts
- Gathering knowledge and anecdotal lessons from others, such as TED talks, family and friends, informational videos, and podcasts

Sandra Flippo, SPHR (retired)
Major: Environmental Engineering | **Goal:** Entry-level position in environmental engineering
Notable: Without relevant experience or internships to showcase, this resume concentrates on skills and projects. Hobbies and interests create an interesting footnote to professional qualifications.

VICTORIA LOPEZ

Champaign, IL || 240-618-7623 || VMLOPEZ@gmail.com || linkedin.com/victoria-engineer

SYSTEMS ENGINEER

NASA SPACE TECHNOLOGY FELLOW

Multi-faceted engineer with a background in mechanical, aerospace, solar, and hydroponic areas and experience in both North and South America. Trilingual (English, Spanish, Portuguese) professional who leverages knowledge to contribute to the field through consulting, project management, research, and teaching. U.S. citizen.

KEY STRENGTHS

- Renewable & Solar Energy
- Test Engineering
- Electric Propulsion
- Rocket Propulsion Analysis

COMPUTER SKILLS

- Computer Aided Design (CAD)
- MATLAB
- SolidWorks
- Python

EDUCATION

University of Illinois at Urbana-Champaign   2023

Master of Science Aerospace Engineering – Cumulative GPA 4.0/4.0
NASA Space Technology Graduate Research Fellowship
- Awarded this mark of distinction for proposal: "Novel Particle Approaches for Modeling Electrospray Propulsion Concepts." Selected to develop groundbreaking, high-risk/high-payoff, early-stage space technology.

University of Brasilia – Brazil   Dec 2020

Bachelor of Science Mechanical Engineering – Cumulative GPA 4.4/5.0
- Brazilian National Council of Scientific and Technological Development Fellowship Award
- Young Talents for Science Fellowship Award

RESEARCH & PUBLICATIONS

University of Illinois – Department of Aerospace Engineering   Oct 2021–May 2023

Graduate Research Assistant – Dr. Suse
- In conjunction with *NASA Fellowship Award*, focused on creation of electric propulsion systems for spacecraft, particularly in applying Molecular Dynamics to model electrospray propulsion architectures.

University of Brasilia

Research Assistant   Aug 2019–Dec 2020
- Supported Director of Satellites and Applications of Brazilian Space Agency.
- Research Title: *Development of a Test Bench for Experimental Investigations of Solid Fuel Ramjet*
- Conference Publications:
  o *Experimental Investigation of High Regression Rate Paraffin for Solid Fuel Ramjet Propulsion* – AIAA Energy and Propulsion Forum, Aug. 2021
  o *Experimental Investigation of Hydrocarbon Based Fuels in Solid Fuel Ramjet Propulsion* – 70th International Aeronautical Congress, Oct. 2021

Carolyn Kleiman, CPRW | Kleiman Careers | carolyn.kleimancareers@yahoo.com
Major: Aerospace Engineering (MS), Mechanical Engineering (BS) | **Goal:** Systems engineering role in aerospace
Notable: Research and Publications relate to her target of aerospace engineering, so they are featured immediately after Education and followed by Engineering Experience that is less directly related.

VICTORIA LOPEZ

Champaign, IL || 240-618-7623 || VMLOPEZ@gmail.com || linkedin.com/victoria-engineer

---

University of Brasilia, continued

Research Assistant   Jul 2018–Jul 2019

- Advised by Dr. Ruiz, Department of Mechanical Engineering — Laboratory of Energy and Environment.
- Research Title: *Performance assessment of a parabolic dish concentrated solar power system in Brasilia.*

ENGINEERING EXPERIENCE

Strom Brasil, Rio de Janeiro, Brazil — S*olar energy engineering company*   Jul 2019–Feb 2020
Engineering Intern

- Generated the most available solar energy and optimum performance by designing photovoltaic systems and layouts based on building design and accessible solar paths.
- Performed computational analysis and simulations of photovoltaic solar energy systems of up to 1000 kW.

TECMEC, Sao Paolo, Brazil — *Consulting services in mechanical engineering*   Mar 2018–Jul 2019
Project Manager — Awarded Best Project Consultant

- Managed design and development team of four consultants working on a medical device mechanical project, which had been the largest contract awarded to the company.
- Developed 3D prototypes, identified materials, and tested functionality while verifying product design and ensuring customer requirements were met.
- Executed technical analysis reports; prospected and cultivated relationships with clients.
- Generated and quadrupled company revenue compared to previous fiscal year.
- Developed company's financial plan and prepared accounting reports.

Odebrecht Engineering and Construction, Sao Paolo, Brazil   Jul 2017–Aug 2017
Electromechanical Division Engineering Intern at the Teles Pires Hydropower Project

- Jointly oversaw the assembly of 364 MW Francis turbines (1820 MW of total installed capacity). Tested and performed troubleshooting at installation to ensure performance according to design parameters.
- Managed construction of on-site security checkpoint at new facility.
- Conducted progress and productivity analysis reports of subterranean water pipeline.

LEADERSHIP

University of Brasilia   Mar 2020–Dec 2020
Volunteer Teaching Assistant, Heat Engines Course

- Instructed weekly two-hour class to 40 students, reinforcing concepts and helping with assignments.
- Taught laboratory classes, performing experiments with diesel engines and compressors.

BAJA SAE Project – Piratas do Cerrado Team   Mar 2016–Oct 2017
Leader, Chassis and Ergonomics Division

- Steered team of four in the design, development, and construction of the Baja vehicle's chassis.
- Performed 3D CAD modeling, finite element structural simulations, ergonomics analysis and simulations, and material analysis and selection.
- Manufactured the Baja car, welded roll cage, and utilized additional machinery such as hydraulic presses, mechanical lathes, and milling machines.
- Participated in the 21st BAJA SAE Brazil National Competition.

TIMOTHY B. STAPLETON

Longmeadow, MA 01106 • 413-381-3884 • tbstaples@gmail.com | LinkedIn

CIVIL ENGINEER: HYDRAULIC ENGINEERING
Public Water Supply / Wastewater Management / Water Treatment Systems

Responsible, hard-working **Civil Engineering Major** with field experience through Donovan & Thomas internship and Engineers Without Borders hydrology engineering project in India.

Project leader with demonstrated track record of taking the initiative and following through on commitments. **Quick study,** eager to learn new skills.

→ Keen interest in hydraulic engineering, particularly as it relates to public water supply, wastewater management, and water treatment systems.
→ Solid PC/Mac skills; knowledge of AutoCAD and MS Office. Studied Latin and Spanish (high school).
→ Div. III College Varsity Track (2019–2023); H.S. Varsity Track Letterman (2017–2019); H.S. Varsity Football Letterman (2018, 2019); Varsity Offensive Lineman's Award (2019); All-Area Football Team (2019).

Sat for the **EIT** exam (Jan. 2023, results pending).

EDUCATION & ENGINEERING EXPERIENCE

WORCESTER POLYTECHNIC INSTITUTE • Worcester, MA   May 2023 Graduate (*antic.*)
College of Engineering, Technology, and Architecture

→ **Bachelor of Science Degree, Civil Engineering** (Dean's List Standing)
→ Member, **Sigma Alpha Pi,** National Society of Leadership and Success
→ Member, **Massachusetts Society of Civil Engineers** and **American Society of Civil Engineers**

DONOVAN & THOMAS | Pittsfield, MA   Dec. 2022–Jan. 2023
Engineering Intern | Directly supported Senior Hydrogeologist; used CAD extensively in project designs/revisions.

→ Worked on **plan designs** for Massachusetts public/private schools and assisted in writing **sedimentation and erosion control plan** for Baker Quarry in Stockbridge, MA.
→ **Researched maps, submitted permit applications, pulled USGS maps, corrected topographic maps,** and handled **water samples** for laboratory testing. On behalf of company, made visits to various state agencies (DOT, DEP) as well as town halls and project subcontractors. Organized bridge records for municipalities.
→ Accompanied engineering teams during **water quality testing;** participated in field test of **well-yielding levels.**
→ Attended **project team meetings** with engineering staff and **on-site meetings** with project/site owners.

ENGINEERS WITHOUT BORDERS USA PROJECT • Abheypur, India   Jan. 2022
Hydrology Project Engineer

→ Selected as 1 of 5 engineering students who installed EWB-sanctioned rainwater harvesting and filtration project.
→ Profiled in Autumn 2022 issue of In*Flow*-Line magazine (American/Massachusetts Water Works Associations).

RELEVANT COURSEWORK

Intro to Surveying & Geographic Information	Engineering & Design	Materials Lab; Dynamics
Civil Engineering Materials Lab	Water Quality Engineering	Structural Analysis
Water Resources Engineering	Engineering by Design	Calculus I, II, III
Engineering Computer Applications	Mechanics of Materials	Structural Steel Design
Calculus-Based Physics I, II	Reinforced Concrete Design	Engineering Economics

PRIOR EMPLOYMENT

Laborer / Landscaper / Site Work for Jacob Edwards, Dalton, MA. Year-round, full-time summers (5/2020–5/2023).

Road Crew for the Town of Pittsfield. Full-time summer position/vacations during college (6/2019–5/2020).

Cashier / Stocker for the Pittsfield Market. Part-time weekends; full-time summers/vacations (5/2017–7/2019).

Paid Columnist for the *Town Caller* newspaper. Researched, interviewed, and wrote a weekly sports column covering 3 high school seasons each year (football, indoor track, and outdoor track) (9/2015–6/2019).

Jan Melnik, MA, MRW, CCM, CPRW | Absolute Advantage | janmelnik.com
Major: Civil Engineering | **Goal:** Position in civic/hydraulic engineering
Notable: Education and Engineering experiences are combined into a single super-charged section to position this new graduate as a hydraulic engineer with substantial in-field as well as educational qualifications.

Terry Trempealeau

Boise, ID 83706 • 208.555.1234 • t.trempealeau@gmail.com

Mechanical Design Engineer

Certified Solid Works Professional (CSWP) • Registered Engineer in Training (EIT) • Lean Six Sigma White Belt

Education | Experience | Engineering Qualifications

Idaho School of Engineering • Boise, ID
Honors Bachelor of Science: Mechanical Engineering • Magna Cum Laude   2023
☐ GPA 3.91. ☐ 2023 Outstanding Student Achievement Award – Engineering
- Modeled 11-stage axial compressor in SolidWorks; determined pressure gradients and key instrument locations using SolidWorks Flow Simulation for Westinghouse J34 Turbojet Engine.
- Designed single-input, dual-output gearbox requiring gear, bearing, lubrication, and housing design.
- Engineered small-scale motorized carpet roller for local carpet distributor, automating loading and unloading of various carpet dimensions by a single operator.
- Designed rocket incorporating center-of-pressure analysis and force transducer to determine thrust.

Custom Fabrication, Inc • Meridian, ID
Engineering and Project Management Intern   Feb 2022–Aug 2022
- Increased material control efficiency by 75%, using process engineering to streamline procurement and material tracking by creating Excel database managing ~50,000 line records.
- Gained knowledge of material standards and specifications to select and procure $20M+ of material.
- Met project milestones resulting in multimillion-dollar payments.
- Developed prototype FDM 3D metal printer, integrating custom wiring harnesses and thermal dissipation systems.
- Worked under NQA-1 Quality program for steel fabrication of government project.
- Evaluated and created change orders to drive schedule and contract revisions that increased fabrication efficiency.

ISE Mechanical Engineering Department • Boise, ID
Engineering Researcher   Aug 2021–Jan 2022
- Led project management for all research on Westinghouse J34 Turbojet Engine.
- Designed and verified fabricated components needed to progress research, resulting in 80% cost savings.

NASA BASALT • Hawaii, HI
Martian Studies Intern   Aug 2020
- Analyzed real-time data of simulated Mars missions for planning future missions.
- Maintained and repaired custom communication systems to improve field use.
- Learned new process operations, including sample identification, prioritization, and use of specialized xGDS software to collect samples for biologic and geologic analogous comparison to Mars.

SOLIDWORKS Certifications
- Certified Professional • Certified Professional Advanced – Drawing Tools • Certified Associate – Sustainability
- Certified Associate – Additive Manufacturing • Certified Professional Advanced – Weldments

Organizations

Tau Beta Pi • The Engineering Honor Society, Idaho School of Engineering
Chapter President, 2022–2023 • Corresponding Secretary, 2020–2021   2020–2023

American Society of Mechanical Engineers (ASME) • Member   2021–Present

Teresa Hutton, CPRW | Best Resume Forward | bestresumeforward.com
Major: Mechanical Engineering | **Goal:** Design engineer
Notable: With notable internships (including a Martian Studies internship that is sure to prompt conversation during interviews!), this newly graduated engineer has a solid record of relevant experience.

Byron Schwab

(971) 770–1460 • byron.schwab@email.com • LinkedIn

Mechanical Engineer – Renewable Energy & Sustainability

Award-winning Mechanical Engineer with 4+ years' experience in *Fortune 10* and *startups*. Highly entrepreneurial, underpinned by ~2 years of leading sustainability projects that spawned multidisciplinary engineering design and research projects in renewable energy. **Project leader** who collaborates with interdisciplinary teams and Lean Six Sigma industry professionals to conceive, develop, and test engineering solutions rooted in human-centered design thinking.

—Technical Competencies—

Excel, VBA, Mechademy, Ansys Fluent, Autodesk AutoCAD, Autodesk Inventor, Python, LaTeX, MURAL/MIRO, SOLIDWORKS, Engineering Equation Solver, Esri GIS, MATLAB, OSIsoft PI, Java, C#, Helioscope, RETscreen, Creality 3D

Education & Training

SOUTHERN ILLINOIS UNIVERSITY CARBONDALE (SIUC)
College of Engineering | Carbondale, IL

Bachelor of Science (**BS**), **Mechanical Engineering** (2023)
Major: **Energy Engineering**, *Minors:* **Continuous Improvement, Sustainability & Mathematics**
Senior Thesis: Low-Cost 3D Printing Approach to Small Wind Turbine Rapid Manufacturing

Activities: Senator, SIUC Undergraduate Student Government (Fall 2020–Present) • Vice President, SIUC Engineering Student Council (Spring 2021–Present) • Drone Technical Team Lead, SIUC Robotics Team (Jan 2021–May 2022)

Recognition:

Fellow & University Innovation Guide • UNIVERSITY INNOVATION FELLOWS PROGRAM	Sep 2020–May 2023

Selected to represent the student voice in the global conversation on the future of education. Developed design thinking skills to support innovative activities that created positive change on campus and within the community.

- **Invited as 1 of 8** SIUC students to attend a conference hosted by FH Salzburg (Austria) University of Applied Sciences and help investigate methods to redesign and optimize parking lots at the Urstein campus.

Leadership Coach • LEADERSHIP DEVELOPMENT PROGRAM SIUC	Sep 2018 – May 2020

Nominated and admitted to NSF grant-funded program to lead lean manufacturing projects in collaboration with Lean Six Sigma Blackbelt. Coached and guided new undergraduates in the field and team-based environments.

- **Led 15** undergraduates in improving a plant manufacturing process by identifying 3 projects focused on optimizing tugger train route, inventory usage, and dock system loading and achieving 10x ROI.

Professional Experience

Mechanical Engineering Intern	Jun 2022–Dec 2022
BERKSHIRE HATHAWAY ENERGY PIPELINE GROUP	Lusby, MD	

Used engineering thermodynamics, project management, and Excel skills to improve plant monitoring processes and uptime at the Cove Point LNG Terminal. Assisted the engineering team remotely throughout the academic year.

- **Saved $1.2M+** and decreased consumable ethane levels 50% by developing and implementing an Excel-based tool that monitored refrigerant usage and analytically predicted future use.
- Boosted team productivity and communication by programming various Excel-based macros that interface with the PI DataLink system, resulting in **streamlined data gathering, monitoring, and reporting processes.**

Kate Williamson, MS, CPRW, CRS+ES, CRS+IT, CSBA | Scientech Resumes | scientechresumes.com
Major: Energy Engineering | **Goal:** Engineering role in the renewable energy industry
Notable: This resume backs up Byron's interest in renewable energy with a portfolio of projects and notable recognition for efforts he has already made in his desired industry segment.

Byron Schwab • Page 2   (971) 770–1460 • byron.schwab@email.com • LinkedIn

Project Manager/Founder   Nov 2020–Jun 2022
GREEN ROOF TEAM AT SIU | Carbondale, IL

Transformed an existing green space into a multidisciplinary innovation hub for participatory learning called the SIU Green Roof. **Initiated and led 4 capital projects** and managed 21 students after securing $15,600 in academic grants and crowdfunding. Created the Young Entrepreneur's Podcast and ran social media campaigns to build Green Roof's brand.

Project Experience

CAPITAL PROJECT: MULTIDISCIPLINARY INNOVATION HUB

Procured a $2,200 SIUC sustainability grant to establish a hub that provided SIUC students and faculty with an innovative space to cultivate engineering design passions through research. Fundraised $2,000 for Green Roof Project initiatives.

- **Hosted 3** in-person and **4** virtual design thinking workshops, attracting international attendees and engaging students, faculty, and community members in **building a project vision** during the COVID-19 pandemic.
- **Recognized** with the *Southern Illinois University System's Distinguished Student Service Award* and the *Illinois Innovation Award* in 2022 for leadership demonstrated in the Green Roof Project.

CAPITAL PROJECT: TEMPORARY WIND TURBINE

Secured a $4,125 SIUC sustainability project grant to design and manufacture a mount for a self-ballasted, vertical-access wind turbine and managed strategic relationships with multiple SIUC project stakeholders.

- Achieved the **first wind energy generation** on campus by implementing the wind turbine design in May 2022.
- **Recruited** and **led 24** undergraduates and early career engineering professionals, 25% remote at other universities, and facilitated virtual discussions using various online tools, including MURAL.

CAPITAL PROJECT: PHOTOVOLTAIC SYSTEM

Initiated a campus solar feasibility project to identify prime rooftop real estate for solar energy generation and inspire students' interest and faculty curiosity around the Green Roof Project. Oversaw a $3,400 sustainability grant.

- **Pioneered** a student-led design and installation of a photovoltaic system on SIU's Agriculture Building and Student Center and **published** solar power feasibility simulations in Helioscope and GIS.
- **Coached 5** freshman students in design thinking principles and collaborative teamwork in a university setting.

CAPITAL PROJECT: SMART IRRIGATION SYSTEM

Awarded a $2,500 research grant from the SIUC Research Enriched Academic Challenge to assess the feasibility of AI and machine learning in monitoring a highly volatile climatic region for the SIU Green Roof Project's irrigation system.

- Oversaw the installation of a Raspberry Pi control system in May 2022 that used remote sensing and automation to perform system checks on soil temperature and moisture content and **reduce water consumption**.
- **Won** the *Best Beginner Hack* at Treehacks 2022 after submitting the hardware design and setup for the automated garden watering system that released water when soil moisture dipped below 40%.

Alex Riordan

555-678-1332 • alex.riordan@gmail.com • LinkedIn Profile • Boston, MA

Aspiring
Process Engineer, Oil & Gas Industry

Senior Northeastern student pursuing full-time employment immediately upon graduation (May 2023).

- **ACADEMICS:** Dean's List student; President's Award for Outstanding Academic Achievement.
- **INTERNSHIPS:** Valuable and successful internships with oil & gas (ExxonMobil) and chemical refining firms (Primo Chemical).
- **INTANGIBLES:** Dedication, work ethic, enthusiasm, and positivity. Ability to work in teams with multi-cultural colleagues.

Education
NORTHEASTERN UNIVERSITY, Boston, MA
Chemical Engineering Major | BS anticipated May 2023
- GPA 3.75
- Dean's List—all semesters
- President's Award for Outstanding Academic Achievement
- Senior Project: *"Greening" Diesel Production*

GREELY HIGH SCHOOL, Cumberland, ME
Diploma May 2018
- Class Valedictorian
- Maine Medal of Achievement in Math and Science, 2018

Lab Skills
- Safety measures, chemical preparation, titrations, and documentation

Computer Skills
- Tableau, Alteryx
- MS Excel, Word, and PowerPoint

Campus Leadership
- **Peer Mentor** | Spring 2020–Spring 2022
- **External Events Coordinator, EcoScholars** | Fall 2019–Fall 2021
- **Social Media and Events Coordinator, Frisbee Golf Club** | Spring 2020

Professional Experience
EXXONMOBIL—**Process and Optimization Co-Op**   Houston, TX | January 2022–August 2022
Gained hands-on engineering experience within refinery processing units. Learned and used 2 new software programs (Tableau and Alteryx) to complete 10 projects, including:
- Performed and analyzed Cooling Water Tower efficiency and pressure survey for 1500 ft Blowdown line piping system.
- Performed Trasar study and analyzed Cooling Water Tower chemical distribution.
- Developed Tableau Dashboards for Gasoline Metrics and Product Offtake.

Supervisor Endorsement: "Alex Riordan was a Day One asset to the ExxonMobil Refinery Team. His technical knowledge, attention to detail, and positive attitude helped accelerate several projects to a successful conclusion ... He tackled a very challenging set of tasks with zeal." **Earned top intern rating (#1 on 5-point scale).**

PRIMO CHEMICAL—**Technical Center Co-Op**   Buenos Aires, Argentina | January 2020–July 2020
Pursued international co-op opportunity, seeking a challenging professional and cultural workplace.
- Developed the Stain Test Protocol on polymer products for the Electronic Market.
- Researched and developed a dimensional analysis study on polymers for the Electronic Market.
- Worked cross-culturally with colleagues in Argentina and at other Primo R&D centers in France, India, China, and US.

Supervisor Endorsement: "Alex displayed a maturity and autonomy that are very rare among university students ... He identified very quickly the priorities and challenges of his missions and provided high quality work ... Alex demonstrated an excellent ability to adapt to a multi-cultural work environment." **Invited to return for internship the following year.**

NORTHEASTERN UNIVERSITY—**Chemistry Teaching Assistant**   Fall 2020–Present
One of a handful of undergraduates chosen as Teaching Assistants, roles primarily held by graduate students.
- Teach a general chemistry lab section to help students apply classroom concepts through experiments. In charge of conducting the class, grading papers, and ensuring students understand the material.

Multicultural Background
- **International Living:** Buenos Aires, 2020 | Lisbon, 2009–2012 | Macau, 2005–2009 | Barcelona, 2003–2005
- **Amigos da las Americas—Trainer and Participant:** Built community consensus and led a well-building project.
- **Languages:** Highly Proficient Spanish | Basic Portuguese

Louise Kursmark, MRW, CPRW, JCTC, CEIP, CCM | Best Impression Career Services | louisekursmark.com
Major: Chemical Engineering | **Goal:** Process engineer in the oil and gas industry
Notable: Two co-op jobs are the highlights of Alex's professional experience, and success on the job is supported by exceptional endorsements from supervisors. The Summary is succinct and powerful.

NATE ANDREWS

(555) 555-5555 ◆ andrews22@cmu.edu
www.linkedin.com/in/andrews22 ◆ Pittsburgh, PA 15201

AEROSPACE ENGINEERING GRADUATE STUDENT → *Leveraging technical, computer science, research, communication, and problem-solving skills to advance aerospace engineering initiatives.*

High-achieving, collaborative aerospace engineer with experience in NASA-funded space weather research and corporate engineering proposal development pursuing January 2024 full-time position.

Skill, Competencies, and Relevant Coursework

MATLAB • Spacecraft Design • Space Weather • Astro mechanics • Orbit Determination • GPS Theory & Design
Computer Science Logic • Propulsion Systems • Thermodynamics • Aero/Hydrodynamics • AutoCAD • Inventor
Research • Client Proposals • Presentations • Interdisciplinary Collaboration • Technical Writing • MS Office

EDUCATION AND HONORS

M.S. in Aerospace Engineering – CARNEGIE MELLON UNIVERSITY - *Expected* Dec 2023
GPA: **4.00** • Accelerated Graduate School Program • NASA-Funded Research Project Assistant

B.S. in Aerospace Engineering – CARNEGIE MELLON UNIVERSITY – May 2021
GPA: **3.75** • Honors College • Dean's List with Distinction • **AIAA Senior Capstone Spacecraft Design Team Leader**

Eagle Scout – 2015 • **AMERICAN INSTITUTE OF AERONAUTICS AND ASTRONAUTICS (AIAA)** – Member Since 2019

PROFESSIONAL EXPERIENCE AND RESEARCH

CARNEGIE MELLON, COLLEGE OF ENGINEERING – *Pittsburgh, PA*

Graduate Research Assistant – NASA-Funded Space Weather Thesis   **Aug 2020–Present**
Analyzing magnetospheric and solar wind data to identify signatures with periods matching atmospheric planetary waves. Compiling relevant characteristic data, interpreting and presenting findings, and preparing for publication.
- Relate planetary waves to space weather waves and how they affect ionosphere where ICON Mission is positioned.
- Confer with NASA engineers and university professor to review project status and determine next steps.

Undergraduate Research Assistant – Orbit Determination with Laser Radar Data   **Aug 2019–May 2020**
Proved use of laser radar data to track unknown satellites and space debris without corner-cube retro-reflectors under specific conditions by coupling laser range data with optically derived angular data; presented findings to peers.
- Created MATLAB algorithm to track space objects, ascertained initial orbit data, and compared to known location.
- Evaluated satellite laser ranging data to determine true photons reflecting off known spacecraft.

Undergraduate Research Assistant – NASA ICON Mission   **Aug 2018–May 2019**
Developed remote sensing geometry tools (MATLAB Scripts) currently utilized by NASA satellite to aid in validation and collaboration of data collection for interactions between Earth's atmosphere and the space environment.
- Visualized timeline of maneuvers for satellite and used Mighti A and B, FUV, and EUV space weather instruments.
- Identified opportunities for collaboration between ICON satellite, TIMED satellite, and ground stations.

ENGINEERING ASSOCIATES OF MORRISTOWN – *Morristown, NJ*

Engineering Intern – Reported to Head of Architectural Engineering   **May 2018–Aug 2018**
Drafted proposals, conducted field work, and created AutoCAD drawings for NJ Office of Homeland Security and Preparedness, NJ Department of Property Management and Construction, pharmaceuticals firms, and NJ schools.
- Designed secure government rooms and collaborated with mechanical, electrical, civil, and structural engineers.

Julie Wyckoff, MEd, Certified Career Transition Coach, YouMap Coach | Custom Career Solutions | customcareersolutions.com
Major: Aerospace Engineering (MS and BS) | **Goal:** Aerospace engineer
Notable: The Professional Experience and Research section is rich with relevant roles and activities that show this new graduate's longtime interest in space science.

CHRIS CALUMET

Fond du Lac, WI • (555) 555-9876 • chris.calumet@email.com

Upcoming Manufacturing Engineering graduate and Certified SolidWorks Associate. Experience in process improvement, time studies, cost reductions, and fixture design and fabrication.

MANUFACTURING ENGINEERING EXPERIENCE

Manufacturing Engineer Intern | American Tool and Engineering | Hartford, WI   April 2023–Present
Engineering, Stamping, Fabrication and Welding, ISO 9001:2000 Registered Company

- Designed pegboard carts to hang punch-press shaker trays, reducing time to locate the size needed.
- Modeled floorplan to calculate space available for future equipment arrangements.
- Reworked welding ventilation from overhead vents to backdraft tables to mitigate unhealthy Hexavalent Chromium gas releasing into workspace.

Lab Assistant | UW-Springfield Machining Lab | Springfield, WI   Jan 2022–Present
Manual & CNC Mill | Manual & CNC Lathe | Drill Presses | Pedestal Grinders | Horizontal & Vertical Bandsaw

- Diagnosed and fixed issues with the machines; kept equipment running well via proper maintenance.
- Managed tool crib inventory, reordered tools when needed, and organized tools for quicker access.
- Mentored students in safe operation of equipment, enabling successful completion of class projects.

Manufacturing Engineer Co-op | All Equipment Corp. | Plymouth, WI   May 2021–Jan 2022
Design, Engineering, and Manufacturing Solutions for OEMs

- Created and updated work instructions in collaboration with the people using the document.
- Designed and fabricated part fixtures for the paint line, increasing throughput and saving money.
- Welded fixtures to prevent parts from loading incorrectly, decreasing cycle time.
- Executed time studies that led to fixture updates and task reordering process improvements.
- Reduced costs by communicating effectively with paint masking supplier, investigating alternative masking, and monitoring inventory levels.

EDUCATION

University of Wisconsin-Springfield | BS Manufacturing Engineering | Springfield, WI   Dec 2023
Academic Honor Society, Spring 2021 | Chancellors Award 2019 & 2021 | Current GPA: 3.23/4.0

Material Removal & Forming Process • Engineering Graphics Solid Modeling • Controls and Instrumentation • Design of Jigs, Fixtures, and Tooling • CAM for Manufacturing Engineers • Lean Manufacturing Systems • Manufacturing Process Engineering • **Capstone: Manufacturing System Design**

Lake Technical College | Entry-Level Fire Fighter – Part A, Part B | Sheboygan, WI   Dec 2021

ADDITIONAL EXPERIENCE

Pump Installer & Well Driller's Assistant | ABC Well Drilling | Village, WI   May 2022–Jan 2023
Well Drilling, Pump, Water Testing for Residential, Commercial, and Agriculture

Volunteer Fire Fighter | Village Volunteer Fire Department | Village, WI   Spring 2021–Present
Department Services 158 Square Miles and Population ~10,000

General Laborer | DEF Corp. | Eau Claire, WI   Sep 2020–Apr 2021
Manufacturer Reflective Sheeting, Specialty Fibers & Composites, Ceramic Wire, Personal Care Products

Farm Hand | Custom Heifers Farm | Village, WI   Jun 2015–Sep 2020
"We raise them, you milk them"—Raising and Breeding ~350 Holstein Heifers

Teresa Hutton, CPRW | Best Resume Forward | bestresumeforward.com
Major: Manufacturing Engineering | **Goal:** Engineering role in a manufacturing environment
Notable: In addition to solid engineering experience gained through internships and on-campus activities, this resume showcases other experience that is interesting and demonstrates a strong work ethic.

DARCY VILLAR

Los Angeles, CA 90001 | 888-555-1212 | Email | LinkedIn

TARGET: PRODUCTION LEAD | TRAINING LEAD
Leadership & Training ➤ Performance Improvement
Drive High Quality Production Through Leadership & Training

- ☑ **Selected as an acting team lead** of 15 employees less than 6 months after employment. Lead team stretches, train new employees, perform offline and rework.
- ☑ **Create and execute daily action plans** that consider production team's strengths, weaknesses, and goals.
- ☑ **Facilitate hands-on training and instruction** in one-on-one, group, and classroom environments.

TRAINING:	Training Facilitation, Coaching, Interpersonal Communication Skills, Group Presentation Skills, Hands-On Training, Classroom Management, MS Suite (Outlook, Word, Excel & PowerPoint)
PRODUCTION:	5S Standards, Team Oriented Leadership, Continuous Improvement, Safety, Quality, Productivity, Cost & Resource Management, Standard Operating Procedures, Performance Monitoring

PROFESSIONAL EXPERIENCE

Production Associate – Trainer | ELECTRIC CAR INC. | Los Angeles, CA   Feb 2022–Current

Perform as **Acting Lead** for Production Line that produces approximately 700 finished units per day.

Offline & Rework | Training | Planning & Organizing | Collaboration | Analysis | Attention to Detail

- ☑ ZERO missed days since hire in a production area that suffers from high absenteeism. Deliver consistent high-quality effort and collaboration. Selected to provide line leadership and training.
- ☑ Utilize initiative and leadership to organize team for daily optimal performance to goal. Stagger lunches, monitor performance, and adjust to fill gaps to keep the line moving.
- ☑ Actively monitor the 15-person team for equipment and line problems. Work quickly to assess and resolve problems or escalate for technical repair as needed.

Teaching Assistant | COMPTON CHILD CARE CENTER | Los Angeles, CA   Sep 2020–Jan 2022

Delivered instructional services including curriculum development, lesson planning, classroom management, and instruction for up to 22 students.

Hands-On & Classroom Facilitation | Presentation | Classroom Management | Curriculum Development

- ☑ Created engaging hands-on lesson plans and science projects. Recognized by the Academic Director as "Most Creative" of 12-teacher group.
- ☑ Developed and facilitated engaging age-appropriate curriculum aligned with student learning objectives.

EDUCATION

Associate of Science (AS): Early Childhood Development, PIERCE COLLEGE, Los Angeles, CA — Dec 2022

DISCstyles LEADERSHIP ASSESSMENT

Strengths: Demand high performance from self and others. Excel at initiating activity and providing direction for the team. Have excellent group presentation skills. Bring a poised, confident, and engaging message to any audience. Set high goals, then work hard with people to achieve those goals.

Natural Behaviors and Traits: Assertive. Determined. Self-Reliant. Confident. Friendly. Generous. Poised. Eager. Flexible. Autonomous. Independent. Firm. Persuasive. Embraces New Concepts. Mover and Shaker. High Energy. Engaging.

Robert Rosales, NCRW, NCOPE, CDCC | EZ Resume Services | ezresumeservices.com
Major: Early Childhood Development | **Goal:** Training and leadership position in manufacturing
Notable: Darcy shifted from teaching to training and wants to stay in her new field—specifically in a manufacturing production environment. Her Headline and Summary make that goal crystal clear.

MARIA BELLINGHAM

CONTACT

Worcester, MA
413.456.7890
mbellingham@mail.com
linkedin.com/in/mbellingham

AREAS OF EXPERTISE

- Programming
- Web app development
- Data analytics
- Leadership
- Critical thinking
- Problem-solving
- Collaboration

EDUCATION

B.S., Computer Science • GPA 3.39
Longwood University, 2023

TOOLS & TECHNOLOGIES

- **Software:** LaTeX, Qt framework, React Native, Vim Editor, GIT, Expo
- **Languages:** C/C++, Python, HTML, JavaScript, Bash scripting, jQuery, SQL, CUDA
- **Programming tools:** GNU Debugger (GDB), Valgrind
- **Operating systems:** Linux/UNIX (Ubuntu, Debian, Arch Linux), Windows 7, 10

**SOFTWARE DEVELOPMENT
PROJECTS AVAILABLE AT:**
https://github.com/MBellingham

SOFTWARE ENGINEER

Recent graduate pairing 4 years of academic and independent C++ experience with an excellent work ethic and leadership skills. Course work included computer network security and cryptography. Successful in both independent and Agile team environments.

Experienced project leader, combining diligence in achieving goals with a demonstrated ability to mentor others.

MAJOR PROJECTS

Senior capstone project: Whiteboard for hand drawing/writing on screen
- Developed front-end in C++.
- Developed user stories.
- Applied Qt framework for user and network interface.
- Collaborated in Agile team environment.

Junior project: Majella—a women's fertility tracking and charting app
- Developed using JavaScript via React Native and Expo client.
- Created a multi-use share system.

PEER LEADERSHIP & ACTIVITIES

President, Assoc. of Computing Machinery Student Club   9/2022–5/2023
Longwood University
- Assisted faculty in the coordination and execution of annual activities.
- Led workshop on Vim Editor; assisted in development of Git workshop.
- Organized and led monthly video game nights and social events.

Vice President/Student Leader, Catholic Campus Ministry   8/2019–5/2023
Longwood University
- Coordinated events with clergy and arranged for speakers.
- Managed financial resources.
- Encouraged students and helped them build peer relationships.
- Planned and led campus-wide activities and programs.

EMPLOYMENT

Delivery Driver • *Domino's Pizza, Worcester, MA*   6/2020–8/2020
Kids Zone Attendant • *Polar Park, Worcester, MA*   Summers 2017–2019

Linda Bartone, CPRW | Cornerstone Resume Services | cornerstoneresumeservices.com
Major: Computer Science | **Goal:** Software engineer
Notable: The graphic and two-column format create a modern presentation, while projects and leadership activities demonstrate professional skills.

CRAIG DEVITO

303.226.3087 • messageme@gmail.com • Denver, CO 80213

STAFF FIRMWARE ENGINEER

Enthusiastic entry-level professional with software, firmware, and hardware engineering knowledge, including circuits, electronics, and embedded systems. Solve issues using completed coursework knowledge in firmware, operating systems programming, scrolling LEDs, FPGA functions, temperature measuring, debugging, and data transfer via Bluetooth. Offer basic understanding of Linux virtual machines and Windows Subsystem for Linux. Contribute to cross-functional teamwork and welcome diversity.

Courses	Technical Proficiency
Data Structures & Analysis	Embedded Systems
Linear Systems	C / C++ / C#
Programming	Assembly
Electronics Design/Microelectronics	MATLAB
Discrete Structures	System Verilog
Circuits & Circuit Design	Python / JavaScript
Embedded Software Engineering	Operating Systems / Real Time OS
Fundamentals of Computer Security	Security
Digital Systems	FPGA—*RTL /VHDL*
Operating Systems / Real Time	RISC V
FPGA Design	Debugging / Testing

EDUCATION & CERTIFICATIONS

Bachelor of Science, Electrical Engineering and Computer Engineering, University of Colorado, 2023
Worked full-time while attending school, building impeccable work ethic.

Microsoft Certified Professional (MCP), 2022
Nimsoft Certified Administrator, 2021
Lifeguard, CPR, and First Aid Certifications, Colorado Red Cross, 2015–Present

CLASS PROJECTS

System Architect, Medtronic Capstone Project, 2023
- Unified hardware and software by programming system component integrations, including autonomous robot, functioning servos, and customized Intel microcontroller. Created firmware to manipulate simple hardware functions while streamlining the user interface.
- Oversaw product integration between two project subsystems, resulting in multiproduct options.
- Contributed to outcomes, working with 12 team members to ensure a complete project design.

LKM and Linux Device Drivers, Operating Systems, Fall 2022
- Revealed hardware and software alignment by creating a character device driver, using system calls, and creating loadable kernel modules in Linux.
- Designed thread-safe application code in adherence to schedule and project requirements.

Ruth Pankratz, MBA, MRW, NCRW, CDCS, CHJMC, CHCLC | Gabby Communications | gabbycommunications.com
Major: Electrical Engineering and Computer Engineering | **Goal:** Firmware engineer
Notable: Six class projects are detailed to show diversity of skills and ability to work with teams. Full-time employment during school is also included to demonstrate work ethic and leadership skills.

CRAIG DEVITO

303.226.3087 • messageme@gmail.com • Denver, CO 80213

CLASS PROJECTS (CONTINUED)

Inverted Pendulum Game, Real Time Operating Systems, Fall 2022
- Developed a real-time physics game using an Inverted Pendulum model.
- Managed tasks using Semaphores and Mutexes.
- Used message queues for inter-process communication.

FPGA Design and Integration Projects, Fall 2022
- Enhanced product options by designing 1080p VGA driver displaying vertical lines and creating 720p VGA driver producing color images.

Computer Security Fundamentals, Spring 2022
- Identified and stopped network and scripting attacks using techniques such as executing man-in-the-middle solutions, implementing hash function with SQL injection, and performing buffer overflows to analyze x86 assembly in GDB.

Bluetooth Temperature Sensor, Embedded Systems, Fall 2021
- Expanded Bluetooth capabilities by collecting temperature sensor data using I2C and sending temperature data to phone via Bluetooth.

EXPERIENCE

City of Fort Collins–Mulberry Pool, Fort Collins, CO   2017–2022
FULL-TIME LIFEGUARD (2020–2022)
Responsible for daily indoor pool operations and safety for 50+ daily visitors. Maintained constant pool area watch, enforced rules, and kept pool and pool are clean. Protected swimmers, managed risks, provided emergency procedures, and defused tense situations. Maintained pool chemical readings and records. Completed daily reports.
- Ensured swimmer safety. Remained calm and responded quickly while under pressure to complete five saves.
- Gained leadership skills teaching 10+ staff swim safety and pool process lessons.

SEASONAL PARK WORKER (2017–2020)
Contributed to safe and clean public spaces and parks. Achieved daily goals and participated in team efforts. Developed strong verbal and written communication and interpersonal skills.
- Conducted daily park safety inspections, including maintenance tasks, reporting, and trash removal.
- Managed 15+ customer service inquires daily by listening to needs and providing solutions.
- Served as team lead in mentoring, coaching, and training 17 seasonal staff.

Frank L. Weston

Fairfax, VA 22030 | 703-555-8876 | frankweston@gmail.com | linkedin.com/in/frankweston

Entry-level Information Security/Cybersecurity Professional

- Highly self-motivated; recently attained **associate of applied science degree in cybersecurity**; currently pursuing **CompTIA A+ certification.**

- Exceptional work ethic (20+ years with one company), characterized by impeccable record of safety and attendance.

- Excellent listener with knack for communicating clearly and concisely with managers/supervisors, business customers, and fellow team members.

- Keen planning, prioritizing, and time management skills, working independently as well as contributing to larger team goals.

- Systematic, deliberate, and persistent in approaching a job; maintain stable and predictable pace in completing complex or specialized projects.

Education, Projects & Certifications

A.A.S. Cybersecurity, Laurel Ridge Community College | May 2023
- Phi Theta Kappa Honor Society Inductee; G.P.A. 3.5

Special Projects

- **Hands-on training, Johns Hopkins University (JHU):** Selected among student peers to participate in program sponsored by National Science Foundation, assisting with research conducted by students and faculty at Johns Hopkins University Information Security Institute.

- **Participant, National Cyber League (NCL) competition:** Applied expertise in password cracking, collaborating with team that placed in top 10 among community colleges across Virginia.

- **Information Technology Intern:** Patriot Federal Credit Union, Ashburn, VA

Certifications

- **CompTIA A+,** CompTIA CertMaster
- **Advanced Network Security**

Technical Competencies
Cloud Computing
UNIX/Linux Scripting
Ethical Hacking Fundamentals
Tactical Perimeter Defense
Advanced TCP/IP Concepts
Windows/Mac OS
IPsec/VPN Design
Intrusion Detection/Prevention
IT Ethics
Penetration Testing
Computer Forensics

Tools
Wireshark, John the Ripper, Aircrack-ng, RainbowCrack, Cain & Abel, VMWare

Employment

SEALY, Middleburg, VA   *Truck Driver | 2000 to 2022*

Worked in team setting and independently, delivering products to regional customer base across 5 states. Managed multiple tasks and priorities. Trusted with daily handling of inventory valued at $150K–$300K.

- Nurtured cross-functional relationships, communicating regularly with shipping and receiving supervisors, store managers, scheduling and manufacturing managers, drivers, and dock workers.

- Served as primary liaison between customers and Sealy, assessing needs, troubleshooting service problems, and remaining diligent in finding solutions.

- Maintained computerized daily logs, records, and reports, which required learning and applying new technology through 4 major logistics systems upgrades.

- Spotted opportunity to achieve substantial operations cost savings and provided data that convinced management to invest in prepaid DOT fees, with annual ROI of ~$50,000.

Additional experience included supervising team of 10+ dock workers at Consolidated Freight for 2 years, while simultaneously maintaining employment at Sealy.

Norine Dagliano, NCRW, NCOPE | EKM Inspirations | ekminspirations.com
Major: Cybersecurity | **Goal:** Entry-level cybersecurity or information security job
Notable: Frank recently completed a degree enabling a career shift to cybersecurity—highlighted with a bold graphic. Both education and work experience are detailed to show broad skills and accomplishments.

JASON KING

✉ 888 Meakin Drive, Windsor, Connecticut 06095
☎ 555.871.0902
✉ jasonking08@gmail.com
🌐 linkedin.com/in/jason-king08

IT | CYBERSECURITY PROFESSIONAL

Goal-driven and highly motivated professional, seeking a challenging IT/Cybersecurity role to utilize knowledge honed from education, certification, and hands-on training. Versatile and quick learner, able to understand different technical components required to manage interactive computing system, troubleshoot network systems, and implement necessary security protocols against cyberattacks. Accustomed to applying new skills to meet organizational goals. Effective at multitasking, with dedication to accomplish tasks while ensuring strict compliance with standards.

CERTIFICATIONS

Coursework in Cybersecurity
Springboard

IT Fundamentals (ITF+) Certification
CompTIA

Coursework in Fundamentals of Networking, Computer Systems Networking, and Telecommunications
Porter and Chester Institute

COURSES

Unix Essential Training, 2022
Cybersecurity Foundations, 2022
Introduction to Ethical Hacking, 2022
Threat Modeling: Spoofing In Depth, 2022
LinkedIn

Technical Support Fundamentals, 2022
Coursera

Introduction to IoT, 2022
Introduction to Cybersecurity, 2021
Cisco Networking Academy

ADDITIONAL TRAINING

Hack The Box (HTB)
Online Cybersecurity Training Platform

TryHackMe (THM)
Cybersecurity Training

INE: Expert IT Training for Networking, Cybersecurity, and Cloud

Cybrary: Free Cybersecurity Training and Career Development

EDUCATION

B.S. in Information Technology/Computer Science (*Anticipated June 2023*)
Full Sail University, Winter Park, FL

Coursework toward Associate's Degree in Cybersecurity, 2021
ECPI University, Richmond, VA

CORE COMPETENCIES

✓ **Understanding** of fundamental components of detecting and responding to threats in a corporate environment, involving threat and vulnerability management, security monitoring, threat emulation, incident response and forensics, malware analysis, and reverse engineering.

✓ **Exposure** to the functions of common operating systems and software applications, as well as use of security and web browsing best practices.

✓ **Competence** in evading endpoint protection and bypassing common security features using different advanced phishing techniques.

✓ **Familiarity** in utilizing cutting-edge technologies in making better decisions and improving organization security against threats and vulnerabilities.

✓ **Ability** to analyze and implement defense against real-world cyber threats, attacks, and other related incidents, along with skills in gathering threat actor intelligence and knowledge of emulating adversary TTPs.

TECHNICAL SKILLS

Operating Systems: Windows, Mac OS, and Linux
Microsoft Applications: MS Office Suite (Word, Excel, PowerPoint)

WORK HISTORY

Pipefitter ▪ AEROTEK, FARMINGTON, CT	2020–2021
Pipefitter ▪ ELECTRIC BOAT, GROTON, CT	2017–2020
OTR Truck Driver ▪ REYNOLDS TRANSPORTATION, WINDSOR, CT	2015–2017
Regional Truck Driver ▪ U.S. EXPRESS, WEST HARTFORD, CT	2012–2015

Michelle King | Resume Professional Writers | resumeprofessionalwriters.com
Major: Information Technology/Computer Science | **Goal:** IT/cybersecurity
Notable: The Core Competency list delves deeply into how skills are used. Extensive self-education (in addition to formal education) in IT and cybersecurity is also detailed.

Kayley J. Dumont

908-321-2341 | kayleydumont@gmail.com

- Target -
HELP DESK TECHNICIAN / DESKTOP SUPPORT TECHNICIAN

Self-driven **Computer Networks & Cybersecurity** graduate trained and experienced in:
- Computer Repair and Troubleshooting; Printer Repair and Troubleshooting; Customer Service
- Cloud Technologies, Microsoft Azure, AWS, Microsoft Office Suite (Word, Excel, PowerPoint)

TECHNICAL EXPERIENCE

REPAIR TECHNICIAN
Lightning Support, Bridgewater, New Jersey   2022–Present
- Use troubleshooting skills to repair computer hardware, software, and electronics brought in by customers.
- Entrusted with the business key due to reliability, consistent quality performance, and excellent customer service.
- Provide input on the business' operations strategy in an effort to increase sales.

COMPUTER INSTALLATION TECHNICIAN
Corporate Consultants, Somerville, New Jersey   2020–2022
- Supported a large biopharma client by collaborating with team to install 180 monitors and docking stations daily.
- Garnered positive client feedback while providing effective post-installation customer support.
- Selected to assume temporary lead role during a Covid-19 scare; managed supervisor's workload while connecting and disconnecting computer stations and performing quality checks on workstations.
- Mentored new staff while serving as a calm, dependable, and conscientious subject matter expert (SME) and source of support.

PRINTER TECHNICIAN
Newton Printers, Woodbridge, New Jersey   2019–2020
- Demonstrated flexibility and adaptability while diagnosing and repairing 75 printing kiosks across three campuses of Middlesex County College on an on-call basis.
- Interacted with library staff, digital learning center staff, and the director of auxiliary business while troubleshooting computer and printer problems and fulfilling service requests.
- Mitigated future technical issues by training clients on basic printer kiosk maintenance.
- Inventoried critical printer supplies to ensure a seamless operation for campus' staff, faculty, and students.

COMPUTER TECHNICIAN
The Computer Lab, Old Bridge, New Jersey   2018–2019
- Diagnosed, repaired, and refurbished approximately 300 desktop and laptop computers brought in by low-income families, veterans, and senior citizens.
- Trained and mentored 10 new volunteers to complete the desktop and laptop refurbishing process independently, inspiring one volunteer to enter into the field of IT.

TECHNICAL EDUCATION

Rutgers University, New Brunswick, New Jersey
Bachelor of Science, Computer Networks & Cybersecurity, May 2023

Middlesex County College, Edison, New Jersey
Associate of Applied Science, Cybersecurity, May 2021

Erika Harrigan, CPRW, PCC | LWJ Coaching & Consulting, LLC | lwjcc.com
Major: Computer Networks and Cybersecurity | **Goal:** Help desk technician
Notable: Kayley's resume emphasizes both soft skills and technical training and proficiency. Because she has significant relevant experience, it is positioned above her Education.

James Lee

(971) 770 – 1460 ● j.lee@mail.com ● LinkedIn ● GitHub

TARGET: Software Development Engineer – Backend Services & Cloud Computing

Designing and deploying scalable, next-generation cloud solutions that meet growing business infrastructure and service needs

Software Development Engineer offering a **BS in computer science** and 2 years of internship and project experience in business and academic settings. Proven experience leading and collaborating with software development teams in system-level programming, backend web service development, AI/ML, and application development projects. Regarded for approachability, problem-solving, and communication skills to meet project deadlines.

IT Skills: Python, Java, C#, C++, Google Cloud, MySQL, MongoDB, Nginx, Docker, React JS, JavaScript, HTML, PHP, Linux/Windows Operating Systems, and software development frameworks (Spring, Flask, .NET)

Education

Bachelor of Science (BS), Computer Science, PACIFIC LUTHERAN UNIVERSITY, Tacoma, WA   2023
Activities: Men's Tennis Team (2020 – 2022), *Voted Team Captain (2021 – 2022)*

Key Skills & Attributes

Cloud Computing (Google Cloud)	Technical Leadership & Teamwork	Object-Oriented Programming (OOP)
Computer Science & DevOps Automation	Written & Oral Communication	Software Development Lifecycles (SDLC)
Networking & Distributed Systems	Root Cause Analysis & Problem Solving	Data Structures & AI/ML Algorithms
Backend Services & Load Balancing	Time Management & Organization	Relational Database Systems

Professional and Project Experience

Software Engineer ● Customerville, Valencia, Spain   Jan 2023 – May 2023

Hired by the CTO to intern and work with developer teams on rebuilding outdated applications and rewriting, reviewing, and modernizing code for compatibility with MongoDB and other database technologies.

- Overhauled an outdated service application using C# and wrote a plugin to convert existing XML data files to JSON objects. This allowed older file and metadata storage in MongoDB and software implementation without code refactoring.

Final Senior Capstone Project   Sep 2022 – May 2023

Led a 4-member team on an AI/ML application and web development project that used natural language processing and sediment analysis to evaluate stock value increases or decreases through headline data with XGBoost. Built out the website backend, hosted on Google Cloud; used docker as a container and Nginx as a reverse proxy and load balancer in a MySQL environment.

Student-Tutor Study Groups, Database Class   Feb 2022 – May 2022

Managed and assisted 5 students, with varying computer science skills, in creating a dynamic web application in Java and JSP/HTML, hosted on a MariaDB SQL server, which allowed tutors to create online student study groups for sign-up and attendance.

Go Game, Object & Design Class   Feb 2021 – May 2021

Worked in a 4-member team on a web-based class project and used Java, JavaScript, HTML, Grizzly (HTTP server), Jax-RS programming, frontend/backend servers, and frameworks to design and implement numerous go-style games. Built an application hosted on the department server called Connect Six, where 2 players place 6 black and white pieces in a row in any direction.

Kate Williamson, MS, CPRW, CRS+ES, CRS+IT, CSBA | Scientech Resumes | scientechresumes.com
Major: Computer Science | **Goal:** Software development engineer
Notable: A detailed Experience/Projects section conveys how James applied IT skills and knowledge to real-world application development. His leadership and problem-solving abilities are also highlighted.

MIKELE LORIA

Brooklyn, NY 11201 | 718.330.7724 | mikele.loria@gmail.com | linkedin.com/mikele-loria-IT

PROFILE

Entry-level Information Technology specialist proficient in databases, programming, and software. Ability to leverage coursework in business administration to provide effective and efficient business solutions. Experience in manufacturing and social services industries developed through competitive internships.

EDUCATION

LONG ISLAND UNIVERSITY, Brooklyn, NY
Bachelor of Business Administration, Computer Information Systems   May 2023

HONORS: Dean's List, Spring 2021–Spring 2023 | Beta Gamma Sigma, Fall 2020 | GPA: 3.8

Related Coursework: Web Programming, Business Analytics, Project Management, Systems Analysis, Data Management & Business Intelligence, Programming Theory & Application

TECHNICAL SKILLS

SAP, SCADA Systems, C#, MySQL, HTML, Java, PHP files, Microsoft Office (Word, Excel, PowerPoint)

INTERNSHIP EXPERIENCE

ADVANCED AIRFOIL COMPONENTS (Manufacturer of Parts for Gas Turbine Engines), Gibsonton, FL
Information Technology Intern, Summer 2022

- Used Tableau and Excel to analyze employee data and put forth recommendations on workflow efficiencies; analyzed employee data so managers could develop performance improvement plans accordingly.
- Created reports using proprietary software, Mercury. Built reports by running macros in Excel and then uploading reports to network drive multiple times a day; saved Manager time to work on other projects.
- Improved workflow by automating contract review signature process through project management software.

BEKAERT CORP. INTERNATIONAL (Manufacturer of Steel Wire and Coatings), Shelbyville, KY
SAP/Supply Chain Intern, Summer 2020

- Identified obsolete/excess diamond dye stock using SAP; saved company more than $14K by canceling outstanding orders.
- Redistributed an excess of $42K worth of excess diamond dyes to alternate processes.
- Calculated and adjusted MRP reorder points for all types of dyes to optimize working capital.
- Ascertained 240 dyes below the minimum sizes used that were recut to save an additional $8K+.

MIDWEST HEALTH SERVICES (Social Service Provider), Massillon, OH
Information Technology Intern, Summer 2019

- Performed setup, troubleshooting, and software configuration of desktops, laptops, and iPhones, while demonstrating strong communication skills to assist with identifying technology issues and repairing printers and copiers.
- Collaborated with other employees on large-scale projects, including installing cables and network wiring in a new building, as well as setting up and configuring new computers and copiers in new location.
- Developed documentation and technical writing skills by mapping out where each piece of technology within the company was located.

ADDITIONAL EMPLOYMENT

Peter Luger Steakhouse, Brooklyn, NY
Hostess & Server, Part time during school years and summers 2018, 2021

- Developed ability to work in a fast-paced world-famous restaurant.

Carolyn Kleiman, CPRW | Kleiman Careers | carolyn.kleimancareers@yahoo.com
Major: Computer Information Systems | **Goal:** IT role with a large company
Notable: Valuable internship experience takes up the bulk of this resume and in every role shows how she contributed. Both the Education and Technical Skills sections include critical keywords.

K E N Y A   D E A N

630-694-3024 | Aurora, IL 60506 | kenya@gmail.com | LinkedIn

SOFTWARE DEVELOPMENT ENGINEER

Upcoming 2023 Graduate fiercely focused on fueling progress by using **tech for good** to create a more equitable future. Passionate about collaborating cross-functionally & cross-culturally to innovate inclusive & disruptive technology.

EDUCATION

BS, Computer Science | University of Aurora | expected May 2023
3.7 GPA | 6X Dean's List | 4X Scholarship Recipient

TECHNICAL SKILLS

Software Development: C, C#, Python, Java, JavaScript, Go, Object-Oriented Programming (OOP)
Operating Systems: Windows, Mac OS, Linux

AWARDS

Winner | 2022 Houston Hackathon
Won 1st place—out of ~70 participants—by building mobile app to drive equity in underserved communities

PROFESSIONAL EXPERIENCE

Software Development Engineer | University of Aurora   **May 2022–August 2022**

- Tapped to join exclusive, government-funded project to build first-of-its-kind app impacting 10K military members.
- Liaised with cross-functional stakeholders to gather requirements, strategize scope, and provide weekly updates.
- Developed back-end and front-end of software application leveraging Java and JavaScript in Agile methodology.
- Built and delivered fully functioning feature within 2 months (33% ahead of deadline).

TESTIMONIALS

*"Kenya is **the best of the best**. She **delivered a challenging software feature within 2 months**—far ahead of the 3-month deadline—and spent the remainder of her time supporting her peers in their projects. She **excels in Java development** and is known for being a collaborative consensus-builder."*

- *Maggie Jacobs, Technical Director at the University of Aurora*

*"Kenya is a **leader among her peers** and thrives at **influencing with or without authority**. In addition to her top-notch technical skills, Kenya has a magnetic personality and an unmatched work ethic. She was a **life saver in our software development project**."*

- *Janet Wright, Technical Manager at the University of Aurora*

Chelsey Opare-Addo | Not Your Mother's Resume | notyourmothersresume.com
Major: Computer Science | **Goal:** Software developer
Notable: This resume is a quick read packed with pertinent information. Testimonials at the bottom provide exceptional third-party endorsement of the candidate.

ANDREW GARCIA

(555) 577-3172 ◆ garcia@abcmail.com
linkedin.com/in/andrewgarcia ◆ Los Angeles, CA 25251

HELP DESK SUPPORT TECHNICIAN

Resourceful, solution-driven IT professional adept at mastering technology tools, resolving the root cause of technical issues, and cultivating relationships to sustain business continuity, IT security, and client satisfaction.

Skills, Competencies & Relevant Coursework

Hardware & Software Desktop Support • Diagnosis & Troubleshooting • Physical & Virtual Operating Systems
Malware Security • Network Protocols • Scrum Methodology • Active Listening • De-escalation • Windows & Linux
Active Directory • Google Suite • Zoom & MS Teams • MS Excel • Adobe Creative Cloud • Web Ex • Spanish Fluency

PROFESSIONAL EXPERIENCE

LINKEDIN CORPORATION (A SUBSIDIARY OF MICROSOFT CORP) – *New York, NY*

Help Desk Support Technician Intern   *Jan 2023–Jun 2023*

Ensured end-user productivity and system security by providing first level IT support for 10,000+ employees throughout the U.S. for the world's largest professional social network of 740M members across 200 countries.

- Reduced ticket resolution time 10% through efficient Service Now request classification, assignment, and tracking.
- Troubleshot Slack, Google, and Adobe apps, fielding 15+ client phone inquiries and 25+ email requests per day.
- Maintained 100% accuracy utilizing Active Directory to process shared permissions for distribution and security.
- Reduced malware impacts by promptly running Symantec End Point Protection and ADW cleaner scans.

GAP, INC. – *New York, NY*

Customer Service Associate   *Jan 2022–Jun 2022*

Promoted in 5 months to work in flagship store of apparel retailer due to technical and communication skills.

- Ensured customer satisfaction by processing 100+ returns per day and assisting customers with exchanges.
- Reduced inventory loss 5% by reporting previously undetected shoplifting attempts in fitting rooms.

Retail Sales Cashier   *Aug 2021–Dec 2021*

Processed 200+ daily transactions on point-of-sale system and tracked stock replenishment with mobile inventory app.

- Ranked #1 of 12 cashiers for selling the most credit card applications for 3 consecutive months.
- Trained 2 new cashiers in point-of-sale system and stock room inventory control and tracking processes.

SHAKE SHACK – *New York, NY*

Host Cashier   *2019–2021*

Served hundreds of customers per day, 40 hours per week. Greeted patrons, processed orders, collected payment, and served meals in a fast-paced environment for one of the most rapidly growing food chains in the U.S.

- Provided service to 500+ guests per day, ensuring order accuracy, food safety, and timeliness.
- Selected to cross-train on each station due to demonstrated ability to pitch in, quickly learn, and cover all roles.

EDUCATION AND RECOGNITION

College-Level Business Education Program – Information Technology Concentration – YEARUP – 2022–2023
Selected for competitive national program of 6-months of intensive business training and 6-month internship.
Relevant Coursework: Computer Applications, Project Management, MS Excel, Communications, Customer Service
Awards: Earned **YearUp Student of the Month Award** for Training Colleagues in New Technology Tools

Julie Wyckoff, MEd, Certified Career Transition Coach, YouMap Coach | Custom Career Solutions | customcareersolutions.com
Major: Information Technology | **Goal:** Help desk support role
Notable: Andrew completed a nontraditional educational program, YearUp, that included a valuable internship with LinkedIn. His prior experience demonstrates exceptional workplace skills.

Douglas Cornwall

Chicago, IL 60601 | doug.cornwall@mail.com | 312-222-5412 | LinkedIn

Innovative Marketing and Project Management Professional

- Demonstrated strength in accurately interpreting and conveying client intentions to achieve exceptional results.
- Reputation as a quick study, learning and mastering new technology and skills to make contribution to organizations.
- Solid work ethic complemented by employing an "above-and-beyond" approach to every assignment and project.

Advertising & Digital Marketing | Project Management | Content Creation | Team Leadership
Social Media Marketing | Brand & Marketing Strategy | Photography

Education

NORTHWESTERN UNIVERSITY | Evanston, IL
Bachelor of Science Degree (2023)
Major: Marketing | Minor: English

Course Highlights
Advertising, Sports Marketing, International Marketing, Consumer Behavior, News Writing, Social Media, Digital Journalism, Music Industry

Technology
SPSS, Social Media (Instagram, Twitter, Facebook), WordPress, Microsoft Office (PowerPoint, Excel, Word), Adobe Lightroom, Sony a7R II camera, ABBYY FlexiCapture

Select Marketing Projects

- **GLOBAL MARKETING RESEARCH PROJECT:** Led team that analyzed market and competition for new Indian soap launch in Egypt and created comprehensive marketing plan, distribution and pricing strategy, and multipronged promotional tactics.

- **SOUTH SIDE DELI:** Collaborated with Chicago-area business to develop expanded social media presence on Instagram/Twitter/Facebook to increase local patronage among university students in the vicinity.

- **JACK'S:** Designed radio and print advertising that boosted traffic and attracted more customers for Evanston restaurant/bar.

Internship Experience

Intern | THE AKERS GROUP | Chicago, IL   **Jan–May 2023**

Secured internship providing exposure to numerous real estate management transactions. Shadowed company president and management staff on corporate property visits. A privately owned real estate development and private equity organization, The Akers Group specializes in commercial and industrial acquisitions.

- Crafted the firm's first digital marketing strategy and detailed plan for execution (to launch Fall 2023).
- Organized real estate documents for Vice President, Facilities; proofed transactions in Excel spreadsheets.
- Attended weekly President's meetings discussing companywide project status.

Intern | SOUTH BEND CUBS | South Bend, IN   **Mar–Sep 2022**

Proactively targeted and created own internship with the High-A affiliate of the Chicago Cubs.

- Shadowed Assistant General Manager and other staff, gaining experience in front-office operations.
- Assisted Marketing Manager by writing ad copy, designing flyers, and brainstorming promotional ideas.

Additional Work Experience

Accounts Payable Clerk | MIDWEST FINANCIAL SERVICES | Chicago, IL   **Summer 2022**

- Captured invoice data using ABBYY FlexiCapture, then organized and recorded data using Excel.
- Tested in top percentage of employees on mandated Excel test—scored a full 10 points above average.

Front End Supervisor | DEAL$ DISCOUNT STORES | Chicago, IL   **Summer 2021**

- Managed 5 cashiers, delegated work assignments, and handled a broad range of customer service issues.
- Developed problem-solving skills and worked effectively to defuse angry customer situations.

Activities

Activity Chair, Northwestern Marketing Club | **Captain,** Club Volleyball | **Volunteer,** Greater Chicago Food Bank

Jan Melnik, MA, MRW, CCM, CPRW | Absolute Advantage | janmelnik.com
Major: Marketing | **Goal:** Entry-level marketing
Notable: Because Douglas is not targeting a specific industry, his various projects, internships, and employment are given equal weight to show the diversity of his background—and his contributions in every role.

Marta D'Sousa

415-445-1909 | marta.dsousa@gmail.com

Digital Marketing • Social Media Management • Multimedia Content

- **Analytical and insightful marketing professional** with experience developing marketing strategies and content, managing social media accounts, and collaborating with team members on market analysis and product development.
- **Effective communicator,** personable and comfortable interacting with prospects, customers, and colleagues.
- **Diligent, hard working, and highly productive** whether working on site or remotely.

Skills and Tools
MS Excel | MS Office | Google Suite
Social Media Platforms (TikTok, Instagram, Facebook, Twitter) | SPSS Statistical Software | Video Editing

Education

BS Marketing | SANTA CLARA UNIVERSITY, LEAVEY SCHOOL OF BUSINESS   Santa Clara, CA | 2023

Business & Technology Emphasis | Global Theme

- *Global Theme Capstone Project:* Analyzed the effect of a global economic force—climate change and sustainability—on a market sector (transportation) and a specific company (Tesla). Conducted deep-dive research that revealed Tesla's primary sectors are technology and energy rather than transportation. Co-presented findings with partner; earned A grade for both analysis and presentation.
- *New Product Development:* Brainstormed with team members to identify a new high-potential product for Coca-Cola and develop start-up and marketing strategies to bring idea from concept to market introduction. Earned grade of A.
- *Marketing Case Analyses:* Reviewed numerous Harvard case studies, examined different market factors, and recommended marketing and advertising strategies that would be most effective for reaching stated business goals.

Professional Experience

Social Media Manager | SANTA CLARA UNIVERSITY WOMEN'S LACROSSE CLUB   Aug 2021–May 2023

Built visibility and engagement for club team that went on to win its league championship.

- Implemented social media best practices: Followed influencers, maintained updated stats, and posted videos, stories, and game announcements.
- Introduced weekly "Throwback Thursday" event that boosted engagement and merchandise sales with alumni.
- Increased Instagram following from less than 100 to 700+ in less than 2 years.

Marketing & Sales Intern | WEST & McCARTHY LAW GROUP   Remote | Jun 2022–Nov 2022

Brought on board as first intern and sole dedicated marketing/sales person for specialized bankruptcy law firm.

- Analyzed lead sources, creating an Excel spreadsheet to calculate ROI. Recommended shifts in marketing and advertising outreach to focus on most valuable sources.
- Created the firm's Instagram account and managed all social media content and marketing.
- Generated an average of $20K weekly revenue, closing 50%–60% of sales calls.

Additional Experience

Café Staff | TOWN FARE CAFÉ AT OAKLAND MUSEUM OF CALIFORNIA   Oakland, CA | Jun 2021–Aug 2021

- Interacted with and assisted more than 50 customers each day. Handled money and processed card transactions.

Senior Counselor | YMCA OF SAN FRANCISCO SUMMER CAMP   San Francisco, CA | May 2020–Aug 2020

- Supervised groups of 20 campers. Led activities and kept campers on schedule. Worked with other counselors to keep campers safe and resolve any conflicts.

Louise Kursmark, MRW, CPRW, JCTC, CEIP, CCM | Best Impression Career Services | louisekursmark.com
Major: Marketing | **Goal:** Digital marketing and social media management
Notable: An on-campus volunteer role and a remote internship provide ample evidence of Marta's professional skills. Relevant class projects are also highlighted.

SHERYL GRAYSON

202.456.7890 | sgrayson@gmail.com
https://www.linkedin.com/in/grayson-sheryl

VALUE PROSPECTUS PROFILE

Top-performing **FLOOR DIRECTOR** who brings to the table a solid understanding of what is required to produce live events. Multi-year experience with broadcast equipment/studio operations. Demonstrated ability to seek out unique content/talent that will enhance show impact while keeping quality of audience experience in mind.

SIGNATURE STRENGTHS

- **Clear focus on target audience,** bringing together different viewpoints and ideas into cohesive programs.
- **Strong visual style** related to video editing, motion graphics, video format standards, and live production.
- **Editorial/creative leadership,** building segments and developing storyline ideas from inception to production while ensuring content meets standards for both journalistic and production quality.

CORE COMPETENCIES

Video/Film Editing | Needs Assessments | Business-to-Business Relationship Management

PROFESSIONAL EXPERIENCE

FLOOR DIRECTOR (Non-paid) **| Fairfax Public Access (FPA) Television Station,** Fairfax, VA | Mar 2013–Present

Perform in multiple roles at FPA, an independent 501(c)(3) non-profit organization that provides residents of Fairfax County and the Washington Metropolitan area both training and tools to create non-commercial television and radio programming that expresses their viewpoints and perspectives at large. Station currently airs 2K hours of original programming annually.

- **Television Producer.** Coordinate action items for writers, other directors, and managers throughout production process. Research production topics utilizing all available informational sources. Review footage to ensure compliance with production and broadcast standards.
- **Camera Operator.** Operate stationary, track-mounted, or crane-mounted television cameras to record scenes for television broadcasts. Confer with other directors, sound/lighting technicians, electricians, and other crew members. Determine studio set, filming sequences, desired effects, camera movements, film stock, and audio/lighting requirements.
- **Technical Director.** Coordinate and schedule studio/editing facilities for producers and engineering/maintenance staff. Discuss filter options, lens choices, and visual effects with photography directors and video operators.
- **Audio Operator.** Monitor strength, clarity, and reliability of incoming and outgoing signals. Control audio equipment to regulate volume and sound quality during television broadcasts.
- **CG/Graphics Operator.** Operate studio graphics software/components.
- **Lighting Equipment Operator.** Create visual lighting effects using color filters, dimmer boards, computerized effects, and switches.
- **Set Designer.** Direct the building of sets that conform to design, budget, and schedule requirements. Establish production style, tone, and atmosphere. Collaborate with lighting and electrical crew on construction details.

EDUCATION AND PROFESSIONAL DEVELOPMENT

AFA Cinema | Northern VA Community College, Alexandria, VA **|** 2023

Additional Training: Location Lighting Workshop | Interview Workshop | Studio Lighting Workshop | Social Media Workshop | TV-IOI Studio | Producer Workshop | Studio C (Tricaster) | Technical Directing | Field Camera Package | JVC Seminar Workshop | Adobe Premiere Pro Edit | Adobe Premiere Pro Level 2 | CG Workshop | Audio for TV | On-Camera Talent | Make-Up for TV | Studio Camera | Directing | Production Assistant | Audacity Audio Editing

INDUSTRY AFFILIATIONS/CERTIFICATIONS

Arlington Independent Media, **Since 2021** | Television, Internet & Video Association of DC (TIVA-DC), **Since 2017**
Women in Film & Video of Washington, DC (WIFV), **Since 2015** | Fairfax Public Access, **Since 2013**

VTC/SOFTWARE/HARDWARE PLATFORMS

Video Production Hardware: JVC/Canon/SONY/MEVO 4K Streaming Cameras | Mackie Audio Mixer |
DataVideo Switcher | Newtek Tricaster | Shure/CountryMan/Audio-Technica Mics

Software: MS Office Professional 2013 | Windows 10 Professional | Adobe Premiere Pro CC |
Cisco WebEx/Skype/Google Hangouts | Audacity | Avid Deko Teleprompter | Studio Binder | Celtx

Phyllis G. Houston | The Re$ume Xpert | rezxprt.com
Major: Cinema | **Goal:** Television director
Notable: Seeking to transition from long-time volunteer to a paid position in TV production, Sheryl showcased her extensive experience along with her recent degree.

GRACE SWIFT

(922) 555-4396 ◆ gracemswift@gmail.com ◆ www.linkedin.com/in/graceswift/ ◆ Reynolds, PA 42596

MULTIMEDIA PRODUCER & SOCIAL MEDIA COORDINATOR

Creative, organized, and adaptable assistant producer and social media manager with a passion for storytelling and experience producing, directing, writing, and promoting 30+ student films from development through distribution.

Production Development & Execution ● Social Media Marketing ● Procurement & Logistics ● Adobe Creative Cloud
Videography ● Photography ● Screenwriting & Editing ● Event Coordination ● Staffing & Scheduling ● Microsoft Office

EDUCATION

Dual Bachelor of Arts (BA) in Media Studies and TV/Film | VILLANOVA UNIVERSITY – *Philadelphia, PA* **| 2023**
Dean's List ● TV/Film Department Ambassador ● National Society of Leadership and Success Member (NSLS)

PROFESSIONAL EXPERIENCE

ACT 1 DIVISION OF PERFORMING ARTS – *Philadelphia, PA*
<u>**Social Media Intern, Division of Performing Arts & TV/Film Department**</u>　　　**Aug 2022–Present**
Plan and execute social media marketing campaigns to increase visibility and participation across the 'Nova community.
- Grow following and engagement by writing relevant copy customized for Instagram, Facebook, TikTok, and Snapchat.
- Promote programs by creating graphics and videos using Photoshop, Illustrator, Premiere, Lightroom, and Canva.
- Serve as Head of Social Media Team for Villanova University Film Festival, collaborating with marketing and digital media teams to capitalize on social media trends, create compelling videos, and craft promotional content.

CAREER DEVELOPMENT CENTER, VILLANOVA UNIVERSITY – *Philadelphia, PA*
<u>**Career Ambassador**</u>　　　**Aug 2022–Present**
Develop and implement career center events, podcasts, and blogs and provide one-on-one career coaching to students.
- Curate and deliver career curriculum and workshops to address the unique needs of performing arts students.
- Produce and host "Career Chat" podcast, including guest recruitment, research, and promotional content creation.
- Write for *Seeking Success* blog and provide university students with career resources and resume review.

VILLANOVA UNIVERSITY TELEVISION STUDIO – *Center Valley, PA*
<u>**Station Manager**</u>　　　**Aug 2021–Present**
Promoted to coordinate staffing, training, scheduling, equipment, and procedures for television studio. Lead team orientation and training, create weekly schedule, and maintain equipment and COVID safety protocols.

<u>**Studio Technician**</u>　　　**Aug 2020–May 2021**
Assisted TV/Film students with in-studio productions and monitored and repaired equipment.

PCM PRODUCTIONS – *Denver, CO | Orlando, FL | Philadelphia, PA*
<u>**Production Assistant, The Food Exchange National Conference**</u>　　　**Jul 2017, 2018, 2019, 2021**
Facilitated backstage logistics for 3-day national corporate conference, engaging 300+ attendees, executives, and actors in a scripted, live multimedia event. Filmed and edited executive speeches for 2021 virtual event.

CONRAD EVENTS, LLC. – *Philadelphia, PA*
<u>**Event Production Team Member, Philly Festival of Books**</u>　　　**Oct 2018, 2019**
Set up community events and escorted high-profile authors across 7 venues for 2-day annual book festival.

Julie Wyckoff, MEd, Certified Career Transition Coach, YouMap Coach | Custom Career Solutions | customcareersolutions.com
Major: Media Studies and TV/Film | **Goal:** Multimedia producer / social media coordinator
Notable: Page 1 can serve as a standalone resume providing an overview of skills and experience; or it can be accompanied by page 2, which details specific film projects during Grace's years at university.

GRACE SWIFT ◆ (922) 555-4396 ◆ gracemswift@gmail.com ◆ www.linkedin.com/in/graceswift/

ACADEMIC FILM PROJECTS

ASSISTANT PRODUCER & SOCIAL MEDIA MANAGER – "The Wedding" – 2023

Assisted Producer with all production needs including budget, schedule, location, transportation, casting, and crewing.

- Created and executed content plan for Facebook and Instagram to promote film, build following, and direct donors to Indiegogo page, resulting in the film exceeding fundraising goal by 18%.
- Coordinated daily production reporting, onsite logistics, and 25 cast and crew to complete project under budget.
- Acted as right hand to producer over 6-month process from pre- through postproduction.

DIRECTOR – "Summer" – 2023 – Awarded *Best Director* and *Best Performance* by industry adjudicator Jennifer Sutton

Directed film for 48-Hour Screendance Festival.

- Collaborated with choreographer to convey sensitive theme of sexual assault.
- Partnered with cinematographer to set up shots keeping match-cut editing in mind across 6 different dancers.
- Customized choreography to fit each unique space and ensure safety during partner work.

DIRECTOR & WRITER – "He Loves Me" – 2023

Developed and executed cinematic vision and created storyboards on tight budget to meet submission deadline.

- Collaborated with cinematographer, production designer, and gaffer to design and execute overall tone of the film.
- Oversaw post-production editing, coloring, and sound design to ensure consistency throughout the film.

PRODUCER – "The Open Door" – 2023

Planned and executed 40-minute dramatic film over 12-month period.

- Secured contracted locations and ensured owners' requests were met.
- Trained new producers on proper practices, recruited crew members, and organized casting process.
- Ensured physical and COVID safety of 20-person crew and 10-person cast including safety during fight choreography.

PRODUCER & 1ST ASSISTANT DIRECTOR – "Alice's Revenge" – 2022

Scheduled and organized entire filmmaking process to meet submission deadline under budget.

- Directed 15 extras to create realistic funeral atmosphere.
- Secured locations and scheduled filming days to ensure smooth and efficient filming process.

1ST ASSISTANT DIRECTOR – "Runaway" – 2022

Directed 20+ extras in 3-minute one-shot film.

- Ensured fight choreography was executed appropriately to maintain both physical safety and COVID protocols.
- Secured location and ensured a quiet space for cast and crew during takes.

PRODUCER – "Forever Young" – 2022

Organized preproduction process and shooting schedules for 20-minute dramatic short film.

- Recruited crew and cast and ensured film finished under budget and on time.

DIRECTOR & CO-WRITER – "Lilies for Kyle" – 2021 – Lead nominated for "Best Actress" at PIMA Filmmaker Showcase

Wrote script and executed creative vision as Director in collaboration with cast and crew.

- Recruited and placed crew and organized casting process.
- Oversaw production design and cinematography.

PRODUCER & 1ST ASSISTANT DIRECTOR – "The Delivery" – 2021

Scheduled, organized, budgeted, and recruited for one-shot film with stunts and fight choreography.

SOCIAL MEDIA MANAGER – "Just for You" – 2021

Conducted on set interviews with cast and crew to promote film and updated donors via Instagram and Facebook.

JANE A. DERRY

Savannah, GA 99999 | 999.999.9999 | janeaderry@gmail.com
LinkedIn | janeaderry.com | behance.net/janeaderry

ANIMATION — MOTION DESIGN — GRAPHIC DESIGN

Passionate Animator — Leveraging intrinsic desire to go beyond the core curriculum and learn new industry skills.

Adaptable Team Player — Positive and open-minded with the ability to synthesize feedback and make appropriate adjustments on projects while supporting and advocating for team members.

> ➢ **Won 1ˢᵗ place** in the 2022 Vans Custom Culture competition at Savannah College of Art & Design.
> ➢ **Awarded 2ⁿᵈ place** for contemporary graphic design at the 2021 Pratt Institute Art Show.

COMPETENCIES

Motion Graphics | Project Management | Cross-Functional Collaboration | Relationship Management | Adaptation | Design Fundamentals | New Project Ideation | Storytelling | Exploration | Editing | 2D & 3D Animation | Adobe Suite | After Effects | Illustrator | Photoshop | Premiere Pro | Cinema 4D | Audition | InDesign | MS Office | Verbal and Written Communication

EDUCATION

Bachelor of Fine Arts (BFA) in Motion Design — *Savannah College of Art & Design* | Savannah, GA   2023
   GPA: 3.9 | Dean's Scholarship | Coursework: 2D Design and Animation, 3D Design and Animation, Drawing, Graphics

Associate of Fine Arts & Associate of Arts — *Glendale College* | Glendale, CA   2020
   GPA: 3.82 | Graduated with High Honors | George Henniker Fine Arts Scholarship

Animation Course —*Tokyo University of the Arts* | Tokyo, Japan   SUMMER 2020

PROFESSIONAL EXPERIENCE

ARTIST'S ASSISTANT | *ART BASEL MIAMI* | MIAMI, FL   2018
Assisted artist in crafting customized printing blocks/ink stamps for attendees at one-day art festival.
   • Collaborated with artist to produce artwork in real-time, interact with audience, and arrange the art show.
   • Learned new art style and taught the audience how to create the art themselves.

PUBLICATIONS

Erudite Literary and Art Journal — *Glendale College*   SPRING 2019
Contributed to journal design and collaborated with team of three to execute the book's development and production.

EXHIBITIONS

Vans Custom Culture Competition — *Savannah College of Art & Design* | Savannah, GA   2022
Pratt Institute Art Show — *School of Design Gallery* | New York, NY   2021
Annual Glendale College Student Art Show — *Glendale College* | Glendale, CA   2019 & 2020
"Like and Share" Artist's Portfolio Exhibit — *The Pit Gallery* | Glendale, CA   2019

PROFESSIONAL ASSOCIATIONS

Sigma Iota Rho: International College Honor Society   2020–PRESENT

Gabrielle Maury, CPRW, CDCS | Refined Resumes LLC | refinedresumesllc.com
Major: Motion Design | **Goal:** Animation and motion designer
Notable: The centerpiece of this beautifully designed resume is the shaded box highlighting notable awards. Jane's involvement in professional activities and associations is also notable.

ASHER CHANNEL

🌐 Baltimore, MD 21208   ☎ 410-555-1212   ✉ asher.channel@ymail.com

BROADCASTING   WEB   TV   RADIO   BRAND BUILDING

★ Recent college graduate with nearly 10 years of broadcast and promotions experience from US Army (Honorable Discharge) and 2 academic internships.
★ Videographer, Creative Writer, and Audio Producer. Strong creative vision. Adaptable to project goals.
★ Project Manager experience in video/audio segment writing, producing, and editing.
★ Liaison between creative services and online content for brand awareness/promotions on all platforms.
★ Roadmap creator for workflow, content, and competing promotional output process deadlines.
★ Advanced user of Microsoft Office, Photoshop, social media platforms, music and video editing applications.

CRITICAL SKILLSET

Production Shoots	Media Relations	Strategic Brand Management
Video Editing	Project Management	Budget Oversight
Script Research	Presentation Skills	Timeline Management
Shot and Scene Planning	Talent Acquisition	Work Planning and Prioritizing
Copyediting and Proofing	Prop Shopping	Production Operations

EDUCATION

BA Degree – Broadcast and Mass Media | Towson University—Towson, MD   2023
AA Degree – Communications | Baltimore City Community College—Baltimore, MD   2019

PROFESSIONAL EXPERIENCE

PROMOTIONAL ASSISTANT | Charm City Media—Baltimore, MD   08/2020–09/2022
- Project manager with end-to-end promotions accountability for successful and profitable outcomes.
- Assisted Promotions and Marketing departments with promotional activities for station, clients, and events.
- Coordinated/oversaw appearances, collaborating across multiple departments to create/execute remotes, on-site events, street team activities, and van hits from conception to completion.
- Executed business administration functions, updated website, and managed staging elements.
- Recorded promotional station event videos, audio segments, social media posts, and photography.
- Prepared contest rules, waivers, and release forms for on air, digital, and social medial contests.
- Supervised prize inventory and in-studio prize sheets. Completed winner fulfillment and release forms.
- Transported/operated audio and production equipment. Managed event signage.

TECHNICAL ASSISTANT INTERN | Baltimore City Community College—Baltimore, MD   09/2017–08/2019
- Assisted instructors in the Video Production Studio. Oversaw operations for high productivity levels.
- Co-managed audio/visual equipment, resources, programs, and video equipment operation.
- Executed hardware/software system troubleshooting and end-user issues via remote tech support.
- Managed and archived record, identifying and resolving discrepancies.
- Analyzed students' technical/network issues and provided guidance for self-solutions.

BROADCAST JOURNALIST SUPERVISOR | U.S. Army—Fort Benning, Columbus, GA   06/2013–06/2017
- Public Affairs Broadcast Specialist for Armed Forces Radio and Television Service.
- Writer, reporter, videographer, producer, editor, and program host for radio and TV productions.
- Created, filmed, and hosted news and entertainment video and audio broadcasts.

Michelle McCann Kelley, CPRW, NCOPE, IJCTC | CareerPro, Inc. | careerprousa.net
Major: Broadcast and Mass Media | **Goal:** Career in broadcasting
Notable: Relevant experience from the U.S. Army and two college internships paint the picture of a highly qualified candidate.

JUSTINE BALSER

Chicago, IL 60623 • 971.770.1460 • justine.balser@email.com • LinkedIn • **View My Portfolio**

DIGITAL MARKETING, SOCIAL MEDIA & GRAPHIC DESIGN ACCOUNT MANAGER

- Bachelor's in **digital media design & strategy** in sports and entertainment and **2+ years of experience** leading graphic design, social media, advertising, and creative marketing projects.

- Drive **increased engagement, brand visibility, and revenues** by managing creative marketing campaigns across diverse business verticals, from initial concept and setup to execution and review.

- Possess strong communication, teamwork, and relationship management skills underpinned by **exposure to B2C marketing services and the B2B agency selection process.**

- **Technology:** Adobe (Photoshop, Illustrator, After Effects, Premiere Pro, Creative Cloud), Facebook, Instagram, Twitter, Snapchat

CORE SKILLS & ATTRIBUTES
Digital Media & Graphic Design
B2B/B2C Marketing Campaign Lifecycles
Creative Project Management
Social Media & Marketing Analytics
People Management (12+ staff)
Search Engine Optimization (SEO)
Photography & Video Editing
Content Management Systems (CMS)
Communication & Presentation
Customer Relationship Management

EDUCATION & CERTIFICATIONS

Bachelor of Arts (**BA**), **Digital Media Design & Strategy (Sports & Entertainment)**   2023
UNIVERSITY OF CONNECTICUT (UCONN), Storrs, CT

CERTIFICATIONS: Hootsuite Platform Certification (May 2022) • Google Analytics (May 2021) • Inbound Marketing Certified (HubSpot Academy, February 2021) • Google Ads Display (March 2021) • Google Ads Search (March 2021)

PROFESSIONAL EXPERIENCE

Bearings Manufacturing Company – Chicago, IL   Jan 2023 – Feb 2023
Marketing & Social Media Advisor

Served in an unofficial advisory role during the B2B agency selection process. Attended presentation meetings and provided input on digital marketing proposals for improving the website, email, and inbound marketing strategies.

UCONN, Athletics Department (The Pound) – Storrs, CT   Aug 2021 – Dec 2022
Co-lead & Content Producer • Social Media Intern

Joined a digital media team to conceptualize, design, and launch unique social media marketing campaigns that increased student-athlete engagement. Leveraged Facebook, Twitter, and Instagram to increase UConn student-athlete engagement.

- **Grew and co-led** the team from 7 to 12+ social media and content developers and managed and guided the implementation of Music Mondays and the Newlywed Game, which boosted followers and fan engagement.
- **Guided interns** in *The Pound's* brand persona and **mentored** one individual to continue leading creative projects to grow the account in preparation for my upcoming departure following graduation.

Chicago Sky, WNBA – Chicago, IL   May 2021 – Aug 2021
Creative Services Intern

Acquired sports-related graphic design experience by supporting a 10-member creative services team in designing and editing graphics and videos for social media marketing, sponsorship activation materials, and e-newsletter campaigns.

- **Increased ticket sales** by designing and circulating 2 game-day flyers to connected hotels and businesses.

Kate Williamson, MS, CPRW, CRS+ES, CRS+IT, CSBA | Scientech Resumes | scientechresumes.com
Major: Digital Media Design & Strategy | **Goal:** Digital marketing
Notable: Justine's internships exposed her to both B2C (business-to-consumer) and B2B (business-to-business) marketing spaces—a valuable perspective. Note the link to her web portfolio at the top of the resume.

BRANDYN WASHINGTON

Creative | Collaborative | Curious

brandynw@mail.com
(555) 555-5555
LinkedIn
New York, NY

DIGITAL MARKETING COORDINATOR

- **Increased customer acquisition and/or social media followers up to 30%** and outperformed peers for all internships, work experience, and leadership positions.
- **Developed first-of-their-kind promotions and omnichannel strategies** for expanding wellness company that broadened brand awareness and attracted new clients beyond set goals.
- **Elected as Vice President of Phi Chi Theta,** a co-ed business fraternity. Oversaw 10-member marketing team and planned/coordinated well-attended, bi-weekly events for 300+ members, adhering to all Covid-19 requirements.
- **Drove $150K in charity donations** in 1 year through community outreach, business partnerships, corporate matching gifts, and alumni engagement.
- **Worked 2 marketing jobs during senior year while attending college full time and making Dean's List.**

CORE SKILLS:

Advertising & Marketing Campaigns	Content Management	Graphic Design
Asset Creation	Customer Acquisition	Incentive Marketing Campaigns
Business Intelligence	Digital / Social Media Marketing	Omnichannel Marketing
Brand Awareness	Excel (Advanced)	Reporting & Analytics

🎓 EDUCATION

B.S. in Business | Dual Minor: Psychology, Marketing | Pennsylvania State University | University Park, PA
Graduated: May 2025 | GPA: 3.7 | Dean's List all 4 years

Academic Leadership
- **Vice President, Phi Chi Theta Business Fraternity** – Led 10-member marketing team; exceeded social media goal 20%.
- **Public Relations Chair,** Penn State Prime Marketing Organization – 1 of only 20 students selected to enroll in 2022.
- Member, Penn State Speech & Debate Society, **2X national qualifier.**

💼 EXPERIENCE

Lead Marketing Intern | Brooklyn Wellness Center | Brooklyn, NY *(100% Remote)*   **May 2022–Jan. 2023**

Developed digital marketing strategies, assets, ecommerce pages, social media plan, client attraction activities, and brand awareness campaign for established wellness center and grand opening of new site. Engaged target audience by creating quality content, robust schedule, interactive posts, targeted hashtags, and incentivized giveaways.

- Promoted within 3 months to supervise 5 marketing interns. Established plans and campaigns for each intern to follow and implemented weekly team status meetings.
- Increased social media presence 30% within 5 months, surpassing target of 20% and outperforming previous interns.
- Expanded overall clientele 20% within 5 months by introducing company's first interactive giveaway, partnering with local businesses, and strengthening social media campaigns.

Marketing Associate | PennState Productions | University Park, PA   **Aug. 2020–May 2022**

Promoted music, entertainment, in-person, and virtual productions ranging from 2K to 10K attendees each. Created print and online assets, interactive and shareable social media graphics, and digital and advertising campaigns.
- Contributed to 18% YOY ticket increase by initiating and overseeing organization's first TikTok marketing campaign.
- Exceeded team goal of increasing social media followers 15% through research and redirection of outreach.

Lucie Yeomans, NCOPE, CEIC, CGRA, OPNS | Your Career Ally | yourcareerally.com
Major: Business | **Goal:** Digital marketing
Notable: Brandyn's resume exudes his own personal brand, starting with the three-word tagline under his name. His experience includes specific achievements and results.

JAMAL BISHOP

New York, NY 10023 ▪ 347.555.7960 ▪ jbishop30@gmail.com

ENTRY-LEVEL MARKETING ASSOCIATE / ACCOUNT MANAGER

Self-starter with strong competitive edge.

Excellent at initiating activity and providing direction for a team or organization.

Skilled in interacting with diverse peers, management, vendors, and customers.

Thrive in fast-paced, results-oriented environment with variety of projects.

✓ Experience in the technology, marketing, advertising, virtual training, and digital space.

✓ Passion for console, cloud, PC, Esports, mobile, VR gaming.

✓ Technical knowledge of online community platforms, systems, and software and social networking tools/trends.

✓ Proficient with MS Office (Word, Excel, PowerPoint).

EDUCATION

Bachelor of Science, Marketing Communication
SUNY Empire State College (2023)

EMPLOYMENT EXPERIENCE

Starfish Digital Agency: MEDIA ANALYST INTERN (Jan 2022 to Dec 2022)
A digital media agency specializing in defining, managing, and executing online marketing strategies.

Secured part-time paid internship in Analyst Department while completing degree. Assisted with gathering data related to consumer demographics, preferences, buying habits and overall market conditions and producing detailed reports of buyer habits/preferences for client companies.

▸ Developed and distributed online marketing surveys; compiled and converted data and findings into tables and charts for use in future product development.

▸ Assisted staff with creating and running digital marketing campaigns, including drafting marketing copy.

Association of National Advertisers (ANA): MARKETING COORDINATOR (Jan 2021 to Nov 2021)
The advertising industry's oldest trade association in the U.S. with over 600 member companies representing 25,000 brands.

Supported numerous accounts by managing logistics for workshops/training programs hosted by ANA for member companies throughout the U.S. Handled multiple administrative tasks, from preplanning through program delivery.

▸ Created and emailed registration links to participants.

▸ Coordinated distribution of post-workshop surveys through SurveyMonkey. Developed Excel spreadsheets to track responses and provided feedback to member companies.

▸ Served as primary point of contact for instructors/trainers, facilitating mock sessions to acquaint them with the training platform (Zoom or Adobe Connect) and providing technology support during live streaming.

▸ Initiated recommended response to Covid-related business changes, which resulted in $15,000 savings in printing and shipping costs by replacing hardcopy workshop materials with electronic files.

Exclusive Concepts, Inc.: TERRITORY MANAGER (Aug 2020 to Jan 2021)
A technology partner specializing in development and execution of marketing strategies for Fortune 50 companies.

Served as face of Verizon Communications, marketing telecommunications services to homeowners and renters throughout Manhattan territory, covering Harlem to SoHo. Set up and managed kiosk in different locations to provide information about services, answer questions, take applications, and schedule installations.

▸ Proactively engaged in conversations, adjusting communication to ethnic, socio-economic, and age diversity.

FREELANCE WORK: Manage successful Twitch channel, ranking in top 1% of live streamers broadcasting video gaming, with average daily following of 200–300 viewers. Promote stream through social media and engage with audience through real-time communication, including asking questions and responding to chats. Solicit and secure company sponsors/affiliate opportunities and promote various products/brands through channel advertising.

Norine Dagliano, NCRW, NCOPE | EKM Inspirations | ekminspirations.com
Major: Marketing Communications | **Goal:** Marketing associate
Notable: In addition to relevant internship and employment experience, Jamal had interesting freelance work that adds interest—and even more qualifications—to his resume.

George Harris

Austin, TX 73301 • 512.555.5555 • georgeharris@gmail.com • <u>LinkedIn</u>

ADVERTISING GRADUATE TARGETING ENTRY-LEVEL MARKETING POSITIONS

⊙ Flexible and resourceful advertising graduate with minor in business, interested in entry-level marketing and brand promotion positions. Well-versed in **social media management, branding,** and **customer acquisition** from internship and virtual merchandising and training manager experiences.

⊙ At ease in **start-up organizations.** Able to prioritize multiple projects and meet deadlines in fast-paced, high-pressure environments while driving continuous improvement. Strong in business processes, best practice development, and marketing campaign conception, execution, and measurement.

⊙ Skilled at collaborating and communicating with cross-functional associates, vendors, and internal and external stakeholders from various cultures and backgrounds. Willing to travel.

CORE STUDIES & EMERGING SKILLS

Product Marketing • Marketing Campaign Development • Multi-Channel Marketing • Google Ads
Print Production • Social Media Management (Facebook, Instagram, Pinterest, Quora) • Copywriting
In-Store Signage • Creative Collateral Development • Category Marketing • Vendor Management
Project Management • Forecasting • Budget Management • Online & Offline Marketing • Branding
Paid Marketing Strategy • Email Campaigns • PPC Campaigns • Customer Acquisition Strategy

EDUCATION & CERTIFICATIONS

BACHELOR OF SCIENCE, ADVERTISING & MASS COMMUNICATION – *Texas State University*　　　2023
GOOGLE ANALYTICS – *Google*　　　2023
GOOGLE ADWORDS FUNDAMENTALS – *Google*　　　2022

PROFESSIONAL EXPERIENCE

VISUAL MERCHANDISING & TRAINING INTERN – *OneStep*　　　2022–2023; Austin, TX
Collaborated with design teams on new product displays and promotions. Developed digital social media content and promotional signage to support branding and in-store events. Aided lead designers with creation and implementation of promotional campaigns.
<u>Select Accomplishment</u>:

• Created digital and print promotional signage packages for launch of joint service between OneStep and Nest. Signage selected for multiple store display and secured **first** customer sign-ups.

SOCIAL MEDIA CONSULTANT – *Independent Contractor*　　　2021–2022; Austin, TX
Created and managed social media accounts to attract new clients and foster positive customer relationships. Aided in creating branding, including logo design, website, and online advertising. Developed content for and monitored metrics for Facebook and Instagram advertisements.
<u>Select Accomplishment</u>:

• **Tyson's Tacos:** Increased Instagram followers by **1,187+** and Facebook likes by **443** over four months.

CONTENT INTERN – *Music Events Now*　　　2020; Austin, TX
Authored creative content for website and social media accounts to promote consumer engagement. Supported music event promotion, including the **South by Southwest Music Festival (SXSW).**

Andrea Adamski, CPRW | Write For You Resumes | writeforyouresumes.com
Major: Advertising & Mass Communication | **Goal:** Marketing and social media management
Notable: Two internships are enhanced by additional freelance work as a social media consultant. The "Core Studies & Emerging Skills" heading allows the incorporation of many valuable keywords without overstating expertise.

Zander Wilson

617-334-5090 • zanderwilson@gmail.com

Career Target: **Sales • Account Management • Marketing**

Business/Marketing Graduate pursuing sales opportunity that will benefit from exceptional competitive drive, work ethic, communication skills, and people orientation.

Value Offered

- **Hands-on experience** creating business-building and social media plans for companies in diverse industries.
- **Leadership and initiative** demonstrated on the soccer pitch and in the locker room, throughout team projects, in coaching and mentoring roles, and in business settings.
- **Resourcefulness and persistence** in identifying and using sources to find answers and craft solutions.
- **Teamwork orientation** in business, academic, and athletic environments—collaborating, contributing, building consensus, and inspiring team members to complete tasks and set high goals.
- **Microsoft Office** skills and experience—Word, Excel, PowerPoint.

Education

BS Business | BOSTON COLLEGE, Chestnut Hill, MA   Anticipated May 2023
Major: Business Management • Minor: Marketing • GPA: 3.3/4.0

Academics: Project Highlights

- Created diversified marketing plan using $5K budget to increase customer base for a fitness organization. *Semester-long project; team of 5.* ***Client adopted all recommendations; 2 years later, business is thriving.***
- Guided a local B&B in its first foray into social media. Crafted a marketing strategy centered on online recommendations. ***B&B currently has 4.5- to 5-star ratings and detailed reviews on TripAdvisor, Yelp, Facebook, Expedia, and other travel sites.***
- Designed a program to build social media presence for a pop-up retailer, focusing on unique image and personality through photos, videos, and an Instagram account. ***Elevated social media presence from zero.***

Athletics: 3-year Starter, Boston College Soccer Team

- Instrumental performer on 2021 and 2022 teams that advanced to the NCAA tournament.
- Honed individual skills and motivated teammates to reach top performance.
- Maintained a high grade point average while balancing academic schedule and extensive athletic activity.

Leadership: Member of BC Soccer Leadership Group

- One of 8 teammates selected by head coach as part of inaugural Leadership Group.
- Met weekly and provided input on a range of topics—game strategy, team building, team management.

Marketing and Leadership Experience

Marketing Intern | METRO-WEST REAL ESTATE SOLUTIONS, Waltham, MA   Summer 2022
Worked with a team of 3 commercial real estate developers/brokers, performing detailed research and assisting with property evaluations and recommendations.

- Sat in on team meetings; conducted site visits; researched rules, regulations, and restrictions for individual parcels; met with city officials to discuss property access and easements.
- Built knowledge of real estate industry and the importance of relationships, resources, and referral networks.

Trainer | BROOKLINE YOUTH SOCCER CLUB, Brookline, MA   Summers 2016–2022
Provided skills training and leadership development for soccer players aged 6 to 11.

- Designed training activities to develop skills while keeping sessions fun and engaging.
- Learned to interact with and motivate players with different personalities and behaviors.

Tutor and Mentor | JEAN McGUIRE K-8 SCHOOL, Boston, MA   Summer 2017
Worked with students at a public school in a financially challenged area of Boston.

- Helped students complete class assignments and tutored them on difficult activities.
- Became a mentor and a trusted advisor students could talk to about their problems.

Additional Work Experience

Team Member | Domino's, Brookline, MA   Fall 2022
Warehouse Associate/Order Picker | Amazon, Dedham, MA   Summer 2021

Louise Kursmark, MRW, CPRW, JCTC, CEIP, CCM | Best Impression Career Services | louisekursmark.com
Major: Business | **Goal:** Career in sales
Notable: The Education section is quite robust, highlighting three distinct areas where Zander excelled—and gained valuable workplace qualifications. His internship and work experiences are also detailed.

Maria Lopez

Seattle, WA 98107 | 206-627-4509 | maria-lopez@gmail.com | linkedin.com/in/maria-lopez08

Project & Account Management Professional | Risk Management/Insurance Industry

Expert account management skills complemented by commitment to customer service that goes above and beyond

Highly resourceful, proactive, and customer-centric professional with track record of *consistently exceeding customer requirements and performance expectations.* Excel in *building collaborative relationships,* incorporating *relationship management strategies.*

- **Exceptional work ethic:** "Doing whatever it takes to be successful." **Highly value integrity and honesty.**
- **Adept in quickly learning new skills,** from product knowledge and customer/account needs to new software.

Innovative & Solution-Focused Problem Solver | Polished Communicator & Public Speaker

Professional Experience & Accomplishments

INTERN, Energy Services | SEATTLE MUTUAL, Seattle, WA   Feb 2023–Present

Hired as integral member of 3-person team supporting new Energy Services unit, marketing whole-property insurance products to independent and private renewable energy power producers across the Northwest.

- **Collaborate with 4 policy underwriters** in developing policies/registering premiums throughout highly detailed manual process required for the customized nature of policies with multiple values and specialty coverages.
- **Develop and methodically maintain library of contractual language and documents** addressing a variety of specialty clauses (Excel database, MSWord, PDFs).

INTERN, National Accounts | SPECIALTY LIGHTING GROUP, Seattle, WA   Jun 2022–Sep 2022

Managed customer service and coordination of strategic accounts for high-end corporate/commercial lighting firm (30+ employees, privately held).

- **Worked closely with sales manager** to develop custom lighting package solutions meeting architectural specifications. **Added value, tailoring "cost-and-design" service contributions to individual customers.**
- **Met customers' urgent deadline requirements,** managed procurement, expedited logistics, negotiated costs and delivery dates, priced custom orders, and sourced product from specified manufacturers or alternate vendors.

INTERN | WESTERN INSURANCE COMPANY, Tacoma, WA   Sep 2021–Jan 2022

Gained exposure to professional sales, marketing, and management practices for the insurance industry. Supported 3 top-performing sales professionals marketing a wide range of individual and group products and services: life, disability, and long-term care insurance; annuities and mutual funds; retirement and estate planning.

- **Used networking, direct mail, and face-to-face marketing strategies** to generate new prospects.

Education & Professional Development

UNIVERSITY OF WASHINGTON | Seattle, WA – **Bachelor of Science degree, Marketing** (2023)

- Minor in Political Science

SEATTLE MUTUAL | Seattle, WA – **Regular Program Participant** (2023–Present)

- Extensive continuing professional education: Computer system training, general insurance practices, risk management, portfolio book of business seminars, etc.

Jan Melnik, MA, MRW, CCM, CPRW | Absolute Advantage | janmelnik.com
Major: Marketing | **Goal:** Account management in the insurance industry
Notable: Three internships—two in her desired insurance industry—are the focal point for this resume and position Maria as an attractive candidate. Because she does not have outstanding grades, her GPA is omitted.

Danielle F. Ye

New York City • danielle-f-ye@mail.com • (212) 367-0090

Aspiring Financial Advisor/Investment Manager

Goldman Sachs & JPMorgan Experience

Academic and employment top performer. Campus leader and natural relationship builder.
Technology Skills: Microsoft Word, Excel, PowerPoint. **Language:** Fluent in Mandarin Chinese.

Education

WELLESLEY COLLEGE • Wellesley, MA

Bachelor of Arts, Dec. 2023 • **Major:** Politics • **Minor:** Legal Studies
Major GPA: 3.9/4.0 • **Dean's List;** graduated in 3.5 yrs.

Relevant Work & Campus Leadership Experience

Intern • GOLDMAN SACHS • New York, NY • Jan.–July 2023

- Directly supported 4 financial advisors in wealth management practice working with high-net-worth clients.
- Created client portfolio proposals, including recommended fund allocations; revised Excel documents to reflect up-to-date calculations.
- Managed coordination and attendance by top 50 mutual fund wholesalers and preferred clients at biweekly financial advisor luncheon and dinner events.
- Created promotional flyers for a "Financial Advisors Networking Event."

Mediator • OFFICE OF ATTORNEY GENERAL LETITIA JAMES • New York, NY • Aug.–Dec. 2022

New York State Public Inquiry & Assistance Center (PIAC)
- Provided voluntary mediation between consumers and businesses.
- Reviewed written complaints and determined appropriate office to handle resolution.
- Achieved resolution in 70% cases in which both parties participated voluntarily.
- Maintained neutrality and established trust and rapport while listening attentively and communicating effectively.

Research Intern, ESG Investing • JPMORGAN CHASE • New York, NY • May–Aug. 2021

- Conducted deep-dive investigation into corporations' ESG (Environmental/Social/Governance) claims and practices.
- Presented detailed research summaries to team of senior investment advisors specializing in ESG funds.

WELLESLEY COLLEGE • Wellesley, MA

Office of Development and Alumni Relations
- **Student Ambassador Interviewer** (Mar. 2022–Dec. 2023): Represented Wellesley in new Student Ambassador Informational Program designed to re-engage alumni with their alma mater. Conducted in-person interviews with select alumni. Generated weekly reports reflecting updated information.
- **Student Caller** (Jan.–Dec. 2020): Developed, maintained, and strengthened relationships with alumni and donors. Promoted philanthropy in a responsible, ethical manner. Garnered most pledges of 6+ rookie student callers.

Fall Fest Weekend
- **Marketing Coordinator** (Sep.–Nov. 2022 and 2023): Created on-campus marketing program designed to boost student participation. Oversaw branding; instrumental in selection of theme and development of logo. Ensured implementation of theme in all marketing collateral (from T-shirts and posters to social media messaging).

Jan Melnik, MA, MRW, CCM, CPRW | Absolute Advantage | janmelnik.com
Major: Politics | **Goal:** Career in financial services
Notable: Without the traditional educational background for financial services, Danielle highlighted her blue-chip internships with two major players in the industry. Her on-campus leadership is also showcased.

TAMEKA ROLLINS

tamekarollins@email.com | 404.555.3456 | Atlanta, GA | linkedin.com/in/tamekarollins

TARGET ROLE: ASSOCIATE ACCOUNT MANAGER, NONPROFIT
Market Research | Customer Service | Technical Aptitude | Data Analysis | Copywriting

Emotionally intelligent communications and marketing professional poised to deliver value as associate account director. Strong communication, writing, and critical thinking skills, with ability to work collaboratively in teams or independently.

Self-motivated and highly accountable—strong work ethic and hustle mentality. Fresh blend of creative mindset, attention to detail, and quality control. Completed demographics research; developed and presented messaging campaigns.

- Team Collaboration
- B2C Message Creation
- Ad Campaign Strategy
- Communication Strategies

- Interpersonal Communications
- Critical Thinking & Analysis
- Presentation Creation & Delivery
- Multimedia Communications

- Website SEO
- Detail Orientation
- Problem Solving
- Creative Thinking

Technical Strengths: Claritas ▪ Statista ▪ R Programming Language ▪ Affinity Designer ▪ Adobe Photoshop ▪ Adobe Illustrator ▪ Microsoft Office ▪ Google Drive ▪ Mac OS ▪ Logic Pro X ▪ Waves Mastering Plugins ▪ VST Plugins ▪ Zoom

LinkedIn Learning Credentials: B2B Marketing Foundations ▪ Google Ads Essential Training ▪ Learning to Write Marketing Copy ▪ SEO Foundations ▪ Google Docs ▪ Leadership Communications ▪ Designing Better PowerPoint Slides

EDUCATION

BA, Communications – Georgia State University, Atlanta, GA; GPA 3.69. Graduation: 12/2023

Academic Theory: Multimedia communications, advertising messaging and methods, building connections between people and brands, managing client relationships, and relationships between communications and public audience.

Learning Application: Completed demographics research using Claritas and Statista. Facilitated in-person targeted segment interviews. Led focus groups via Zoom. Created framed message campaigns focused on nonprofit / developmental causes. Presented campaigns using customized PowerPoint themes and layouts.

Relevant Coursework: Marketing Research, Communication and Social Influence, Campaign Strategy, Creative Advertising, Brand Creation, Critical Communication Theory, Communication in Developing Countries.

PROFESSIONAL EXPERIENCE

COWLEY MARKETING– Atlanta, GA   05/2022 – 08/2022
Marketing firm specializing in strategies for nonprofit organizations.

Client Services Intern
Provided employee technical support for office hardware and software.
- Completed IT service requests to maintain business productivity.
- Performed entry-level data analysis and website search engine optimization (SEO).
- Mapped client experience through new social media channels.

Takeaways: This experience strengthened my level of professionalism, taught me accountability for organizational assets, how to effectively track long lists of client data, and how to develop meaningful relationships with clients.

DISCSTYLES™ COMMUNICATION AND BEHAVIORAL STRENGTHS ASSESSMENT

Profile Summary: Excellent listener, able to get along with wide variety of people. Values diplomacy. Supportive and analytical. Manages workloads and delegates when necessary. Patient, detailed, with high quality control standards.

Cathy Lanzalaco, MBA, CPRW, CPCC, NCOPE, SPHR, SHRM-SCP, RN | Inspire Careers | inspirecareers.com
Major: Communications | **Goal:** Account management
Notable: Tameka's Experience "Takeaways" and DISC assessment results are unique features of her resume. The Education section loads keywords into three different categories.

CYNDI OKSANA

781-445-1210   Greater Boston Area   cyndi.oksana@email.com

ACCOUNT MANAGEMENT

Client Service & Support — Territory Management — Needs Assessment & Proactive Problem-Solving

High-energy, proactive account manager with recent BA in Business/Marketing and a 5-year record of providing exceptional service, sales, and support to key accounts—enhancing the client relationship and delivering bottom-line business benefits.

Polished presenter before groups of all sizes and at all levels of the client organization, from technology-system end-users to senior executives. **Relationship builder** who partners effectively with clients, distributors, and colleagues to achieve business objectives. **Consistent top performer** eager for new professional challenges.

EXPERIENCE AND ACHIEVEMENTS

KJK Distributors, Quincy, MA • 2019–2023
Market-leading supplier of electrical distribution, industrial control, and automation products, systems, and services.

SALES ENGINEER, Industrial Channel, Jan. 2022–Jan. 2023

> **Rapidly turned around underperforming 3-state territory, building from 84% of quota to 101% of goal in just one year.** Serviced over 100 accounts through a major channel of distribution, focusing efforts on building strong business relationships and partnering with distributor sales force to meet customer needs.

- **Advanced powerful partnership with distributor sales representatives, encouraging their commitment to KJK and helping to drive sales growth.**
  - Made joint sales calls to identify customer needs and develop new revenue opportunities.
  - Organized and led product-training and open-house events to build knowledge of and enthusiasm for KJK products.
- **Finished year as #3 performer among 18 nationwide.**

PREMIER ACCOUNT REPRESENTATIVE, Inventory Systems, Feb. 2019–Dec. 2021

> **Brought on board to introduce new inventory-management system to the company's #1 distributor, a national account representing millions of dollars in annual sales volume.**

- Completed successful roll-out on schedule, visiting account sites in 49 states.
- Delivered extensive end-user training and numerous informational presentations to the distributor's senior management team.
- Built exceptional account relationships through proactive problem resolution and careful attention to unique needs of their business.

XYZ International, Cincinnati, OH • 2017–2019
Provider of voice and data telecommunications services to business accounts

ACCOUNT MANAGER

> **Maintained a $500K book of business,** providing attentive account service and ensuring each account had the most appropriate and cost-effective telecom plan.

- Named to "President's Circle," 2018, for excellence in customer service.

PERFORMANCE EVALUATIONS

"Her ability to catch on quickly, her experience and ability to meet customers' needs enabled Cyndi to hit the road running from Day 1."

"Cyndi has had a major impact on the team. She has displayed high motivation and productivity."

"...outstanding performance... The quantity and quality of her field visits enabled [us] to meet a very ambitious plan."

"She always puts the best interest of the company first..."

"Cyndi consistently performs above the required level for her position."

EDUCATION

Bachelor of Business Administration (BBA), Marketing Concentration, June 2023
University of Massachusetts, Boston, MA

- 4.0 GPA; Dean's List all semesters. Until final semester, worked full time while attending school.
- Managed all aspects of individual and team projects: marketing strategy development, SWOT analysis, research methodology, data collection and analysis, report preparation, and presentation of findings.

Louise Kursmark, MRW, CPRW, JCTC, CEIP, CCM | Best Impression Career Services | louisekursmark.com
Major: Business Administration | **Goal:** Account management
Notable: Cyndi pursued her BA part-time for nearly five years while building an excellent record in account management. Now that she's completed her degree, she's ready to move up in her career.

SEAN BROWN

Lawrence, KS 66049 ● 785.555.3456 ● seanbrown@gmail.com ● LinkedIn

Applied Behavioral Science Major Targeting Business Development

❖ Creative, resourceful and adaptable candidate offering unique combination of professional skills and experience developing entrepreneurial businesses and **customer relationships**.

❖ Enthusiastic and detail-oriented professional with keen sense of **urgency to timelines**. Strong ability to understand others' perspectives and **influence** them to action.

❖ Competitive, **decisive,** and committed to professional growth, continuous learning and improvement. Willing to travel.

Core Competencies

B2B Relationship Building • Consensus Building • Personal Finance Consulting • Lead Generation
Account Management • Sales Process Design • Upselling • POS Systems • Qualtrics Survey Software
PRiSM • Quick Books • Fishbowl • R Computing Regression • Jack Henry Banking

EDUCATION

Bachelor of General Studies in Applied Behavioral Science – Minor in Psychology   Anticipated Dec. 2023
University of Kansas – Lawrence, KS   **Major GPA: 3.77**

Emphasis on basic research and behavioral economics with certifications earned in research experience, leadership studies, and global awareness.

STUDENT CAREER HIGHLIGHTS:

❖ Chosen as sole undergraduate for **prestigious research associate internship** for *Seven Pillars Institute for Global and Financial Ethics* for 2023. Developed two publication-ready financial ethics articles: Ethics in a Time of Cuts; Behavioral Ethics: Developing Business in a New Age.

❖ Selected as a **featured dual presenter** at *2023 Society for the Quantitative Analyses of Behavior Conference* in Chicago, Illinois: Behavioral Psychology Goes to the Arcade: Tests of Artificial Intelligence in Simulated Sports.

❖ Selected as **second author presenter** at *2022 Mid-American Association for Behavior Analysis Conference* in Milwaukee, Wisconsin: Schenk, M.J., **Brown, S.D., Collier, S.C., & Reed, D.D. (October 2022). Behavior analytic tests of artificial intelligence in simulated sports: An application of the generalized matching law. Poster presented at 14th annual conference of the Mid-American Association of Behavior Analysis, Pewaukee, WI.

WORK EXPERIENCE

Personal Finance Consultant / Teller I   2020–Present
MidWest Bank, Lawrence, KS

Advise clients on financial plans using knowledge of tax and investment strategies, securities, insurance, pension plans, and real estate. Assess clients' assets, liabilities, cash flow, insurance coverage, tax status, and financial objectives. Promote growth by initiating and offering new products and services to clients.

❖ Consistently exceeded company goal of less than $20 in discrepancies per month by **$2** on average.

❖ Received **100%** on all mystery shop evaluations, consistently surpassing the branch goal of 87%.

❖ Nominated by customers and coworkers for the **Central Star Customer Service Award**.

ADDITIONAL EXPERIENCE

Bookkeeper / Beverage Control Associate   2018–2020
Replay Lounge, Lawrence, KS

Assistant Manager / Bartender   2016–2018
The Cave at the *Oread Hotel,* Lawrence, KS

Sales Representative   2015–2016
Orscheln Farm & Home, Iola, KS

Andrea Adamski, CPRW | Write For You Resumes | writeforyouresumes.com
Major: Applied Behavioral Science | **Goal:** Business development
Notable: For this new graduate seeking career advancement, the resume equally emphasizes personal characteristics, strong academic performance, and outstanding results in his current position.

DAVID THOMAS SMITH

713.222.7222 | dtsmith@gmail.com | www.linkedin.com/in/david-smith-dts/

Seeking Customer Service Roles

★ Nearly a decade of experience in customer facing roles, both in retail and service-oriented industries.

★ Recognized for proactively addressing / resolving problems and providing positive customer experiences.

★ Entrusted to handle high-profile security detail and safe armored transport for large organizations and financial institutions.

EDUCATION

Bachelor of Applied Arts & Sciences (BAAS) | Organizational Leadership | University of Texas | 2023
Honors: 3.90 GPA | President's List

Associate of Science | General Studies | Harris County College | 2022

AREAS OF EXPERTISE

Organizational Leadership | Guest Services | Customer Service | Customer Education | Conflict Management |
Process Improvement | Operational Efficiencies | Risk Mitigation | Compliance | Workplace Improvement |
Security Detail | Incident Report Management | Background Checks | Customer Focus |
Proactive Problem Solving | Attention to Detail | Integrity & Reliability | Teamwork |
Results Orientation | Multi-Task Management | Performance in High-Pressure Situations

Conversational Spanish, Russian, German, and Chinese

ACADEMIC ACHIEVEMENTS	PROFESSIONAL ACHIEVEMENTS
Graduated Magna Cum Laude	Recognized by leaders for Outstanding Job Performance
Completed two degrees while working part-time	Recognized by peers for Best Team Player
	2X Employee of the Month recipient

WORK HISTORY

TRUE EXPRESS | NORMAN, OK   11/2021 TO 04/2023
Delivery Driver

- Responsible for safely delivering packages to customers in a timely manner.
- Leveraged knowledge of GPS and navigation apps to determine most efficient delivery routes.
- Reviewed orders prior to delivery to ensure accuracy and completeness.
- Performed preventative vehicle maintenance checks to identify concerns or potential issues.
- Recognized as *Employee of the Month* for stellar performance.

ACADEMY SPORTS & OUTDOORS | NORMAN, OK   11/2020 TO 10/2021
Team Member

- Entrusted with conducting background checks on customers wanting to purchase firearms.
- Helped customers complete required paperwork.
- Stocked merchandise and managed inventory on firearms and accessories in department.
- Received *Attendance Award* for reliable attendance *and* covering the most shifts for other associates.

Kristi Meenan, CPRW | We Write It Now | WeWriteItNow.com
Major: Organizational Leadership | **Goal:** Customer service
Notable: An extensive work history, from jobs held while attending college, warranted a two-page resume for David—especially because all his experience involved customer service (his current career goal).

DAVID THOMAS SMITH, CONTINUED   713.222.7222

CHOCTAW NATION ENTERTAINMENT | CHOCTAW, OK   01/2020 TO 10/2020
Tribal Security

- Handled all aspects of maintaining a safe and conflict-free environment for customers and staff within the casino. Handled both security incidents and medical emergencies.
- Protected property from vandalism, theft, and other illegal activity.
- Monitored, investigated, and reported on any crimes or damage that occurred on site.
- Developed and documented detailed incident reports; submitted to management team.
- Quickly responded to medical emergencies; administered first aid or other emergency procedures.
- Partnered with tribal police on current investigations.
- Maintained compliance with safety regulations and general casino operations.

GOLD CLASS ARMORED | DENTON, TX   12/2018 TO 12/2019
Armed Driver

- Tasked with operating and controlling armed vehicle to and from delivery locations safely.
- Handled safe transport and protection of products and merchandise valued from $50K–$100M.
- Pursued and achieved level 2 and level 3 security certifications.
- Engaged in clear radio communications with dispatch and other security personnel.

EARLY CAREER PROFILE

Held various part-time roles in retail and/or service environments while pursuing college degrees.

Team Member, Dick's Sporting Goods   **Cashier**, Cabella's
Grocery Clerk, Sprouts Grocery   **Team Member**, Columbia Sportswear

TECHNICAL KNOWLEDGE

Microsoft Word | Microsoft Excel | Microsoft SharePoint | Zoom | Skype

JENNIFER JONES

281.999.4299 | jenniferjones@yahoo.com | https://www.linkedin.com/in/jennifer-jones/

Medical Sales | Pharmaceutical Sales

→ Motivated college graduate with 3+ years' hands-on experience working in medical office settings while managing full schedule of college courses.
→ Committed to helping improve patient outcomes through cutting-edge medical advancements.
→ **Ready to take previous experience in medical settings and transition into an entry-level role in medical or pharmaceutical sales.**

EDUCATION: Bachelor of Science | Kinesiology | Texas Tech University | 2023

KEY STRENGTHS

Strong Communication Skills | Collaborative Mindset | Relationship Building | Customer Service | Sales Presentations | Overcoming Objections | Detailed Follow Up | Patient Advocacy | Patient Education | Drive for Results | Problem Solving | Strong Work Ethic | Administrative Support

WORK HISTORY

DR. RON ROBERTS, MD | LUBBOCK, TX   01/2023 TO 07/2023
Medical Assistant
- Responsible for reviewing and documenting patient history and taking patient vitals.
- Answered questions and addressed patient concerns with empathy and compassion.
- Submitted prescription information to pharmacies.
- Observed and documented patient information and treatment plan.
- Demonstrated excellent communications and detailed follow through when working with patients, families, and physicians.

CARING CHIROPRACTIC | LUBBOCK, TX   01/2021 TO 12/2022
Rehabilitation Therapist (Internship)
- Assisted and guided patients in stretches and strengthening exercises.
- Provided electric stimulation and heat/ice application prior to adjustment by doctor.
- Observed and documented patient responses to prescribed exercises and therapies.
- Educated and informed patients on benefits of various therapies and modalities.

SOCIAL HOUR RESTAURANT | LUBBOCK, TX   05/2020 TO 12/2020
Server / Bartender (Part Time)
- Greeted and seated customers; responded to customer inquiries regarding food and beverage items.
- Gathered food and beverage orders; communicated orders accurately to kitchen staff.
- Anticipated and responded to customer needs; resolved concerns with friendly, positive attitude.
- Assisted other servers to ensure all customers walked away with an exceptional service experience.

THROUGH HIM MINISTRIES | HOUSTON, TX   06/2015 TO 08/2020
Junior Camp Counselor | Senior Camp Counselor (Part Time)
- Initially hired as junior counselor; promoted to senior counselor in 2018 with responsibility for 30+ campers.
- Assisted senior counselors manage daily activities for large group of campers.
- Led small group discussions, encouraging camper participation in positive ways.
- Helped organize and run daily camper activities; monitored camper events to ensure their safety.

TECHNICAL APPLICATIONS

Microsoft Office Suite | Microsoft SharePoint | Microsoft Teams | HubSpot

VOLUNTEERING | LEADERSHIP ROLES

Physical Therapy Aide | Achieve Therapy & Rehab | January 2022 to July 2022
Undergraduate Teaching Assistant | Anatomy & Physiology Lab | August 2022 to May 2023

Page 1 of 1

Kristi Meenan, CPRW | We Write It Now | WeWriteItNow.com
Major: Kinesiology | **Goal:** Medical or pharmaceutical sales
Notable: The Summary clearly conveys the current goal, strong qualifications, and eagerness to move into a new field armed with a recent bachelor's degree. Work ethic and customer skills are highlighted in Experience.

AUBREY DIAZ

AubreyDiaz@mac.com   520.555.2319   linkedin.com/in/aubrey-diaz

PHARMACEUTICAL SALES REPRESENTATIVE
Drive, Tenacity, and Leadership
Bilingual and bicultural: English and Spanish; conversational French

Goal-driven recent college graduate focused on maximizing company sales, revenues, and customer loyalty; adapt easily to changing dynamics, make time-critical decisions, and resolve problems through research. collaboration, and conceptual thinking.

Building Customer Loyalty ↑ Driving Repeat Business ↑ Exceeding Expectations

Offer experience in sales, customer service, and healthcare environments with a firm commitment to high performance and achievement, demonstrating strengths in areas of:

Planning/Research/Analysis ... Training/Education/Communication ... Presentations and Negotiations
Customer Service Excellence ...Client Relationship Management ... Continuous Improvement
Persistence ... Initiative ... Integrity ... Coachability ... Accountability

EDUCATION

University of Arizona, Tucson, AZ – **B.S. SPANISH** – May 2023
Course work included: *Human Anatomy ... Genetics ... Spanish Medical Terminology ...*
Cell Biology ... Intro to Personality ... Leadership in Organizations

EXPERIENCE

Southern Arizona Technology Center, Tucson, AZ   2021–Present
ADJUNCT INSTRUCTOR – CPR/First Aid Safety Training (American Heart Association)
Provide well-planned and practical on-site instruction, assessment, presentation, and leadership, independently employing current BLS CPR Instructor Certification. Consistently earn student evaluation scores of 98% or better.
- Deliver technical instruction in a professional and engaging manner: Integrate real-world experience and challenging activities while modifying teaching approach to accommodate varied learning styles.
  - Travel to medical practices and high schools, presenting 2–3 classes per day, 4–5 days per week with as many as 20 students from diverse ethnicities and backgrounds.
- Celebrate student accomplishment with positive feedback: Evaluate and document student performance, following established AHA guidelines and meeting required timelines.

Hopkins Jewelry, Tucson, AZ   2020–2021
SALES CONSULTANT
Ensured a positive customer experience, offering clients options tailored to diverse needs and requirements in an inviting and welcoming atmosphere. Confidently and enthusiastically offered professional advice and followed through with upselling techniques to meet and surpass sales goals.
- Drove new business: Identified and addressed opportunities to cultivate referral clients, employing a proactive, solution-focused approach to strategically showcase products and ignite sales growth.
- Promoted brand loyalty and repeat business: Leveraged learned knowledge of jewelry and gems, as well as competing brands, to deliver high-impact presentations that demonstrated passion for products, championed brand, and built customer trust.
- Exceeded sales expectations: Consistently rated in top 10% for sales volume with 50% upsell and 75%–80% close rate, using a consultative sales methodology.

Donna Tucker, CPRW, NCOPE | CareerPRO Resume Center | 4greatresumes.com
Major: Spanish | **Goal:** Pharmaceutical sales
Notable: Aubrey's resume paints a comprehensive picture of her marketability for her target role of pharmaceutical sales. She has extensive work experience and has made contributions in every role.

AUBREY DIAZ
Page 2

AubreyDiaz@mac.com   520.555.2319   linkedin.com/in/aubrey-diaz

---

Premier Cosmetic Surgery, Tucson, AZ   2019–2020

INTERPRETER/TRANSLATOR

Provided language services to non-English-speaking patients, conferring with doctors, nurses, and other medical staff and applying knowledge of medical terminology and HIPAA.

- Interpreted and translated an assortment of medical information: Communicated patient information, diagnoses, and or pharmacological instructions in pre-op and post-op situations.

Ardmore Petroleum Industries, Tucson, AZ   2016 – 2017

INSIDE SALES REPRESENTATIVE

Planned and managed outbound cold calls, strategically establishing rapport with trusted clients, then presenting information and statistics on project investments/returns.

- Noted as a leader in call productivity: Handled 100+ calls daily with professionalism and integrity, customizing scripts and answering questions to maximize call quality and sales scheduling rate.
- Mentored struggling representatives: Served as the "go-to" to build/strengthen skills for optimal sales success while contributing to high morale and productivity.
- Recognized for high call conversion: Achieved 30% or better call conversions to sales closers.

Madeline Harper Studio, Oro Valley, AZ   2014–2016

CHEER AND TUMBLING COACH

Coached children from toddlers to 8th grade, both 1:1 (private) and in groups, customizing lessons for both fun and preparation for cheer squad tryouts with attention to physical ability and safety. Contributed to studio enrollment growth of 12% year over year.

- Provided Inspiring leadership and ongoing training support: Placed emphasis on positivity and goal setting, empowering students to grow and excel.
- Kept students challenged and engaged: Listened to ambitions and concerns; promoted teamwork, sportsmanship, and respect for others while learning new routines.
- Received positive feedback from students, parents, and facility staff: Noted as an oft-requested coach based on research of all school tryout requirements and customized programs.

Yummy Treats & More, Tucson, AZ   2014–2016

SALES ASSOCIATE

Vitalized sales by upselling and adding a personal touch to each customer transaction, ultimately raising guest satisfaction scores and average ticket sales 10% or more.

- Promoted continuous improvement in service and quality: Assumed a team leadership role, training and guiding other associates in sales strategy and service excellence.

Extensive volunteer work in medical clinic and women's resource center (see LinkedIn profile for details).

ZION HENRY, Chicago, IL
312-456-7890

zh@gmail.com
linkedin.com/in/zh

CERTIFICATED MEDICAL SALES REPRESENTATIVE
TARGET: **MEDICAL SALES ROLE** in the Medical Devices Sector

RECOGNITION: AWESOME SAUCE LEADERSHIP SCHOLARSHIP, Chick-fil-A Corporation: 2020, 2021, 2022.

Award-winning, enthusiastic, results-oriented sales and marketing professional with *4 years of repeated success at outperforming objectives, transforming operations, and increasing bottom-line profits for employers.*

Supervised 50+ employees in a fast-paced, customer-centric environment. *Resolved customer complaints* across multiple channels. *Self-funded education* through commitment, outstanding time management skills, scholarships, and working full-time while in school. Speak conversational Spanish.

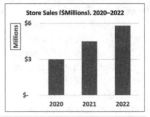

Communication	Sales	Inventory Control
Leadership	Operations Management	Problem-Solving
P&L Management	Customer Service	Technology

EXPERIENCE

Best Accounting Inc., Des Moines, IA *(Small, woman-owned bookkeeping firm)* 1/2023–5/2023

Internship: Research & Development Consultant

- **Remodeled website.** Employed Google Ads. **Interviewed** external accounting and mortgage professionals. **Sized the market** to introduce a new training offering. **Co-authored** an in-depth competitive analysis.
- RESULTS: **Increased leads and weekly web visits up to 16X. Presented** training recommendation.

Chick-fil-A Franchise, Chicago, IL *(Billion-dollar franchise business ; 2,600 restaurants nationwide)* 7/2019–12/2022

Hospitality & Operations Manager | Administration & Finance Manager | Culinary & Quality Manager

Earned rapid promotions with expanded duties, while in college full-time. **Led 50+ employees.** *Ran the business during its busiest hours.* **Collaborated** *with B-to-B distributors and vendors for the smooth running of the restaurant.*

- RESULT: **Grew store sales each year by 18+%.**
- **Partnered** with management colleagues to tailor a marketing plan for December 2022 promotion. RESULTS: Obtained **record-breaking sales** of **$700K** for **month** and **$5.2M** for **2022—a 23% year-over-year increase.**
- **Retrained 50+ staff** to enhance the customer experience. **Revamped the drive-thru** to reduce droves of bottlenecks. RESULTS: **Speeded service customers by 43%. Raised** customer **satisfaction** score to **97+%.**
- **Initiated a food waste system** to monitor kitchen inventory and food waste. **Donated excess waste** to homeless shelters. **Hired, trained, and maintained adequate** kitchen staff. RESULTS: **Decreased daily waste from $300/day to $80/day. Eliminated all overtime hours.** Received **tax benefits** for donations. Held each section responsible for their waste.
- **Remodeled the inventory system** to cut time on inventory control and $3K overspend per month per department. Used software to track expenditures, receipts, and invoices across 5 departments for end-of-month accounting. RESULTS: **Inventory time plunged by 75% to 6 hours/month.** Kept departments accountable.

EDUCATION & CERTIFICATES

BBA Marketing & Management, University of Iowa	2023
Orthobiologics & Regenerative Medicine, Medical Sales College	2023
Certifications: OR Protocol, Aseptic Technique & Infection Control, Bloodborne Pathogens, AdvaMed Code of Ethics, National Patient Safety Goals, HIPAA, Fire Safety, Electrical Safety	2023
Management Training, Chick-fil-A Franchise	2020

Kasindra Maharaj, CELDC, Reach CPBS, Conversational Intelligence® Enhanced Skills Practitioner | KM Career Insights | kasindramaharaj.com
Major: Marketing and Management | **Goal:** Medical device sales
Notable: Because he worked full time while attending school, Zion has an extensive Experience section (filled with results) to support his current goal. An eye-catching chart illustrates his success in sales.

TAYLOR MICHAELS

taylor.michaels@gmail.com | **412.555.5555** | LinkedIn | Pittsburgh, PA

CAREER TARGET: MANAGEMENT CONSULTANT

DATA MANAGEMENT | STRATEGY & ANALYSIS | PROJECT MANAGEMENT | PEER LEADERSHIP

Chemical and biomolecular engineering graduate of University of Pittsburgh, '23

Strong project management and cross-functional collaboration skills developed during Shine Life Sciences internship and as project head at University of Pittsburgh's Jones-Systems Laboratory. Conducted research and created drug modeling credited with reversing disease state in late-stage multiple sclerosis patient. Passionate about tackling toughest enterprise challenges and helping to solve complex issues from strategy to execution, capturing greatest opportunities.

Regard working within diverse teams as key to innovation. Excel in fast-paced team environments. Lead with ethics and integrity. Highly coachable and open to giving and receiving constructive feedback. Outstanding analytical, critical thinking, and technical abilities. Committed to self-development and continuous learning.

Project Management | Report Writing | Time Management | Team Collaboration | Task Prioritization

Biomedical Engineering | Oncology Clinical Research | Biotechnology | Computational Biology | Compliance
Personalized Medicine | Drug Development & Delivery | Artificial Intelligence | Clinical Trials | Machine Learning
Digital Medicine | Cheminformatics | Predictive Modeling | Data Management | Stakeholder Relations

Technical Skills – Microsoft Office Suite, Java, MATLAB, Python, R Coding, Data Analytics, Aspen & Pro II Process Modeling
IR & UV Spectroscopy, Gas, HPLC Chromatography, SAS Programming

EDUCATION

BS, Chemical and Biomolecular Engineering – University of Pittsburgh – Johannes School of Engineering, Pittsburgh, PA. **Graduated, 05/2023**. Cumulative GPA 3.85

Relevant Coursework – Biomolecular Engineering, Thermodynamics, Bioseparations, Biostatistics, Organic Chemistry, Physics, MATLAB, Numerical Methods, Mass Transfer, Heat Transfer

College Entrance Scores – ACT: 35 overall in Math, English, Science | SAT – 1520 with 780 in Math and 740 in English

PROFESSIONAL EXPERIENCE

JONES-SYSTEMS LABORATORY – Pittsburgh, PA   **08/2019 to 5/2023**

Project Head

- **Assisted in driving strategic agenda,** expediting drug development, and delivering enhanced testing credited with reversing course of disease progression in late-stage MS patient including restoration of damaged muscle.
- **Developed artificial intelligence programs** to perform predictive modeling of treatments based on retrospective data sets for 32 disease states. Improved success rates 25% compared to conventional physician treatments.
- **Led multinational group** of US and Taiwanese researchers to develop AI-guided heart transplant software and resultant procedures that increased survival rate by 45% compared to current procedures. Conducted clinical trials working directly with surgeons treating patients under high-stress operating room conditions.
- **Authored NIH grant proposals** that raised over $450K to fund clinical research.

Experience takeaways: I enjoyed patient interaction and working alongside biotech and medical professionals. I liked being called upon to solve unique challenges placed before me.

Cathy Lanzalaco, MBA, CPRW, CPCC, NCOPE, SPHR, SHRM-SCP, RN | Inspire Careers | inspirecareers.com
Major: Chemical and Biomolecular Engineering | **Goal:** Management consulting
Notable: Seeking a position in a highly competitive field. Taylor filled his two-page resume with extensive experience and examples of peer leadership. His "Experience Takeaways" strengthen the distinction of his resume.

PROFESSIONAL EXPERIENCE *(continued)*

SHINE LIFE SCIENCES – Philadelphia, PA   **06/2022 to 09/2022**
Cheminformatics Intern

- **Oversaw implementation of cheminformatics programs** to model drug functions and isolate prospective drug candidates. Saved $1M in annual drug discovery costs by decreasing number of candidates needed to be tested.
- **Developed enhanced workflows** that integrated cheminformatics, inventory, algorithm reliability, and data management technologies.
- **Reduced data collection time by one hour** by integrating inventory and data management technologies into existing workflows to streamline and accelerate the drug discovery process.
- **Enabled implementation of new workflows six months** ahead of schedule by establishing key relationships and strategically balancing stakeholder interests across interdisciplinary departments involved in drug development.

Experience takeaways: The multidisciplinary role I had was a great way to learn the interconnectedness of all departments and stakeholders involved in the drug development pipeline to ensure business needs were met.

CITY AMBULANCE SERVICE INC. – Philadelphia, PA   **01/2021 to 06/2021**
Vaccination Assistant

- **Contributed to 25% of state population receiving COVID-19 vaccinations,** meeting four-month accelerated project timeline as part of emergency response team.

Experience takeaways: This volunteer experience deepened my connection to the community I live in and made me appreciate the role that first responders and public health professionals play in the well-being of those they serve.

PEER LEADERSHIP ACTIVITIES

MENTORSEAS – City Rocks, PA | 09/2019 to 05/2023
Engineering Mentor: Provided advisement, tutoring, class, and career planning to 27 undergraduate engineering students to place them in labs that matched their individual interests and career goals.

THE SABRE EXPERIMENT – City Rocks, PA | 09/2018 to Present
Mentor: Mentor underprivileged middle and high school students in science, coding, and engineering design principles.

AMERICAN INSTITUTE OF CHEMICAL ENGINEERS | 09/2020 to 06/2021
Regional Liaison: Managed university chapters for Carnegie-Mellon University, Duquesne University, and University of Pittsburgh. Increased membership 10% and distributed funds to support chapter operation.

Experience takeaways: I am grateful for the opportunity to give back through mentoring and gain experience in fundraising for an organization that supports the professionals in my industry.

DISCstyles™ COMMUNICATION & BEHAVIORAL STRENGTHS REPORT

Very Outgoing. Persuasive. Influential. People-Oriented. Optimistic. Verbal. Likes Variety. Excellent Team Player.
Action-oriented. Able to handle many projects simultaneously. Strong ability to meet others easily and able to communicate to large and small audiences with equal poise and confidence. Flexible problem solver. (02/2023).

Languages: English (native), Tamil (fluent), German (conversational), Spanish (conversational).

OLIVER PARKER

715.555.5555 | oliverparker-2023@maryville.edu | LinkedIn

BUSINESS MANAGEMENT GRADUATE | BUSINESS ANALYST

Finding Solutions Through Intelligent Data & Research

Senior college student with strong client-facing internship experience. **Ranked #1 Sales Associate, grossing $145K in under 3 months.** Identify problems and initiate process improvements, lead teams, and conduct strategic analyses. Leverage qualitative and quantitative research in developing solutions to increase sales output and drive overall operational improvements and organizational growth.

EDUCATION

Bachelor of Science, Business Management | Leadership & Organizational Effectiveness
MARYVILLE UNIVERSITY | St. Louis, MO | Anticipated Graduation May 2023

Honors & Awards | Dean's List | GPA 3.7/4.0

CORE COMPETENCIES

Qualitative & Quantitative Research	Revenue Generation	Proactive Problem Solving
Organizational Development	Consultative Selling	Strategic Communication
Project Management	Nonprofit Management	Critical Thinking
Client Management	Process Improvement	Analytical

INTERNSHIPS

CLIENT SERVICES INTERN   06/2022 – 08/2022

Expert Connect | Chicago, IL | *Global Leader in Knowledge On-Demand* ✦ *$252M Annual Revenue* ✦ *1,500+ Employees*

Sourced and qualified top-tier professionals to convey knowledge and expertise as advisors to high-level global projects. Acted as key liaison connecting clients and industry experts.

- **Research.** Assisted early-stage industry research and due diligence for medical and life science disciplines.
- **Communication.** Drove business forward by improving client engagement through 1:1 virtual meetings, interviews, in-person meetings, and surveys.
- **Sales.** Generated **$22K,** exceeding goal by 10%.

SALES INTERN   05/2021 – 08/2021

Red Rock Energy Drinks | Englewood Cliffs, NJ | *Healthy Energy Drinks* ✦ *$16.8M Annual Revenue* ✦ *100+ Employees*

Served as key member of Pro Sales Team expanding **Anheuser-Busch's Southern California soft launch** in convenience stores. Built strategic **NBA relationships** to develop partnerships and expand product distribution.

- **Protocols.** Developed time-saving protocols to improve database collection. Conducted 3 database projects for **Anheuser-Busch Distributors nationwide.**
- **Relationships.** Contacted **26 NBA teams'** Head Athletic Trainers to sell Red Rock energy products.

SALES ASSOCIATE INTERN   05/2020 – 08/2020

Sports Courts | Chicago, IL | *Regional Team Sports Program* ✦ *$3.7M Annual Revenue* ✦ *35+ Employees*

Generated **100+** qualified leads for close rate of **~60%** to grow market share and increase gross revenue. Managed sales cycle from opportunities through closing deals selling sports equipment.

- **Ranked #1.** Top Sales Associate grossing **$145K** in under 3 months.
- **Opportunities.** Increased leads **35%,** leveraging trigger marketing on Facebook, LinkedIn, and TikTok.
- **Client-Facing.** Served in dual client-facing role between sales and project management.

ADDITIONAL EXPERIENCE

FOUNDER & EXECUTIVE DIRECTOR   2016 – Present

Home Safety Campaign | Chicago, IL | *Nonprofit* ✦ *Home Fire Safety Program*

Founded 501(c)(3) nonprofit delivering home fire safety education. Planned and developed program and raised funds to purchase products. Offer virtual and in-home fire safety education for seniors.

- **Donations.** Raised **$15K+** from local donations to purchase smoke detectors installed free to seniors.
- **Outreach.** Coordinate informational events, presenting program to **20+** local senior centers annually.

TECHNICAL SKILLS

Microsoft Office Suite | Salesforce

Roshael Hanna, CPRW | Resumes 4 Results USA | resumes4resultsusa.com
Major: Business Management | **Goal:** Business analyst
Notable: Strong internship experience—with impressive results!—is the most expansive part of this resume. A unique additional experience—founding a nonprofit organization—adds leadership qualifications.

CANDACE HUANG

215-345-6789 • candacehuang@mail.com • LinkedIn.com/in/Candace-Huang

GOVERNMENT RELATIONS / PUBLIC ADMINISTRATION
Neighborhood Services Liaison • Office Administrator • PR and Press Aide • Public Policy Analyst

Recent J.D. with several years' experience in political office administration—public and media relations, constituent communications and interaction, scheduling, fundraising, event management. Bilingual English / Cantonese.

Participated in successful grassroots campaign and served as key liaison with Asian community. Demonstrated keen analytical, problem-solving, and follow-up skills to ensure appropriate issue resolution and maintain positive image in important communities.

EDUCATION

TEMPLE UNIVERSITY BEASLEY SCHOOL OF LAW, Philadelphia, PA **Juris Doctor,** 2023
- **Pennsylvania Bar Exam** — May 2023 (admittance to bar anticipated September 2023).
- **Financed 100%** of tuition and expenses, working full-time throughout college and law school.

THE OHIO STATE UNIVERSITY, Columbus, OH **BS Business Administration,** 2017
- **Major: Marketing**

RELEVANT EXPERIENCE

DR. MICHAEL LEE, PHILADELPHIA CITY COUNCIL, Philadelphia, PA 2000–2023
Staff Assistant (Intern), 2022–2023

One of 2 campaign staffers selected for transition/start-up team following Dr. Lee's election to City Council.
- **C**reated an active and effective constituent-response system that was crucial to building and maintaining neighborhood support. Served as initial constituent contact; provided attentive and persistent follow-up to diverse constituent questions, problems, complaints, and issues.
- **O**versaw outreach to and interaction with Asian communities city-wide.
- **A**ttended neighborhood meetings, prepared reports, and delivered briefings. Scheduled public engagements and meetings.
- **S**et up administrative processes and systems to ensure smooth running of office operations and constituent communications.

Campaign Aide, 2000–2002

One of first volunteers for grassroots citywide campaign that resulted in #3 finish among 27 candidates. Participated in fundraising, publicity, public contact, and campaigning.
- **E**ffectively represented the candidate city-wide, personally campaigning door-to-door in more than 30 districts.
- **P**ersonally built volunteer network and voter support through extensive contacts in the Asian community.
- **S**erved as intermediary between prospective constituents and the candidate, building a positive image through proactive problem resolution.

WILLIAM CISNEROS FOR MAYOR CAMPAIGN, San Francisco, CA 1995–1997
Office Manager / Chief Assistant to Campaign Director, Asian HQ

Bolstered the candidate's image and effectiveness in Philadelphia's large Asian community.
- **R**esearched, confirmed, and publicized campaign events and candidate appearances.
- **P**olled event attendees to gather audience-specific information for the candidate.
- **C**oordinated fundraising activities and helped ensure smooth-running events.

ADDITIONAL EXPERIENCE

SHEARSON, LEHMAN, HUTTON, San Francisco, CA 2016–2017
Analyst (Intern)

Independently sought and attained year-long internship with highly regarded investment firm.
- **R**esearched and analyzed clients' portfolio investments, cross-referencing specific stock and bond information to create a comprehensive picture of investment performance.
- **P**repared detailed reports that included performance history, liquidity analysis, and assessment of optimum mix of investments to meet clients' objectives for risk, growth, and liquidity.
- **P**articipated in client meetings, gaining insight into effective presentation of investment material to high-net-worth individuals.
- **D**esigned an automated system to put expiration and "watch" tags on potential red-flag issues.
- **E**arned Series 7 and 63 licenses.

Louise Kursmark, MRW, CPRW, JCTC, CEIP, CCM | Best Impression Career Services | louisekursmark.com
Major: Law (JD), Marketing (BS) | **Goal:** Public administration / politics
Notable: Candace transitioned from early career goals (finance) to her current passion: politics. Her resume features her new law degree and three highly relevant roles, with early financial experience also mentioned.

JOSEPH SPRIGGS

Laurel, MD 20706 | 301.801.3100 | jspriggs@gmail.com

DATA ANALYSIS & MATHEMATICS SPECIALIZATION

Outgoing, rising Mathematician with recent Bachelor of Science in Mathematics and extensive experience collaborating between cross-functional teams to input data and analyze results utilizing statistical analysis modeling software. Presented with honors for superior attention to detail and problem-solving strengths. Able to swiftly learn the ropes by training beneath more experienced peers on tools, techniques, and protocol.

*** Eager to apply newly acquired skills in data analysis and statistical modeling. ***

AREAS OF EXPERTISE

- Mathematical Modeling
- Algebra & Calculus
- Worker's Compensation Claims
- Computer Programming

- Logistics Management
- Performance Improvement
- Charts, Graphs, Spreadsheets
- Problem Solving

- Statistics & Data Analysis
- Team/Relationship Building
- Research Management
- Business Acumen & Reporting

EDUCATION

Bachelor of Science in Mathematics: Morgan State University – Baltimore, MD   2023

- **Dean's List Student**
- **Research Project—Pig Heart Transplant:** Determined whether investments were worthwhile through thoroughly analyzing line graphs documenting cost benefits from the beginning of a pig's life cycle to the end.
- **Coursework:** Introduction to Analysis; Applied Statistics; Calculus I, II, II; Linear Algebra; Transition to Higher Math; Ordinary and Partial Differential Equation; Computer Science I and II; Numerical Methods; Number Theory; Communication in Mathematics; Survey of Algebra

PROFESSIONAL EXPERIENCE

Morgan State University – Baltimore, MD   2022–2023
Student Researcher

Performed in-depth research to determine the cost efficiency of performing pig heart transplantation in place of human heart transplantation on human participants. Collected extensive data on costs involved (e.g., pig feed, property, scientific equipment, cost of aging pigs, etc.) and analyzed findings with linear algebra to determine cost benefits.

Key Accomplishments:
- Acquired extensive experience performing applied statistics, linear algebra, and data analysis.
- Presented data results in a clear, cohesive manner to professors and peers.

Park Landscapes Inc. – Laurel, MD   2018–2022
Landscaper

Visualized and mapped out blueprints on a seasonal basis to capture the attention of the public and gain reputation for aesthetically pleasing landscapes. Performed routine maintenance on all landscaping designs.

Key Accomplishments:
- Honored as the "Best Landscape in the County" for architecturally appealing design and property management.
- Scripted and presented new blueprints every season for the entire 17–20 acres.

Purchasing Prowess – Bowie, MD   2016–2018
Mass Merchandiser

Designed schematic plans and entered data into company-specific software to maintain customer records across a fast-paced, competitive environment. Forecasted inventory levels and assessed stock losses to ensure products remained readily available to the public. Reported service updates to senior management using stellar business acumen.

Key Accomplishments:
- Multitasked and took on additional roles on demand in support of operations.
- Ensured stock remained in full supply while avoiding excess.

TECHNICAL SKILLS

Microsoft Office: Word, PowerPoint, Excel • Keynote • R studio • GeoGebra • Java Programming • MATLAB

Zakiyyah Mussallihullah, CARW, CTW | Andy Thomas Careers Now | andythomascareersnow.com
Major: Mathematics | **Goal:** Data analytics
Notable: "Key Accomplishments" are called out for each position—both an on-campus research role and several unrelated experiences that built strong workplace skills.

KELLY THOMPSON

New York, NY 10030 | 646-234-7939 | Kelly.thompson@gmail.com | linkedin.com/in/kellythompson

FINANCE | ACCOUNTING | AUDITING

Self-motivated Accounting Major dedicated to learning and implementing new systems to increase staff efficiency and boost financial goals. Proficient in using Excel, data validation tools, and bookkeeping techniques to streamline processes and improve user experience. Detail-oriented with experience managing multiple projects while maintaining quality and accuracy.

Bookkeeping | Data Analysis | Invoices | Financial Accounting | Auditing | Finance | Customer Service
Communication | Time Management | U.S Generally Accepted Accounting Principles (US GAAP) | Organization
Relationship Building | Recordkeeping | Critical Thinking | Microsoft Word | PowerPoint | Excel

EDUCATION

CUNY City College | New York, NY   Expected Graduation May 2023
Bachelor of Science: Accounting
   Coursework: Corporate Financial Reporting; Math Analysis in Business; Cost Management; Auditing 101

Bronx Community College | New York, NY   August 2019
Certification: Business

RELATED COURSES & CERTIFICATES

Corporate Finance Institute (CFI) | Remote   August 2021
Excel Crash Course
   ➢ Mastered keyboard shortcuts in Excel, increasing efficiency and productivity.
   ➢ Utilized functions and formulas appropriately to automate spreadsheets and improve user experience.
   ➢ Enhanced financial analysis skills by applying data validation tools, Net Present Value (NPV), and Internal Rate of Return (IRR) functions to spreadsheets.

LinkedIn Learning | Remote   July 2021
Accounting Foundation: Bookkeeping Certificate
   ➢ Learned how to create income statements and balance sheets using financial transactions in ledgers.
   ➢ Gained insight on 4-step bookkeeping process and best practices when managing accounts.

CUNY City College | New York, NY   January 2020–April 2020
Group Team Member: Business Core Applied Semester Experience Course
   ➢ Collaborated with team of 5 to create income statement for Noodles & Company, predicting profit and losses for 4 consecutive years at new location.
   ➢ Created income tracking system in Excel and applied data validation tools to enhance user experience and streamline process.
   ➢ Organized weekly team meetings via Zoom and scheduled reminders to stay on track of assignments.

WORK EXPERIENCE

New York City Market | New York, NY   June 2015–June 2021
Cashier
   ➢ Promoted to cashier after 6 months for delivering exceptional customer service.
   ➢ Trained 25 new employees on store policies and procedures, as well as customer service strategies to maintain 100% satisfaction.

Courtesy Clerk   December 2014–June 2015
   ➢ Successfully enrolled 50 new shoppers into loyalty rewards program.
   ➢ Greeted customers, responded to customer inquiries in timely manner, and maintained store safety.

Kaljah Adams, ACRW | The Career Advising Hub | careeradvisinghub.org
Major: Accounting | **Goal:** Accounting, auditing, or financial management
Notable: The "Related Courses and Certifications" section shows how Kelly dedicated herself to learning even beyond her college courses. Her experience, while unrelated, adds valuable workplace skills.

CRYSTAL WATKINS

555-223-6654   https://www.linkedin.com/in/crystal-watkins   crystalwatkins@gmail.com

ASPIRING AUDITOR/ACCOUNTANT

Competitive | Disciplined | Hard Working | Accountable

→ **Academic and athletic high performer** known for determination, work ethic, and dedication to continuous improvement.

→ **Goal achiever** who approaches challenges with discipline, effective time management, and a daily commitment to accomplishing small details that are the foundation for major wins.

→ **Quiet leader** able to inspire teammates to work together, work hard, and improve performance.

EDUCATION

UNIVERSITY OF MICHIGAN, Ann Arbor, MI
Bachelor of Science in Business, May 2023 | Double Major: Accounting and Economics
GPA 3.533 | Dean's List | Athletic Honor Roll 2021, 2022, 2023 | Big Ten All-Academic Team 2021, 2022

→ **Starter:** *NCAA Division 1 Women's Basketball Team*
Transferred to Michigan to benefit from more intense, competitive athletic environment. Through advance planning, good time management, and clear communication with professors and coaches, maintained high grade point average while balancing a heavy academic schedule and 20+ hours of weekly basketball activities.

→ **Curriculum Highlight:** *Business Audit/Case Study (Accounting Information Systems course)*
Worked with 3 teammates on 5-week project auditing a fictionalized company, creating a report of findings and recommendations, and delivering class presentation. Earned grade of A.

→ **Major Coursework:** *Accounting*—Advanced Financial Accounting | Auditing | Accounting Information Systems | Tax Accounting | Financial Accounting | Cost Accounting | Tax Research Seminar
Economics: Microeconomic Theory | Economics of Sports | World Economic Development History | Labor Economics and Industrial Relations

RUTGERS UNIVERSITY, New Brunswick, NJ
Completed 2 years toward Bachelor of Science in Business | Major: Accounting
GPA 3.429 | Dean's List | Big East All Academic Team 2019, 2020

→ **Starter:** *NCAA Division I Women's Basketball Team*

BREWSTER ACADEMY, Wolfeboro, NH
Graduate, 2019

→ **Performance Highlight:** Elected to attend out-of-state boarding high school to gain a more competitive basketball experience. Advanced from 2nd team to 1st team within 4 months through hard work, intensive skills development, and openness to guidance and feedback from coaches and teammates.

LEADERSHIP AND PROFESSIONAL DEVELOPMENT

→ **She Leads:** One of 3 (out of 15) basketball players chosen to attend university-sponsored program for developing women's leadership skills. Brought leadership lessons back to team.

→ **Apex Leadership Experience:** With entire basketball team, participated in challenging experiential training exercise designed to promote teamwork, build trust, and develop leadership skills.

→ **Team Leadership:** Stepped up to help drive culture and performance change following losing season and coaching turnover. Led by example and used empathy and communication skills to inspire teammates to work together to improve. Resulted in contagious energy in the locker room and an immediate performance turnaround.

WORK EXPERIENCE

Trainer/Coach/Referee: New Brunswick Youth Development Academy   Summers 2016, 2017, 2018, 2019, 2021
Server: McFadden Grill, New Brunswick, NJ   Summer 2020

Louise Kursmark, MRW, CPRW, JCTC, CEIP, CCM | Best Impression Career Services | louisekursmark.com
Majors: Accounting and Economics | **Goal:** Position as an auditor with a Big 4 accounting firm
Notable: Crystal did not have any internships or relevant work experience because she devoted so much time to college athletics. Her resume focuses on leadership, character traits, and overall performance.

MICHAEL JOHNSON

Greater Houston Area ☎ 832.347.2311 ⌨ michaeljohnson_07@gmail.com
🌐 https://www.linkedin.com/in/michaeljohnson_07/

☐ QUALIFICATIONS PROFILE

Highly motivated, performance-focused, and detail-oriented professional, offering solid knowledge of accounting best practices and principles from education background. Interested in pursuing a challenging career to utilize and further enhance skills acquired from education. Excellent in analyzing data and operations processes to identify and execute efficient course of action. Armed with outstanding ability to integrate innovative strategies to boost efficient communication and improve business operations. Technically proficient with Microsoft Office Suite (Word, PowerPoint, Excel, and Outlook) and IDEA.

☐ EDUCATION

MASTER OF SCIENCE IN ACCOUNTING · May 2023
C.T. Bauer College of Business, University of Houston, Houston, TX
Dean's List of Honors (Spring 2022, Spring 2023)

BACHELOR OF BUSINESS ADMINISTRATION IN ACCOUNTING · May 2021
Robert C. Vackar College of Business & Entrepreneurship, University of Texas: Rio Grande Valley, Edinburg, TX
Dean's List of Honors (Fall 2018, Spring 2019, Fall 2020, Spring 2021)

☐ PROFESSIONAL DEVELOPMENT

<u>Examination:</u>	**Passed all 4 sections, CPA Exam · May 2023**
<u>Certification:</u>	**Assurance/Financial Reporting	University of Houston · May 2023**
	**Advanced Internal Audit	University of Houston · May 2023**
	**IT Systems Risk Management	University of Houston · May 2023**

☐ CORE COMPETENCIES

- Solid understanding of global accounting principles.
- Competence in analyzing financial and audit data along with conducting record maintenance and budget assessment.
- Outstanding skills in utilizing spreadsheets and databases, including Excel's PivotTable and VLOOKUP.
- Technically proficient with Microsoft Office Suite (Word, PowerPoint, Excel, and Outlook).
- Familiarity with economics, finance, marketing, and management principles.
- Knowledge of the roles of ethics and public policy in business.
- Adeptness in addressing diverse accounting issues.
- Capability of working professionally and collaboratively with diverse professionals.

☐ ACADEMIC PROJECTS

Role: Team Member | **TOYS R US** (*Financial Statement Analysis*)   Spring 2023
- Gathered past financial data to analyze the feasibility of their corporate strategy to compare with actual results compiled by other research members.

Role: Team Leader | **KRISPY KREME** (*Fraud Examination*)   Spring 2023
- Coordinated with the team on research regarding the company's fraud as well as leading the team in creating a final research presentation.

Role: Team Leader | **RICHARD BOWEN AND CITIGROUP** (*Ethics for Accountants*)   Fall 2022
- Compiled a case study with the team detailing Richard Bowen, Citigroup, the 2008 financial crisis, and financial data.

Role: Team Member | **T-MOBILE AND METROPCS MERGER** (*Advanced Accounting*)   Fall 2021
- Assessed the combined and separate financial statements of the companies to create a financial forecast, compared it with actual results found by other researchers, and worked together to form a proper analysis of the merger.

Michelle King | Resume Professional Writers | resumeprofessionalwriters.com
Major: Accounting (MS and BS) | **Goal:** Accounting
Notable: Highlights of this resume are the Professional Development section—mentioning a highly desirable accomplishment in passing the CPA exam—and Academic Projects describing relevant experience.

JAMES BENNETT DAY

Greenville, SC | 864.541.2345 | bennettday21@gmail.com | linkedin.com/in/bennettday

Versatile and resourceful emerging professional prepared to build on comprehensive experience in **financial management and analysis.** Exceptional communication, interpersonal, and teamwork skills. Known for ability to readily establish rapport with colleagues, customers, and communities. History of exceeding expectations.

"You are wise beyond your years and a special young man. Being part of the BMW Credit Leadership and Development Program, I have met many young folks and I have to say hands down, I have never met anyone who has impressed me as you have." ~ Adam Hamilton, Internship Supervisor, BMW Financial Services Company

EDUCATION

Bachelor of Science (BS), Clemson University, Clemson, SC – May 2023
Major: Financial Management, Minor: Accounting ✦ GPA: 4.00/4.00

UIS Study Abroad Program, Universitat Autònoma de Barcelona, Barcelona, Spain – Spring 2022
Studies focused on finance and entrepreneurship ✦ **GPA: 4.00/4.00**

Morocco Exchange Program, Rabat, Morocco – Spring 2021

PROFESSIONAL & TECHNICAL COMPETENCIES

Data Mining | Data Analysis | Data Visualization | Data Processing | Quantitative Data
Accounting Techniques | Financial Analysis | Fiscal Balance Projection | Value Investment Principles | Mergers
Risk Management | Cost-Benefit Analysis | Cash Flow Management | Statistical Modeling | Bloomberg Terminal
Microsoft Office | PowerPoint | Access | Excel | Adobe Photoshop | SQL | Tableau | Green Belt Training

INTERNSHIP EXPERIENCE

Clemson University, Clemson, SC   Aug 2022—May 2023
DATA ANALYTICS INTERN
- Collected valid, structurally sound data focused on university athletic department revenue streams and analyzed program benefits and potential.
- Created visualizations and decision-ready dashboards to support departmental decision-making.

BMW Financial Services Company, Greenville, SC   Jun—Aug 2021
CREDIT ANALYST INTERN
- Generated profits and mitigated risk by reviewing credit applications, determining customer creditworthiness, and identifying potentially delinquent customers. Assisted in opening $250K—$50M lines of credit.
- Improved employee recognition and morale by determining existing inefficiencies. Collaborated in the development of a proposal for new award and created a prototype for award procedure and prize.
- Analyzed performance of Ford dealerships in the eastern U.S. and detailed action steps for improvement.
- Enhanced consumer engagement and increased online buying experience satisfaction by upgrading website.
- Reduced losses by communicating with customers and dealerships to identify remedies for default payments.

ABC Marketing, Charlotte, NC   Jun—Aug 2019 and 2020
OPERATIONS INTERN
- Reconciled and analyzed completed projects ranging from $50K–$2M.
- Identified ways to reduce shipping and handling costs, expedite order tracking, improve timely delivery.

CAMPUS/COMMUNITY CONTRIBUTIONS & VOLUNTEER WORK

Participant, **Excel & Lead Program** (Clemson multi-year student leadership development program)   2021–2023
Leader, **Be a Star** program (Partnership supporting students with disabilities in recreation and athletics)   2020–2022
Leader, Nueva Vida Barcelona Food Drive for the Homeless   Jan—May 2022
Member, Wall Street South Investment Club   2019—2023

Jean Austin, NCRW, NCOPE, CJSS, CCMC, COPNS, MS | Talents Presented | talentspresented.com
Major: Financial Management | **Goal:** Financial management and analysis
Notable: Three relevant internships provide ample evidence of James' value—which is emphasized by a powerful endorsement from one of his internship supervisors positioned at the top of the resume.

Addison McCall

Staten Island, NY • 718.477.1985 • addison.mccall@gmail.com

Accountant/Auditor

Accounting new graduate pursuing a full-time position
while working towards becoming a Certified Public Accountant.

Education

College of Staten Island, Staten Island, NY
Bachelor of Science in Accounting—May 2023
- **Core Courses:** Advanced Accounting, Auditing, Accounting Info Systems, Cost Accounting

Awards

- **Internal Revenue Service Recognition Award** for outstanding public service contributed through the Volunteer Income Tax Assistance Program
- **United States Coast Guard Leadership Award:** Junior ROTC (high school)
- **Brigadier General Thomas Draude Award** for Superior Integrity and Leadership

Related Accounting Experience

Intern • Clayton and Sanders, CPAs, Staten Island, NY   September 2022–April 2023
Accounting Assistant • Smith & Sons, CPAs, Brooklyn, NY   Summer 2021
- Performed corporate write ups, bank reconciliations, and data entry.
- Recommended new software to partially automate the reconciliation process, saving hours of staff time at the critical end-of-month period.
- Gained insight into client relationships and ways to communicate difficult financial information.

Volunteer Income Tax Provider • Internal Revenue Service   Tax Seasons 2019–2023
- Prepared 1040 forms for low income households and elderly and disabled people.

Additional Employment

Financed 100% of college expenses as a Banquet Waiter throughout high school and college. Worked for Far Hills Country Club, Staten Island, NY, from 2019–2023 and the Garden Club from 2018–2019. In 2020, was promoted to Banquet Captain and managed the activities of 30 wait staff.

Technical Skills

Knowledgeable in QuickBooks, Creative Solutions, Microsoft Word, Excel, PowerPoint, and Access.

Profile

I am a highly motivated individual who loves to work, is willing to learn, and can accomplish tasks of any difficulty. I am a very good communicator and team player as well as team leader.

Beverly Baskin, Ed.S., LPC, MCC, CPRW | BBCS Counseling Services | bbcscounseling.com
Major: Accounting | **Goal:** Accounting and/or auditing position
Notable: Clarity and conciseness are the hallmarks of this resume. Character and soft skills are communicated in the final section, "Profile."

MALCOLM GARRETT

Phoenix, AZ 85001
malcolmgarrett@email.com | 623.766.5410 | linkedin.com/in/Malcolm-Garrett

RISING FINANCE AND MARKETING PROFESSIONAL

JOB TARGET ▶ FINANCIAL ANALYST

University of Arizona honors graduate poised to assume full-time financial analyst position. Internship and special project experiences span private and public companies, nonprofit, and government bureau. Successfully navigated highly competitive application process to participate in rigorous Freedman Reports securities analysis program. Consistently stepped up to assume project leadership and guide peers toward goal accomplishment.

Adaptable under stress and respond positively to quickly changing priorities. Coachable, respectful, and collaborative. Eager to apply strong academic preparation and hands-on experience to help achieve organizational objectives.

AREAS OF SPECIAL ABILITY AND EXPERIENCE

Analytical Skills • Financial Analysis • Marketing Analytics • Business Operations Analysis • Research Methodologies • Data Collection • Complex Data Analysis • Revenue Models • Financial Forecasting • Balance Sheets • Income Statements • Cashflow Statements • Equity Research Analysis • Excel VLOOKUP and Pivot Tables • Detail-Oriented • Peer Leader • Public Speaking • Presentation Development and Delivery • Teamwork • Remote Collaboration Strategies • Complex Problem Solving • Consensus Building • High-Quality Work • Executive Report Creation • Interpersonal Communication

EDUCATION

BS, Business, Finance and Marketing –University of Arizona, Eller College of Management, Tucson, AZ
Graduation 05/2023 *magna cum laude*; **Dean's List recognition all semesters; 3.75 cumulative GPA**
Four-year recipient of Merit of Excellence Scholarship

Community Service Marketing Project – Participated in team to assist nonprofit organization, Higher Love, with marketing efforts and fundraising activities. Analyzed organization's existing marketing strategies and proposed new ideas to expand media reach, increase fundraising, and promote brand awareness.

▶ **Experience Reflections –** *Provided me with a greater understanding of the organization and its mission, along with greater insight into the workings and challenges of sustaining a nonprofit organization.*

PROFESSIONAL EXPERIENCE

Growth Ops Intern | MONTGOMERY SOLUTIONS INC. – Tucson, AZ | 06/2022 – 08/2022

▶ **Experience Reflections –** *Applied theoretical learning to analyze and recommend solutions to real-world marketing challenges. Developing a presentation and reporting findings and recommendations to senior leaders and founder/CEO was energizing and gave me an opportunity to see how much I could push myself to achieve.*

- **Collected and analyzed complex data sets** of closed-won cycle times from 250+ partner practices to optimize growth ops, outreach, and implementation teams. Developed recommendations based on research.
- **Tailored survey questions** and developed target list of practices to support market research findings.
- **Identified procedural opportunities,** suggested process improvements, and presented findings of intensive summer-long project to senior leadership, including founder and CEO.

Cathy Lanzalaco, MBA, CPRW, CPCC, NCOPE, SPHR, SHRM-SCP, RN | Inspire Careers | inspirecareers.com
Major: Business, Finance, and Marketing | **Goal:** Financial analyst
Notable: A clear Headline, strong Summary, and detailed Education and Experience sections paint the picture of a highly qualified new graduate. Two pages are needed to convey all his relevant material.

Research Analyst | FREEDMAN REPORTS – Dallas, TX | 08/2021 – 12/2021

▶ **Experience Reflections –** *This was a highly competitive project and a privilege to be chosen. I learned more in this program than any other class I have taken. The level of critical thinking, teamwork, and collaboration required to achieve our goals was intense, but so valuable. Especially important was navigating team collaboration and communication during COVID and devising creative solutions to the logistical challenges we faced.*

- **Created equity research report** with two peers on upstream oil and gas company, Dunnelle Petroleum Company (NYSE: DPE), headquartered in Oklahoma City, Oklahoma. Led financial modeling aspect of project.
- **Forecasted all income statement,** balance sheet, and cash flow statement items for next 10 years.
- **Applied DCF and multiples methods** to establish company valuation and forecast 12-month target stock price.

Intern | CITIZENS MONETARY PROTECTION BUREAU – Sacramento, CA | 05/2021 – 08/2021

▶ **Experience Reflections –** *This experience strengthened my appreciation for communication and teamwork. Working for a federal government bureau taught me how key communication is, especially when dealing with public-facing documents. Understanding what projects teams are working on can help determine how you interact with them and whether they may need assistance when short-staffed or under time constraints.*

- **Analyzed and categorized** 200+ websites containing advice for senior citizens on reverse mortgages and home equity lines of credit to aid Office of Older Americans. Organized findings in Excel spreadsheet.
- **Reviewed 50 state attorney general websites** to determine level of use of bureau informational content and categorized information in Excel spreadsheet.

Election Advocate | MARICOPA COUNTY – Phoenix, AZ | 9/2018 – 11/2018

▶ **Experience Reflections –** *Prior to taking on this role, I did not fully understand the intricacies of voting laws and how critical a solidly enforced procedure was to ensure the integrity of the democratic process. The extensive training prepared me to carry out the process and gave me better insight to the role of the advocate.*

- **Checked in 500+ voters** using electronic voter registration system and provided voters with ballots.
- **Protected integrity of election process** in accordance with federal and state law.

EXTRACURRICULAR INVOLVEMENT

UNIVERSITY OF ARIZONA – Tucson, AZ
Gamma Pi | 01/2021– 05/2023

- **Participated in biweekly chapter meetings** with brothers of University of Arizona's Gamma Pi chapter.
- **Connected and collaborated** with chapter members and fraternity alumni across country.

Finance Career Management Program | 01/2021 – 05/2021

- **Completed six-week program** to learn effective networking, recruitment, and career development techniques.
- **Researched financial services firm** with five other participants and presented findings to 100+ peers.

BUSHRA SALIH

Miami, FL 33458 | 561.200.1809 | bsalih@gmail.com

Health Informatics Analyst with Quick Wit & Commitment to Excellence!

Dedicated, high-energy professional—a recent Master of Health Informatics who consistently rises to workplace challenges to support ongoing operations and ensure commitment to excellence in health policy and data management. Quick to conform to and master latest protocols, best practices, automated processes, and software.

Skilled at absorbing large quantities of technical data and positioning teams for success through superior written and oral communications, quick thinking, and collaboration. Eager to work with data sets and design SOPs for your organization.

AREAS OF EXPERTISE

- Information/Data Analysis
- Regulatory Compliance
- Screening & Recordkeeping
- Systems Management
- Medical Diagnostics
- Rehabilitative Services
- Chronic & Acute Conditions
- Treatment Planning
- Clinical Environments
- Patient Satisfaction
- Deadline Management
- Relationship/Team Building

TECHNICAL SKILLS

- Microsoft Office: Word, PowerPoint, Excel, Access
- G-Suite
- Zoom
- SQL
- HTML
- SPSS

MEMBERSHIP

Student Physical and Occupational Therapy Society:
- Attended meetings hosting acclaimed occupational therapists.

EDUCATION

Master of Science in Health Informatics
University of South Florida, Tampa, FL: *Pending Graduation August 2023*

- *Capstone Project:* Translated 12 years of regional health data into meaningful projections related to occupancy, staffing needs, and specialty training opportunities for a major health system in South Florida. Identified opportunities to become leading provider of specialty services in 2 emerging areas.

Bachelor of Science in Allied Health
University of Tampa, Tampa, FL: *2021*

Social-Behavioral-Educational Researchers
Collaborative Institutional Training Initiative: *Feb 2020*

Basic Life Support for Healthcare Providers (BLS)
Administering Emergency Oxygen: American Red Cross: *2020*

PROFESSIONAL EXPERIENCE

HORNET MEDICAL CENTER, Tampa, FL: *2020–2021*
Therapist Assistant (Shadowing)

Evaluated and recorded key concepts relating to patient occupational therapy for patients recovering from a wide range of ailments, including stroke, traumatic brain injuries, cancer, and joint replacement.

Witnessed patients regain utilization of limbs during the rehabilitation process. Directly assisted patients with taking steps and other daily activities.

Learned protocols/best practices to record and input data on patient progress.

Key Accomplishment

- Consistently attended training sessions, resulting in building immense rapport among senior healthcare professionals and being assigned additional activities and software training to aid in patient recovery.

CHILDREN'S THERAPEUTIC SERVICES, Tampa, FL: *2019–2020*
Therapist Assistant (Shadowing)

Partnered closely with a team of friendly, upbeat therapists to ensure patients diagnosed with autism, cerebral palsy, and other conditions received optimal care.

Assigned to work directly with patients needing to improve fine and gross motor skills. Built long-lasting relationships while developing skills in therapeutic techniques and best practices for improving the patient experience..

Key Accomplishment

- Acquired immense insight on how to input confidential data using multiple charting systems.

Zakiyyah Mussallihullah, CARW, CTW | Andy Thomas Careers Now | andythomascareersnow.com
Major: Health Informatics (MS), Allied Health (BS) | **Goal:** Informatics analyst
Notable: This resume makes the most of shadowing experience for a new graduate who did not have any formal internships or relevant work experience. Notice the unique headline!

MATTHEW BETTS

303-235-8710 | matthew.betts@gmail.com

Aspiring
DATA ANALYST | ECONOMIC ANALYST

Recent graduate (BS Economics) with skill and passion for identifying, analyzing, and communicating data insights—using data to tell a story that informs and influences organizational strategy and decision-making.

Skills and Strengths

- **Data Research, Analysis, Visualization, and Presentation:** Experienced at identifying and mining data sources to develop accurate and meaningful analyses for businesses and nonprofits.
- **Technology:** Skilled and experienced in using Excel, PowerPoint, R, SQL, Stata, and SAS.
- **Communication:** Effective in sales roles (including cold-calling) and team projects, using both data and persuasion to influence opinions and drive action.

EDUCATION

BS Economics | University of Colorado, Boulder, OH | 2023

Senior Capstone Project: Senior Seminar in Economics

- Independently identified study topic—the effects of climate change on the Colorado ski industry—and created project plan encompassing data research, analysis, and presentation.
- Researched and identified statistical sources and transformed into data using regressions in R and Excel.
- Analyzed findings, prepared report, and presented to the university Economics Department.
- *Of note: Earned "Best Presentation" recognition and grade of A.*

Executive Case Study: Entrepreneurship (Amazon Prime)

- Member of 4-person team conducting semester-long research and SWOT analysis to identify potential new markets and services to expand market share for Amazon Prime.
- Brainstormed ideas and analyzed economics to determine viability and profitability.
- Created and delivered presentation to local business executives.
- *Of note: Our concept—live-streamed remote concerts—became an offering for Amazon Prime and other broadcasters in response to the COVID crisis. Entire team received A grade.*

EXPERIENCE

Sales Associate | Outdoor Outfitters, Boulder CO | Dec 2022–Present

- Hired during busy holiday season, quickly mastered diverse roles and became go-to person when help is needed in any area of store operations.
- Maintain a consistently high level of customer service.

Sales Intern | Rocky Mountain Connections Group, Denver, CO | Aug 2021–Oct 2021

- Honed communications and sales skills, conducting phone and email outreach to build a pipeline of potential customers for nonprofit that manages fundraising raffles and events.

Volunteer | Healthy Denver School & Community Gardens, Denver, CO | Summers 2019, 2020

- Took full responsibility for caring for community garden during several week-long rotations.

Fundraiser | Environment America, Boulder, CO | Feb 2019–May 2019

- Cold-called members and potential donors to raise funds to support environmental causes in Colorado.
- Quickly rose to one of the top fundraisers in the office by building rapport, adjusting communication style as needed, and sharing enthusiasm for environmental causes.
  - #1 in fundraising, 2 consecutive weeks

Diligent and hard working | Collaborative | Flexible and adaptive
Able to relocate | Excellent time manager, comfortable and productive on-site or remote

Louise Kursmark, MRW, CPRW, JCTC, CEIP, CCM | Best Impression Career Services | louisekursmark.com
Major: Economics | **Goal:** Position as data analyst / economic analyst
Notable: Projects are detailed in Education because they showcase highly relevant skills and accomplishments. Experience is less relevant to current goals but conveys work ethic and professional skills. The resume closes with valuable soft skills.